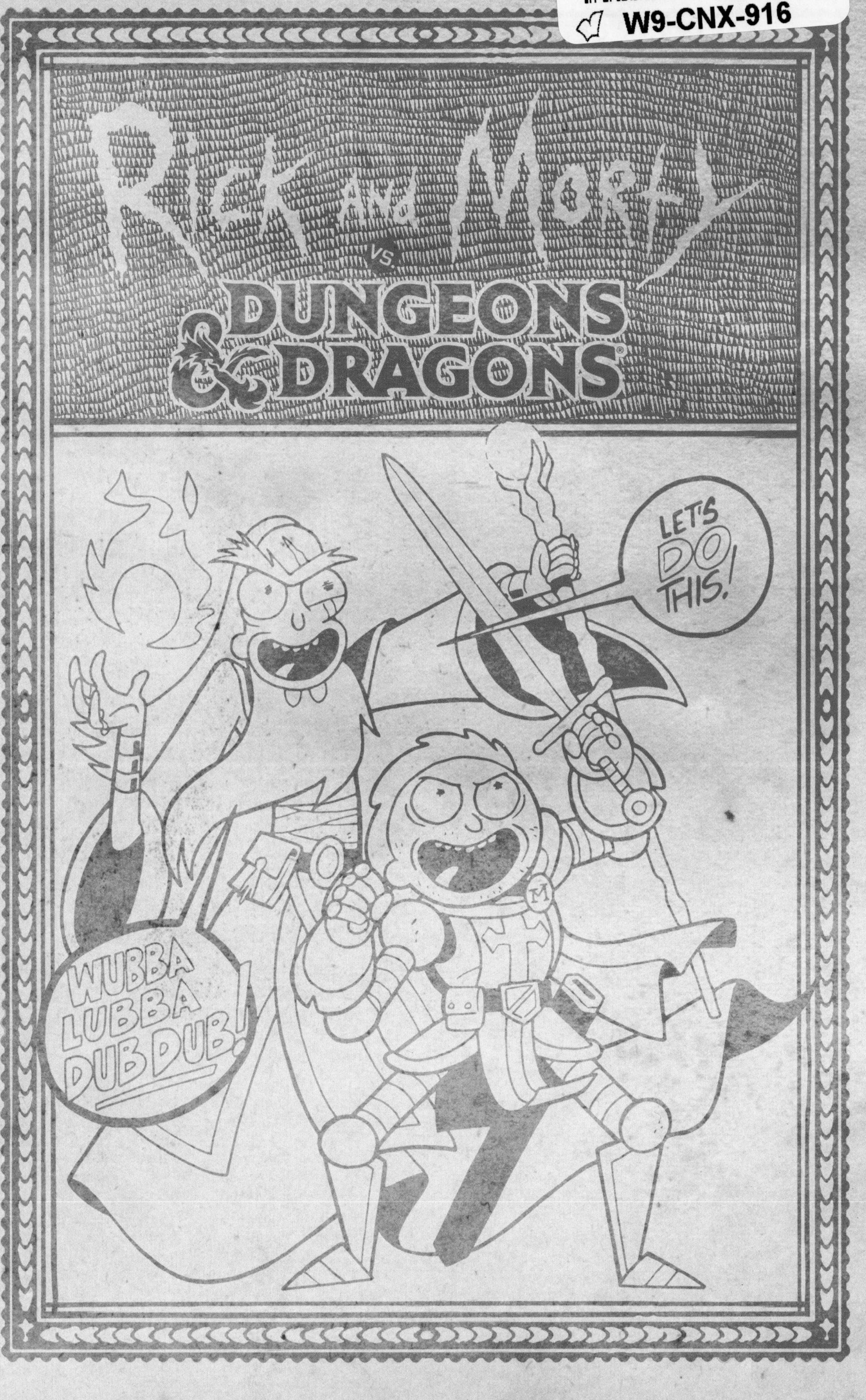
Rick and Morty
vs.
Dungeons & Dragons
LET'S DO THIS!
WUBBA LUBBA DUB DUB!

ISBN: 978-1-68405-416-9   22 21 20 19   3 4 5 6

Special thanks to the D&D team at Wizards of the Coast and to Justin Roiland, Dan Harmon, Marisa Marionakis, Mike Mendel, Meagan Birney, Elyse Salazar, and Janet No.

Originally published as RICK AND MORTY™ VS. DUNGEONS & DRAGONS issues #1–4.

Chris Ryall, President & Publisher/CCO • John Barber, Editor-in-Chief
Cara Morrison, Chief Financial Officer • Matthew Ruzicka, Chief Accounting Officer • David Hedgecock, Associate Publisher
Jerry Bennington, VP of New Product Development • Lorelei Bunjes, VP of Digital Services
Justin Eisinger, Editorial Director, Graphic Novels & Collections • Eric Moss, Sr. Director, Licensing & Business Development

Ted Adams and Robbie Robbins, IDW Founders

Joe Nozemack, Founder & Chief Financial Officer • James Lucas Jones, Publisher • Charlie Chu, V.P. of Creative & Business Development • Brad Rooks, Director of Operations • Melissa Meszaros, Director of Publicity • Margot Wood, Director of Sales Sandy Tanaka, Marketing Design Manager • Amber O'Neill, Special Projects Manager • Troy Look, Director of Design & Production Hilary Thompson, Senior Graphic Designer • Kate Z. Stone, Graphic Designer • Sonja Synak, Junior Graphic Designer Angie Knowles, Digital Prepress Lead • Ari Yarwood, Executive Editor • Sarah Gaydos, Editorial Director of Licensed Publishing Robin Herrera, Senior Editor • Desiree Wilson, Associate Editor • Alissa Sallah, Administrative Assistant Jung Lee, Logistics Associate • Scott Sharkey, Warehouse Assistant

Written by Patrick Rothfuss & Jim Zub

Art by Troy Little

Colors by Leonardo Ito

Letters by Robbie Robbins

Series Edits by Chase W. Marotz & David Hedgecock

and Sarah Gaydos & Ari Yarwood

Rick and Morty™ created by

Justin Roiland and Dan Harmon

Collection Edits by Justin Eisinger and Alonzo Simon

Collection Design by Robbie Robbins and Shawn Lee

Publisher Chris Ryall

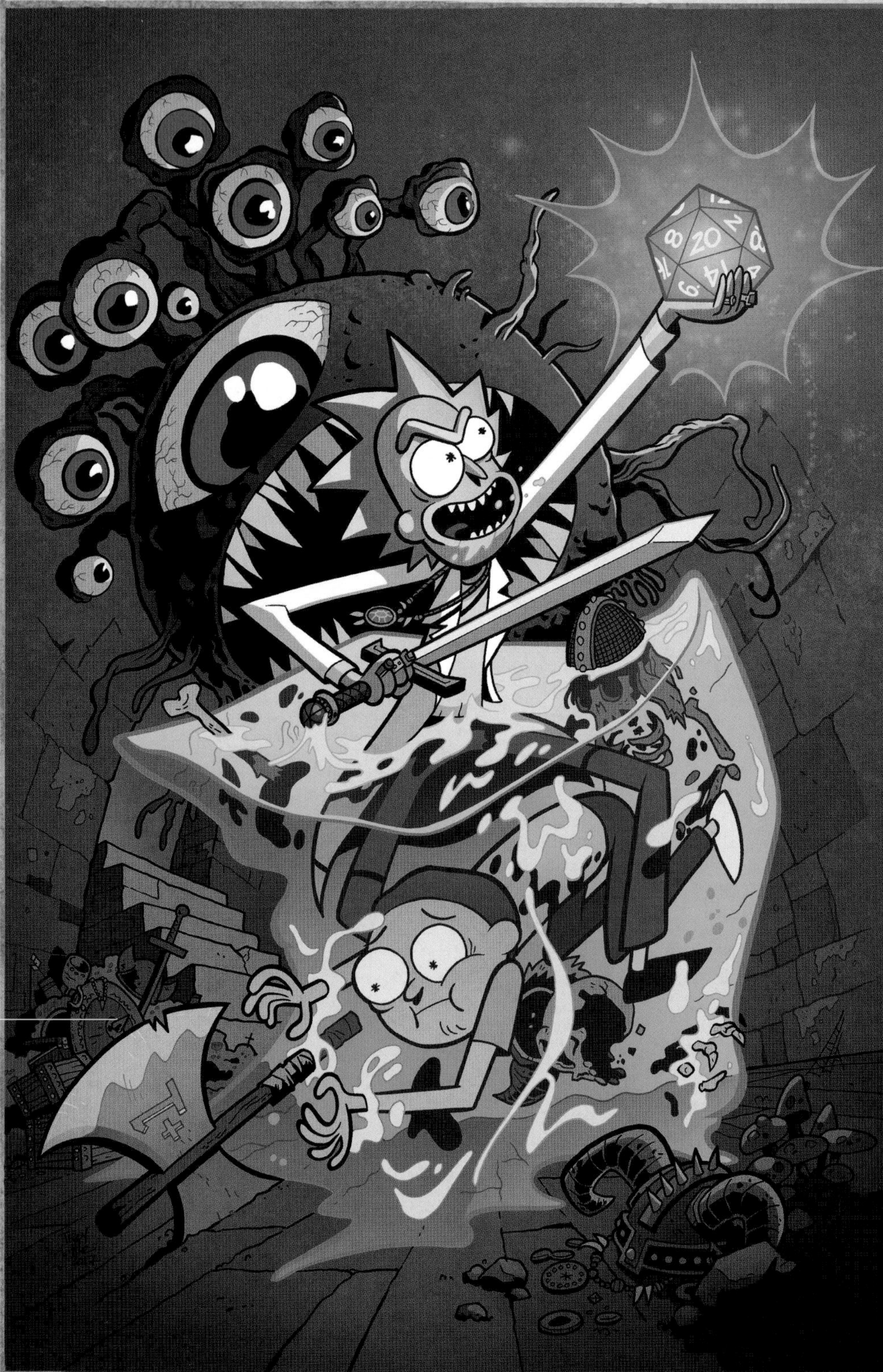

Art by Troy Little

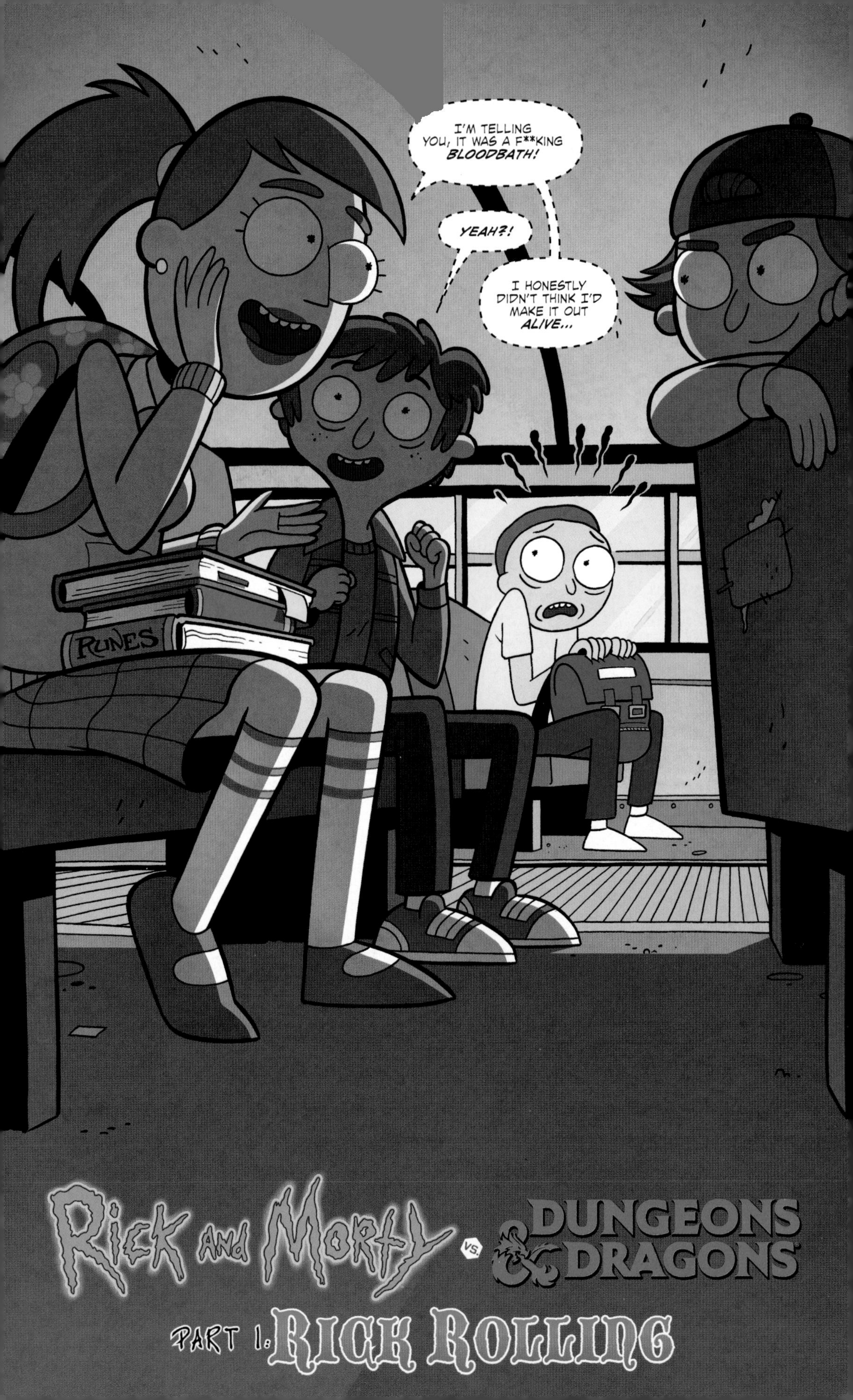

I'M TELLING YOU, IT WAS A F**KING BLOODBATH!
YEAH?!
I HONESTLY DIDN'T THINK I'D MAKE IT OUT ALIVE...
RUNES
RICK AND MORTY VS. DUNGEONS & DRAGONS
PART 1: RICK ROLLING

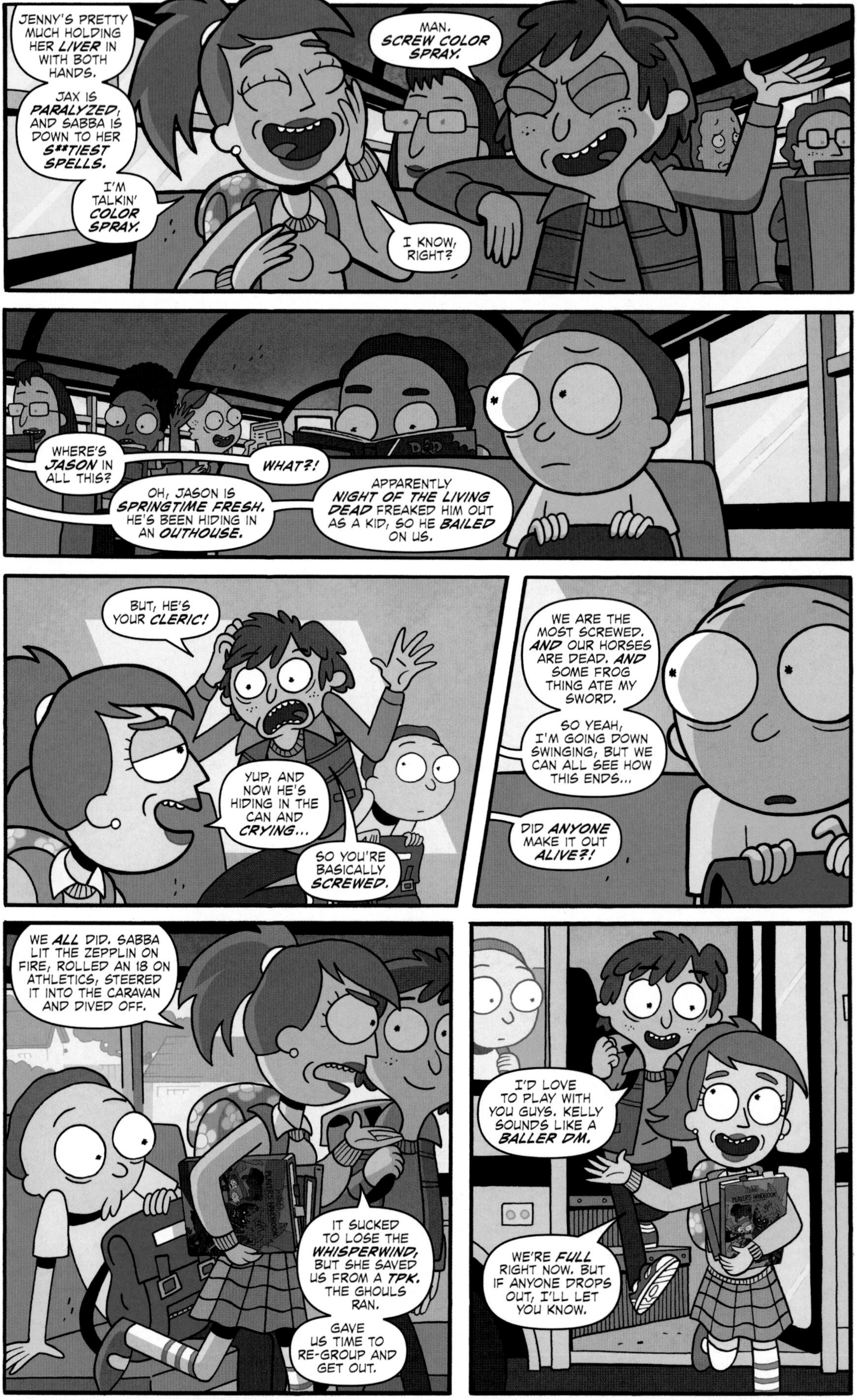
JENNY'S PRETTY MUCH HOLDING HER LIVER IN WITH BOTH HANDS.
JAX IS PARALYZED, AND SABBA IS DOWN TO HER S**TIEST SPELLS.
I'M TALKIN' COLOR SPRAY.
MAN. SCREW COLOR SPRAY.
I KNOW, RIGHT?
WHERE'S JASON IN ALL THIS?
WHAT?!
OH, JASON IS SPRINGTIME FRESH. HE'S BEEN HIDING IN AN OUTHOUSE.
APPARENTLY NIGHT OF THE LIVING DEAD FREAKED HIM OUT AS A KID, SO HE BAILED ON US.
BUT, HE'S YOUR CLERIC!
YUP, AND NOW HE'S HIDING IN THE CAN AND CRYING...
SO YOU'RE BASICALLY SCREWED.
WE ARE THE MOST SCREWED. AND OUR HORSES ARE DEAD. AND SOME FROG THING ATE MY SWORD.
SO YEAH, I'M GOING DOWN SWINGING, BUT WE CAN ALL SEE HOW THIS ENDS...
DID ANYONE MAKE IT OUT ALIVE?!
WE ALL DID. SABBA LIT THE ZEPPLIN ON FIRE, ROLLED AN 18 ON ATHLETICS, STEERED IT INTO THE CARAVAN AND DIVED OFF.
IT SUCKED TO LOSE THE WHISPERWIND, BUT SHE SAVED US FROM A TPK. THE GHOULS RAN.
GAVE US TIME TO RE-GROUP AND GET OUT.
I'D LOVE TO PLAY WITH YOU GUYS. KELLY SOUNDS LIKE A BALLER DM.
WE'RE FULL RIGHT NOW. BUT IF ANYONE DROPS OUT, I'LL LET YOU KNOW.

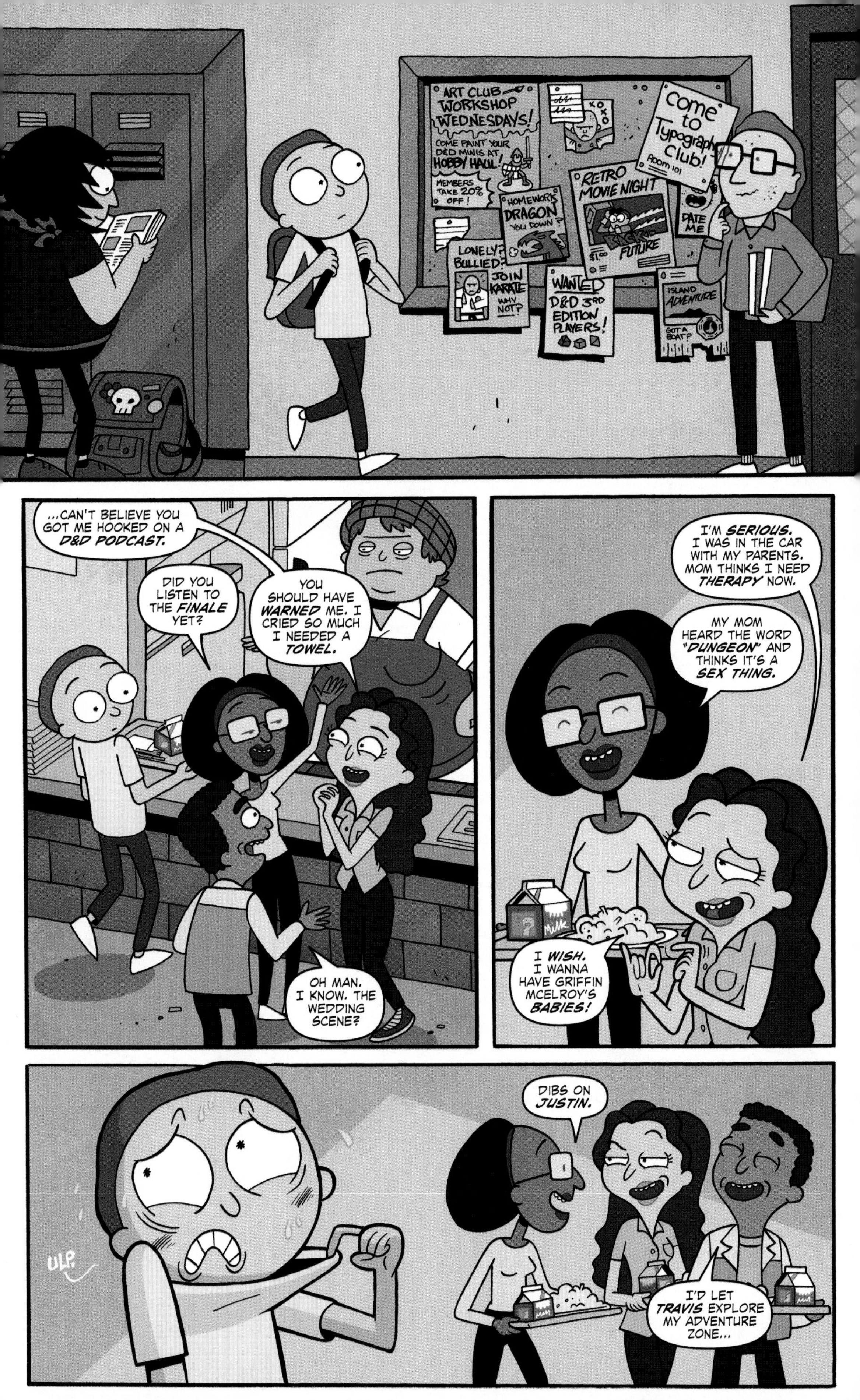
ART CLUB WORKSHOP WEDNESDAYS!
COME PAINT YOUR D&D MINIS AT HOBBY HAUL!
MEMBERS TAKE 20% OFF!
Come to Typography club!
Room 101
RETRO MOVIE NIGHT
$1.00
BACK FUTURE
HOMEWORK DRAGON YOU DOWN?
DATE ME
LONELY? BULLIED?
JOIN KARATE
WHY NOT?
WANTED
D&D 3RD EDITION PLAYERS!
ISLAND ADVENTURE
GOT A BOAT?
...CAN'T BELIEVE YOU GOT ME HOOKED ON A D&D PODCAST.
DID YOU LISTEN TO THE FINALE YET?
YOU SHOULD HAVE WARNED ME. I CRIED SO MUCH I NEEDED A TOWEL.
OH MAN. I KNOW. THE WEDDING SCENE?
I'M SERIOUS. I WAS IN THE CAR WITH MY PARENTS. MOM THINKS I NEED THERAPY NOW.
MY MOM HEARD THE WORD "DUNGEON" AND THINKS IT'S A SEX THING.
I WISH. I WANNA HAVE GRIFFIN MCELROY'S BABIES!
ULP.
DIBS ON JUSTIN.
I'D LET TRAVIS EXPLORE MY ADVENTURE ZONE...

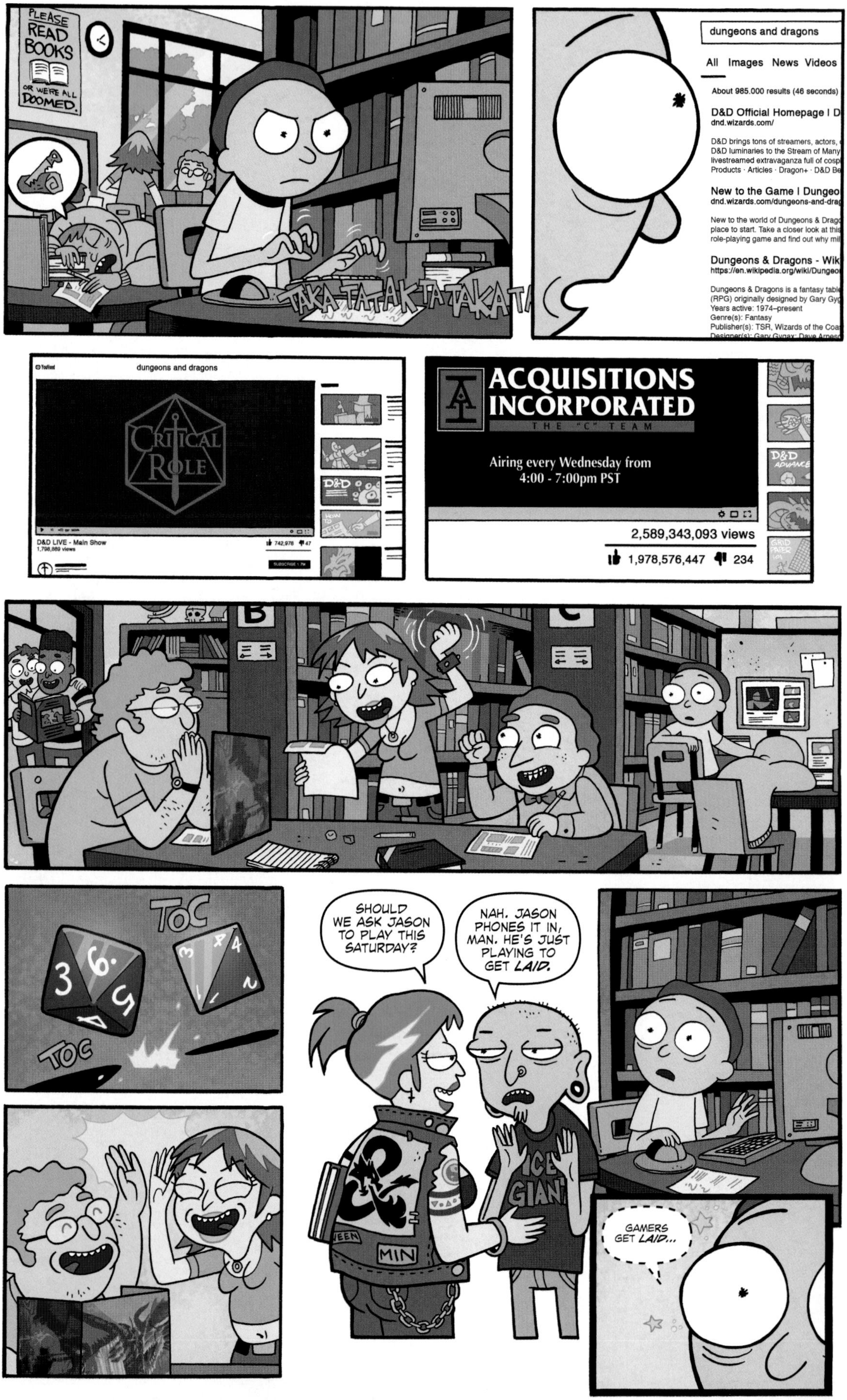

PLEASE READ BOOKS OR WE'RE ALL DOOMED.
TAKA TATAKTA TAKATA
dungeons and dragons
All Images News Videos
About 985.000 results (46 seconds)
D&D Official Homepage I D
dnd.wizards.com/
D&D brings tons of streamers, actors,
D&D luminaries to the Stream of Many
livestreamed extravaganza full of cosp
Products · Articles · Dragon+ · D&D Be
New to the Game I Dungeo
dnd.wizards.com/dungeons-and-drag
New to the world of Dungeons & Drag
place to start. Take a closer look at this
role-playing game and find out why mil
Dungeons & Dragons - Wik
https://en.wikipedia.org/wiki/Dungeo
Dungeons & Dragons is a fantasy tabl
(RPG) originally designed by Gary Gyg
Years active: 1974–present
Genre(s): Fantasy
Publisher(s): TSR, Wizards of the Coa
dungeons and dragons
CRITICAL ROLE
D&D LIVE - Main Show
1,798,889 views
742,978
47
ACQUISITIONS INCORPORATED
THE "C" TEAM
Airing every Wednesday from 4:00 - 7:00pm PST
2,589,343,093 views
1,978,576,447
234
D&D ADVANCE
GRID PAPER
B
C
TOC
TOC
SHOULD WE ASK JASON TO PLAY THIS SATURDAY?
NAH. JASON PHONES IT IN, MAN. HE'S JUST PLAYING TO GET *LAID.*
ICE GIANT
MIN
GAMERS GET *LAID...*

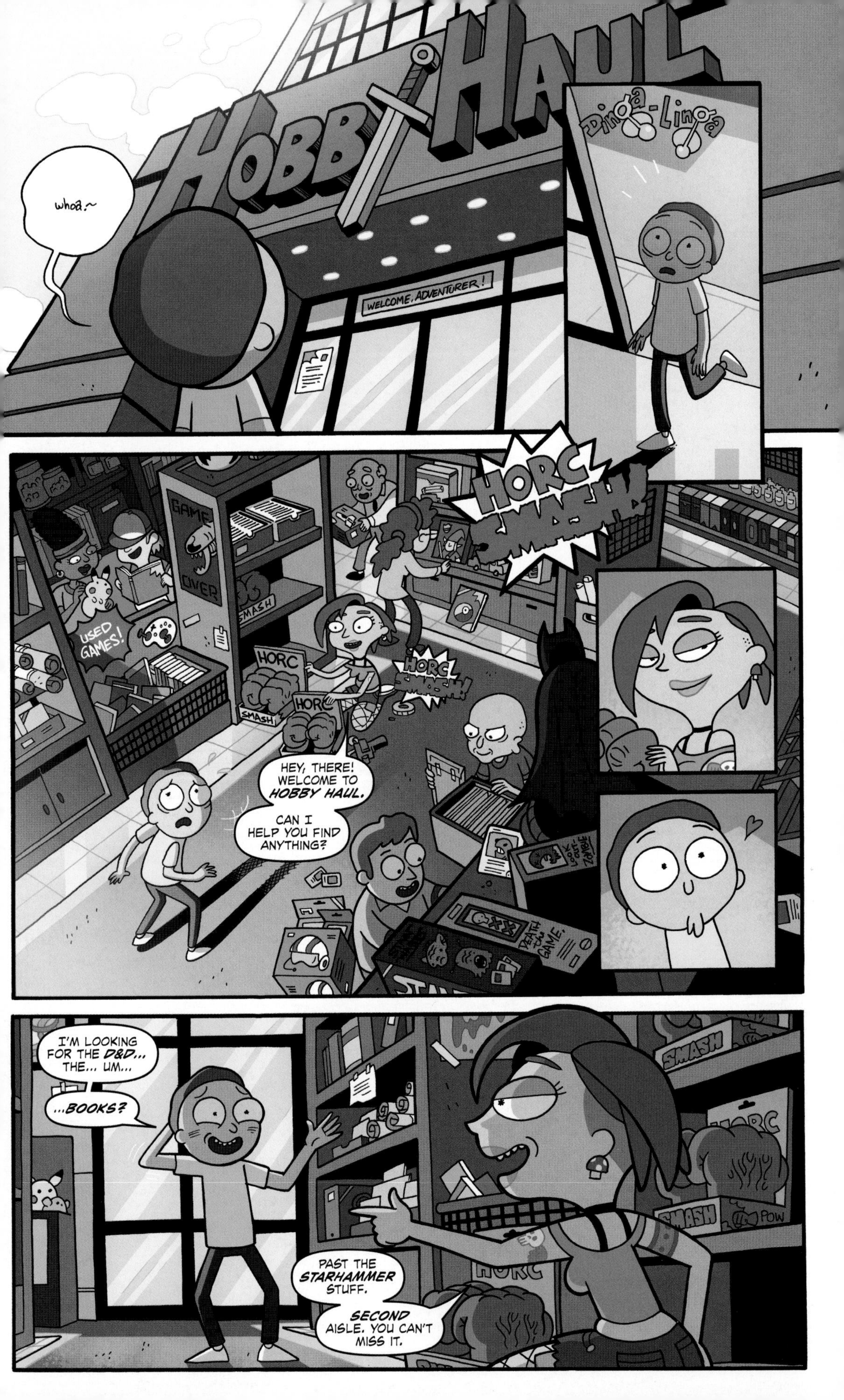
HOBBY HAUL
whoa.~
WELCOME, ADVENTURER!
Dinga-Linga
HORC SMASH!!
GAME OVER
USED GAMES!
HORC
SMASH
HORC SMASH!
HEY, THERE! WELCOME TO HOBBY HAUL.
CAN I HELP YOU FIND ANYTHING?
LOOK OUT ZOMBIE
DEATH GAME.
I'M LOOKING FOR THE D&D... THE... UM...
...BOOKS?
SMASH
HORC
SMASH
POW
PAST THE STARHAMMER STUFF.
SECOND AISLE. YOU CAN'T MISS IT.

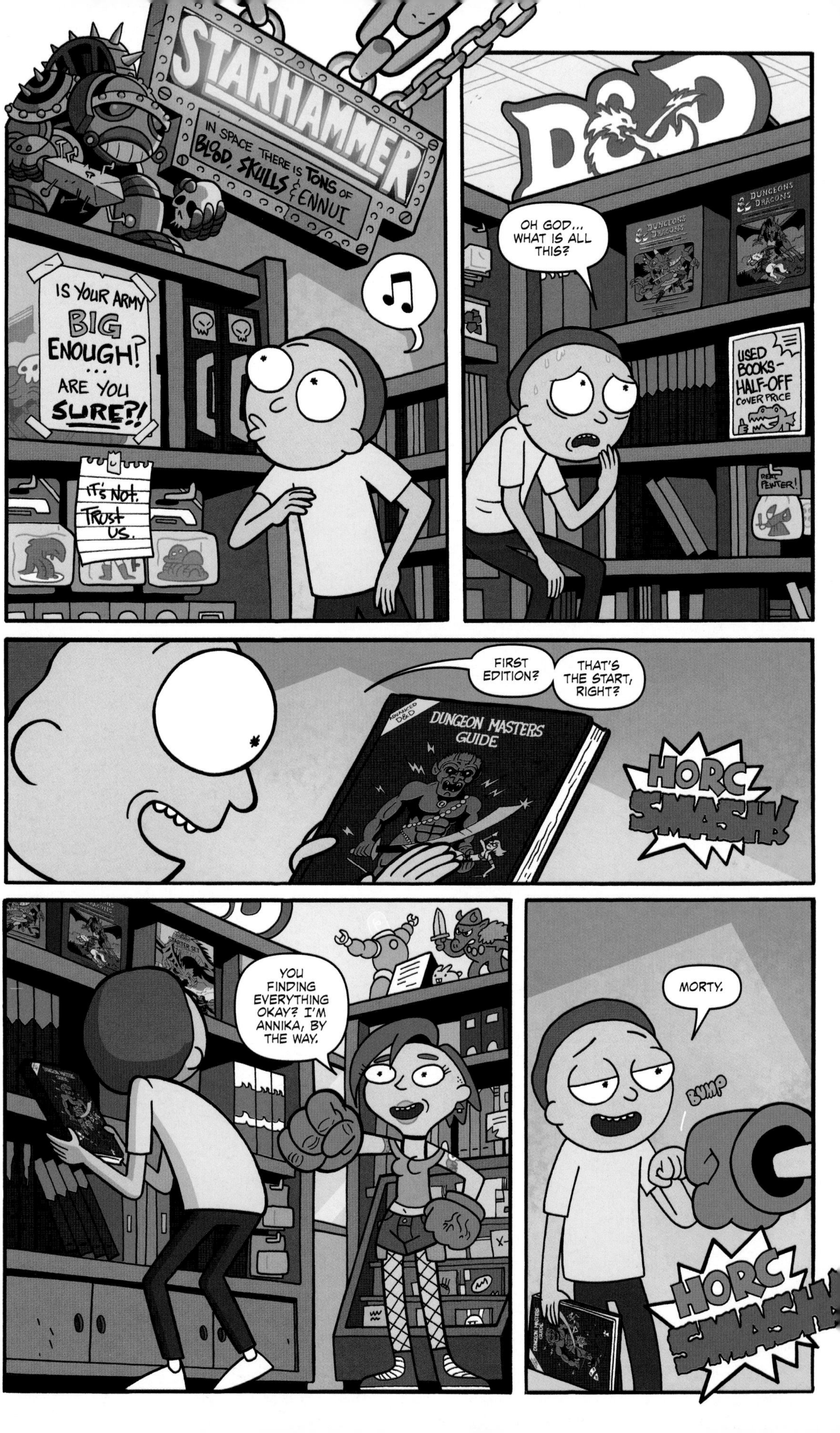
STARHAMMER
IN SPACE THERE IS TONS OF BLOOD, SKULLS & ENNUI
IS YOUR ARMY BIG ENOUGH? ... ARE YOU SURE?!
IT'S NOT. TRUST US.
♫
OH GOD... WHAT IS ALL THIS?
USED BOOKS - HALF-OFF COVER PRICE
REAL PEWTER!
FIRST EDITION?
THAT'S THE START, RIGHT?
DUNGEON MASTERS GUIDE
HORC SMASH!
YOU FINDING EVERYTHING OKAY? I'M ANNIKA, BY THE WAY.
MORTY.
BUMP
HORC SMASH!

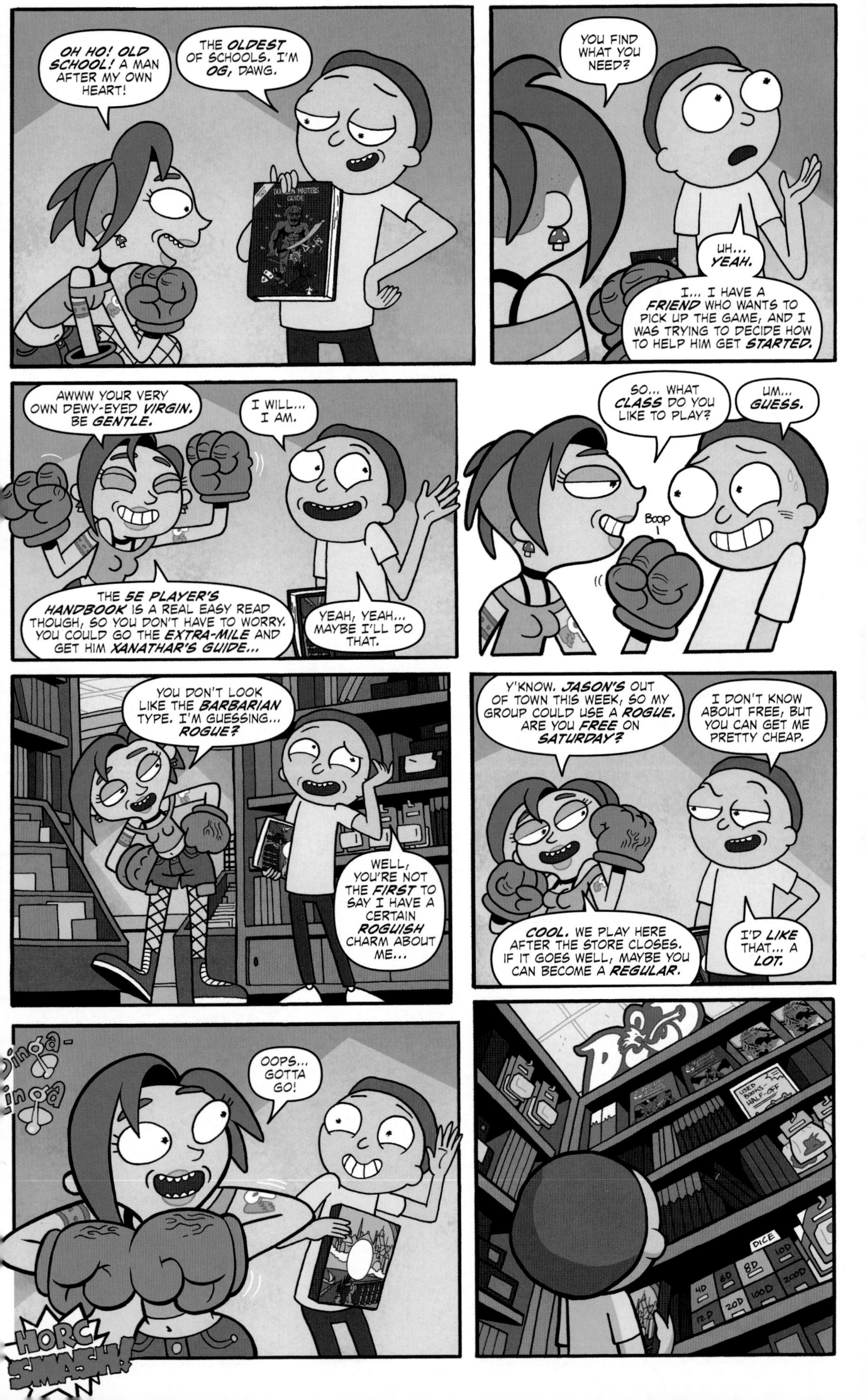

OH HO! OLD SCHOOL! A MAN AFTER MY OWN HEART!
THE OLDEST OF SCHOOLS. I'M OG, DAWG.
DUNGEON MASTERS GUIDE
YOU FIND WHAT YOU NEED?
UH... YEAH.
I... I HAVE A FRIEND WHO WANTS TO PICK UP THE GAME, AND I WAS TRYING TO DECIDE HOW TO HELP HIM GET STARTED.
AWWW YOUR VERY OWN DEWY-EYED VIRGIN. BE GENTLE.
I WILL... I AM.
THE 5E PLAYER'S HANDBOOK IS A REAL EASY READ THOUGH, SO YOU DON'T HAVE TO WORRY. YOU COULD GO THE EXTRA-MILE AND GET HIM XANATHAR'S GUIDE...
YEAH, YEAH... MAYBE I'LL DO THAT.
SO... WHAT CLASS DO YOU LIKE TO PLAY?
UM... GUESS.
BOOP
YOU DON'T LOOK LIKE THE BARBARIAN TYPE. I'M GUESSING... ROGUE?
WELL, YOU'RE NOT THE FIRST TO SAY I HAVE A CERTAIN ROGUISH CHARM ABOUT ME...
Y'KNOW. JASON'S OUT OF TOWN THIS WEEK, SO MY GROUP COULD USE A ROGUE. ARE YOU FREE ON SATURDAY?
I DON'T KNOW ABOUT FREE, BUT YOU CAN GET ME PRETTY CHEAP.
COOL. WE PLAY HERE AFTER THE STORE CLOSES. IF IT GOES WELL, MAYBE YOU CAN BECOME A REGULAR.
I'D LIKE THAT... A LOT.
OOPS... GOTTA GO!
HORC SMASH!
USED BOOKS-HALF-OFF
DICE
4D
6D
8D
10D
12D
20D
100D
200D

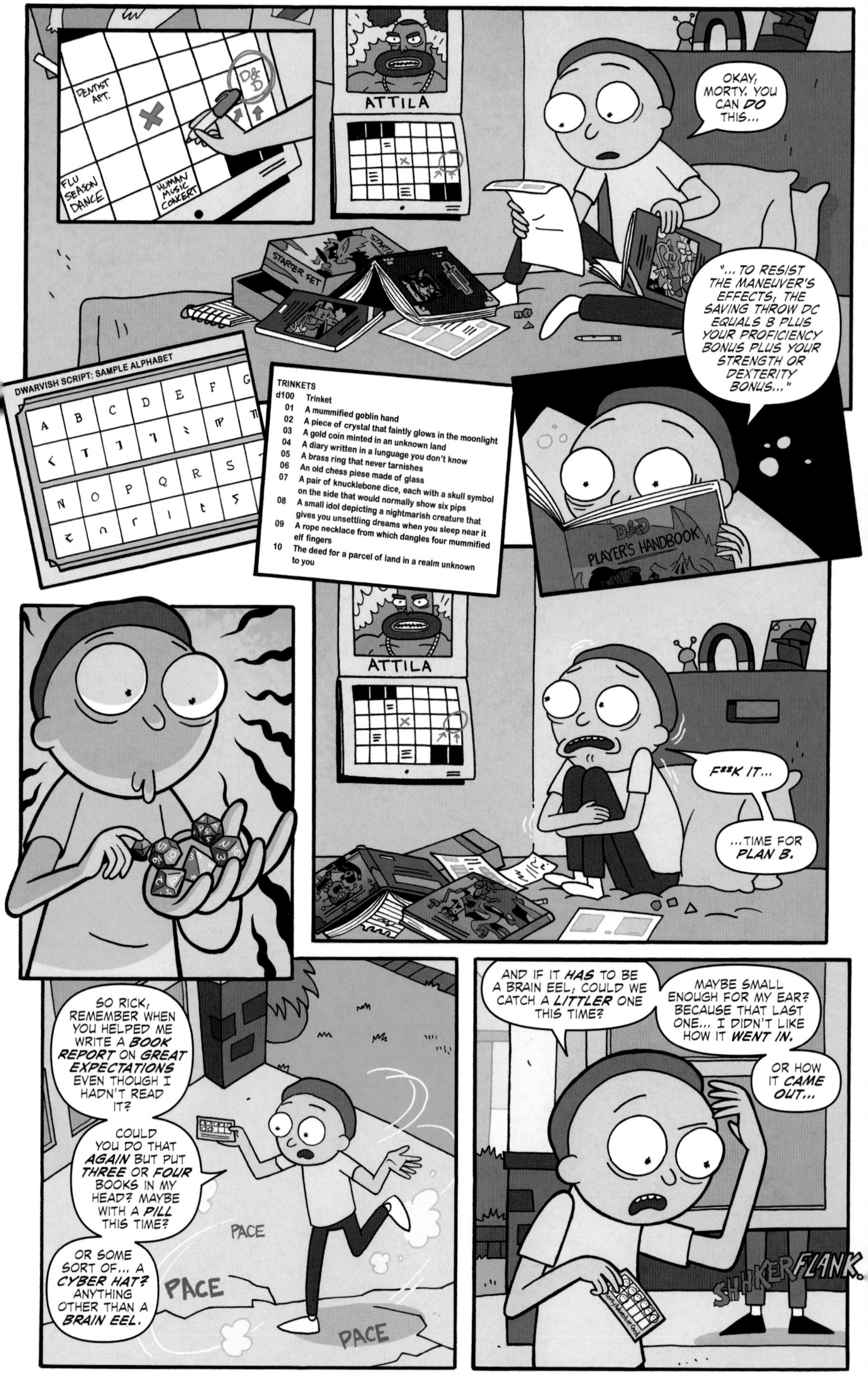
DENTIST APT.
D&D
FLU SEASON DANCE
HUMAN MUSIC CONCERT
ATTILA
OKAY, MORTY. YOU CAN *DO* THIS...
STARTER SET
"...TO RESIST THE MANEUVER'S EFFECTS, THE SAVING THROW DC EQUALS 8 PLUS YOUR PROFICIENCY BONUS PLUS YOUR STRENGTH OR DEXTERITY BONUS..."
DWARVISH SCRIPT: SAMPLE ALPHABET
A B C D E F G
N O P Q R S
TRINKETS
d100 Trinket
01 A mummified goblin hand
02 A piece of crystal that faintly glows in the moonlight
03 A gold coin minted in an unknown land
04 A diary written in a lunguage you don't know
05 A brass ring that never tarnishes
06 An old chess piese made of glass
07 A pair of knucklebone dice, each with a skull symbol on the side that would normally show six pips
08 A small idol depicting a nightmarish creature that gives you unsettling dreams when you sleep near it
09 A rope necklace from which dangles four mummified elf fingers
10 The deed for a parcel of land in a realm unknown to you
D&D PLAYER'S HANDBOOK
ATTILA
F**K IT...
...TIME FOR *PLAN B.*
SO RICK, REMEMBER WHEN YOU HELPED ME WRITE A *BOOK REPORT* ON *GREAT EXPECTATIONS* EVEN THOUGH I HADN'T READ IT?
COULD YOU DO THAT *AGAIN* BUT PUT *THREE* OR *FOUR* BOOKS IN MY HEAD? MAYBE WITH A *PILL* THIS TIME?
OR SOME SORT OF... A *CYBER HAT?* ANYTHING OTHER THAN A *BRAIN EEL.*
PACE
PACE
PACE
AND IF IT *HAS* TO BE A BRAIN EEL, COULD WE CATCH A *LITTLER* ONE THIS TIME?
MAYBE SMALL ENOUGH FOR MY EAR? BECAUSE THAT LAST ONE... I DIDN'T LIKE HOW IT *WENT IN.*
OR HOW IT *CAME OUT...*
SHHKERFLANK.

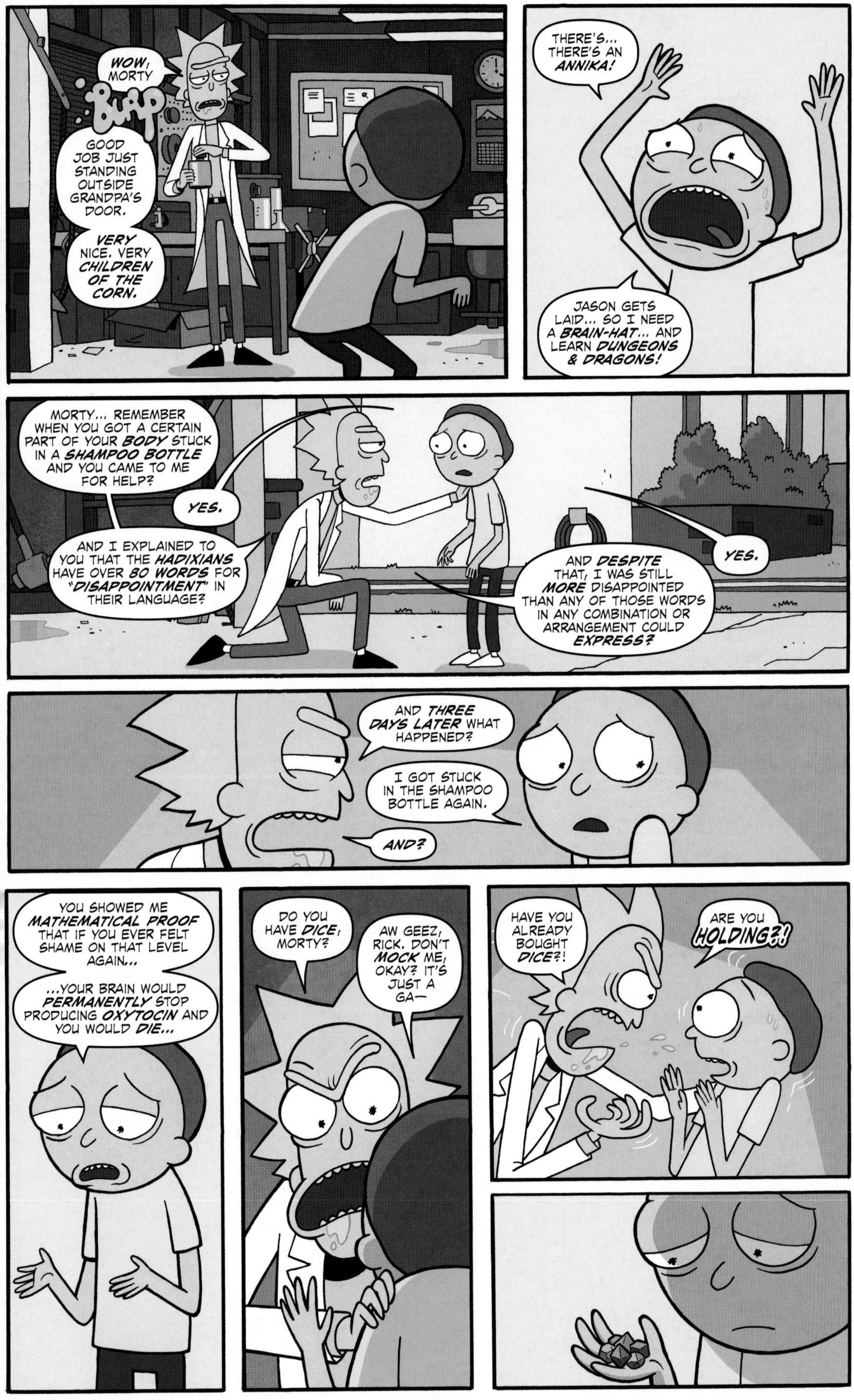
WOW, MORTY
BURP
GOOD JOB JUST STANDING OUTSIDE GRANDPA'S DOOR.
VERY NICE. VERY CHILDREN OF THE CORN.
THERE'S... THERE'S AN ANNIKA!
JASON GETS LAID... SO I NEED A BRAIN-HAT... AND LEARN DUNGEONS & DRAGONS!
MORTY... REMEMBER WHEN YOU GOT A CERTAIN PART OF YOUR BODY STUCK IN A SHAMPOO BOTTLE AND YOU CAME TO ME FOR HELP?
YES.
AND I EXPLAINED TO YOU THAT THE HADIXIANS HAVE OVER 80 WORDS FOR "DISAPPOINTMENT" IN THEIR LANGUAGE?
YES.
AND DESPITE THAT, I WAS STILL MORE DISAPPOINTED THAN ANY OF THOSE WORDS IN ANY COMBINATION OR ARRANGEMENT COULD EXPRESS?
AND THREE DAYS LATER WHAT HAPPENED?
I GOT STUCK IN THE SHAMPOO BOTTLE AGAIN.
AND?
YOU SHOWED ME MATHEMATICAL PROOF THAT IF YOU EVER FELT SHAME ON THAT LEVEL AGAIN...
...YOUR BRAIN WOULD PERMANENTLY STOP PRODUCING OXYTOCIN AND YOU WOULD DIE...
DO YOU HAVE DICE, MORTY?
AW GEEZ, RICK. DON'T MOCK ME, OKAY? IT'S JUST A GA—
HAVE YOU ALREADY BOUGHT DICE?!
ARE YOU HOLDING?!

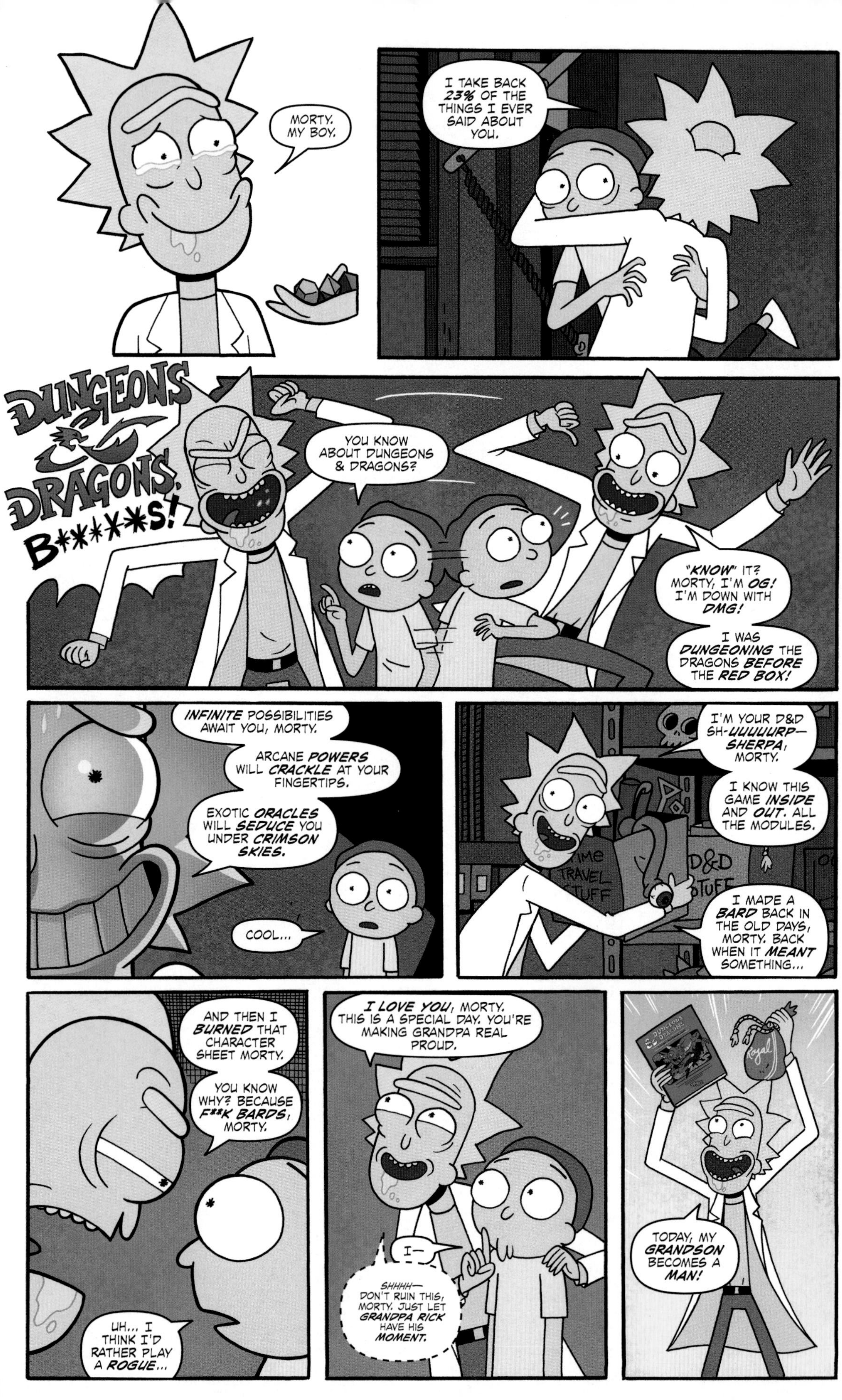
MORTY. MY BOY.
I TAKE BACK 23% OF THE THINGS I EVER SAID ABOUT YOU.
DUNGEONS & DRAGONS, B*****S!
YOU KNOW ABOUT DUNGEONS & DRAGONS?
"KNOW" IT? MORTY, I'M OG! I'M DOWN WITH DMG!
I WAS DUNGEONING THE DRAGONS BEFORE THE RED BOX!
INFINITE POSSIBILITIES AWAIT YOU, MORTY.
ARCANE POWERS WILL CRACKLE AT YOUR FINGERTIPS.
EXOTIC ORACLES WILL SEDUCE YOU UNDER CRIMSON SKIES.
COOL...
I'M YOUR D&D SH-UUUUURP—SHERPA, MORTY.
I KNOW THIS GAME INSIDE AND OUT. ALL THE MODULES.
TIME TRAVEL STUFF
D&D STUFF
I MADE A BARD BACK IN THE OLD DAYS, MORTY. BACK WHEN IT MEANT SOMETHING...
AND THEN I BURNED THAT CHARACTER SHEET MORTY.
YOU KNOW WHY? BECAUSE F**K BARDS, MORTY.
UH... I THINK I'D RATHER PLAY A ROGUE...
I LOVE YOU, MORTY. THIS IS A SPECIAL DAY. YOU'RE MAKING GRANDPA REAL PROUD.
I—
SHHHH— DON'T RUIN THIS, MORTY. JUST LET GRANDPA RICK HAVE HIS MOMENT.
DUNGEONS & DRAGONS
Royal
TODAY, MY GRANDSON BECOMES A MAN!

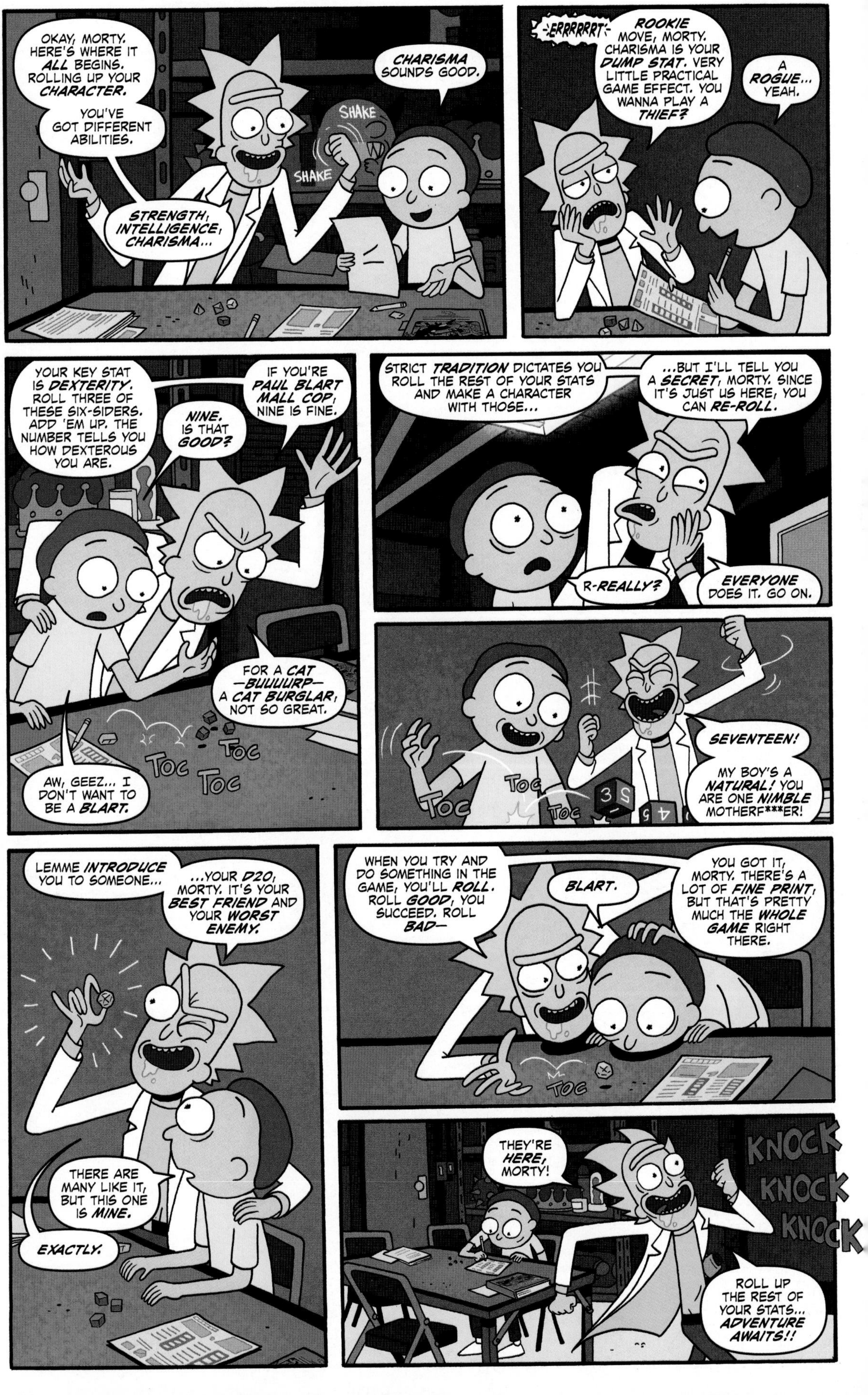
OKAY, MORTY. HERE'S WHERE IT ALL BEGINS. ROLLING UP YOUR CHARACTER.
YOU'VE GOT DIFFERENT ABILITIES.
STRENGTH, INTELLIGENCE, CHARISMA...
SHAKE
SHAKE
CHARISMA SOUNDS GOOD.
-ERRRRRRT-
ROOKIE MOVE, MORTY. CHARISMA IS YOUR DUMP STAT. VERY LITTLE PRACTICAL GAME EFFECT. YOU WANNA PLAY A THIEF?
A ROGUE... YEAH.
YOUR KEY STAT IS DEXTERITY. ROLL THREE OF THESE SIX-SIDERS. ADD 'EM UP. THE NUMBER TELLS YOU HOW DEXTEROUS YOU ARE.
NINE. IS THAT GOOD?
IF YOU'RE PAUL BLART MALL COP, NINE IS FINE.
FOR A CAT —BUUUURP— A CAT BURGLAR, NOT SO GREAT.
TOC
TOC
TOC
AW, GEEZ... I DON'T WANT TO BE A BLART.
STRICT TRADITION DICTATES YOU ROLL THE REST OF YOUR STATS AND MAKE A CHARACTER WITH THOSE...
...BUT I'LL TELL YOU A SECRET, MORTY. SINCE IT'S JUST US HERE, YOU CAN RE-ROLL.
R-REALLY?
EVERYONE DOES IT. GO ON.
TOC
TOC
TOC
SEVENTEEN!
MY BOY'S A NATURAL! YOU ARE ONE NIMBLE MOTHERF***ER!
LEMME INTRODUCE YOU TO SOMEONE...
...YOUR D20, MORTY. IT'S YOUR BEST FRIEND AND YOUR WORST ENEMY.
THERE ARE MANY LIKE IT, BUT THIS ONE IS MINE.
EXACTLY.
WHEN YOU TRY AND DO SOMETHING IN THE GAME, YOU'LL ROLL. ROLL GOOD, YOU SUCCEED. ROLL BAD—
BLART.
YOU GOT IT, MORTY. THERE'S A LOT OF FINE PRINT, BUT THAT'S PRETTY MUCH THE WHOLE GAME RIGHT THERE.
TOC
THEY'RE HERE, MORTY!
KNOCK
KNOCK
KNOCK
ROLL UP THE REST OF YOUR STATS... ADVENTURE AWAITS!!

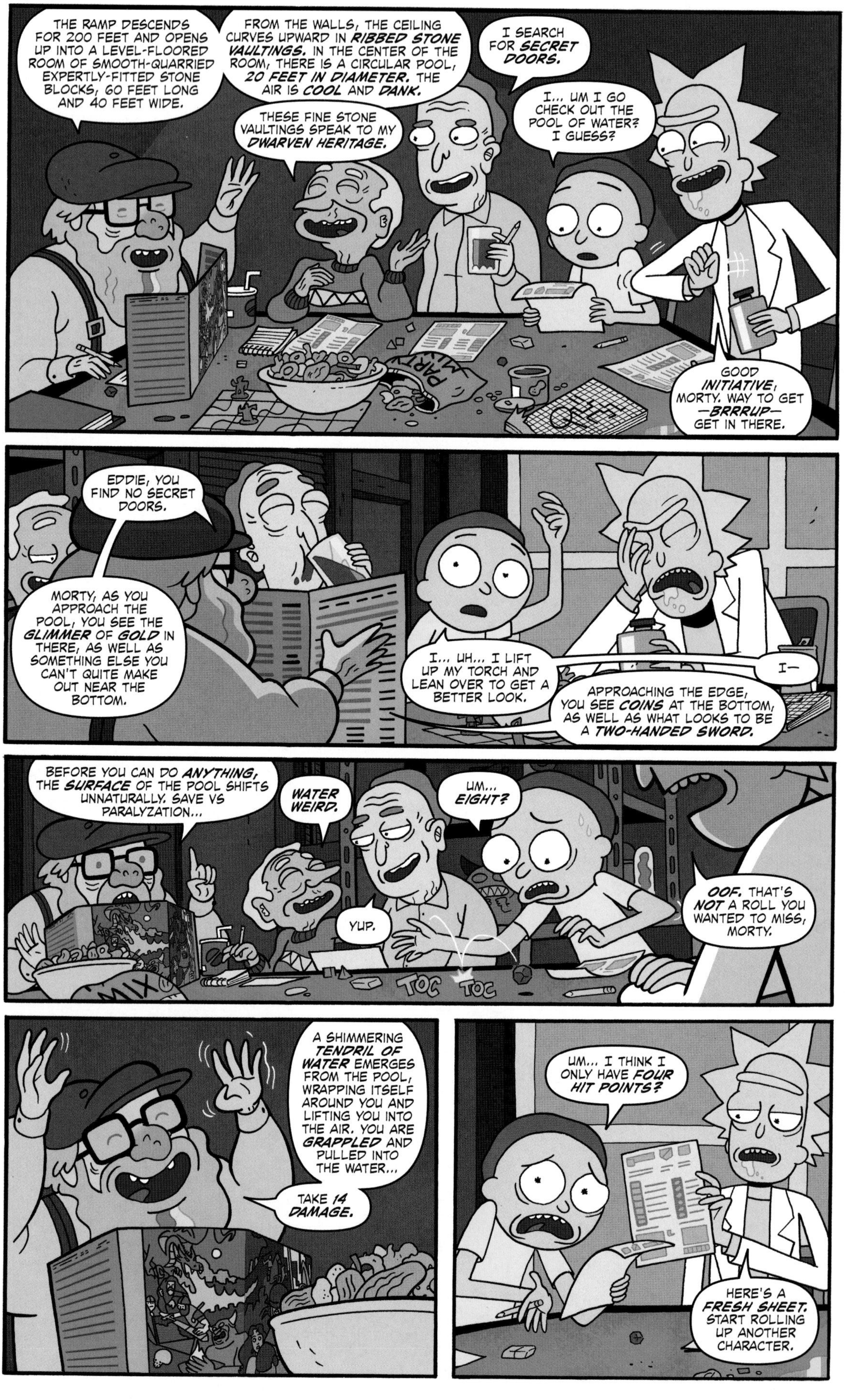
THE RAMP DESCENDS FOR 200 FEET AND OPENS UP INTO A LEVEL-FLOORED ROOM OF SMOOTH-QUARRIED EXPERTLY-FITTED STONE BLOCKS, 60 FEET LONG AND 40 FEET WIDE.
FROM THE WALLS, THE CEILING CURVES UPWARD IN RIBBED STONE VAULTINGS. IN THE CENTER OF THE ROOM, THERE IS A CIRCULAR POOL, 20 FEET IN DIAMETER. THE AIR IS COOL AND DANK.
THESE FINE STONE VAULTINGS SPEAK TO MY DWARVEN HERITAGE.
I SEARCH FOR SECRET DOORS.
I... UM I GO CHECK OUT THE POOL OF WATER? I GUESS?
GOOD INITIATIVE, MORTY. WAY TO GET —BRRRUP— GET IN THERE.
PARTY MIX
EDDIE, YOU FIND NO SECRET DOORS.
MORTY, AS YOU APPROACH THE POOL, YOU SEE THE GLIMMER OF GOLD IN THERE, AS WELL AS SOMETHING ELSE YOU CAN'T QUITE MAKE OUT NEAR THE BOTTOM.
I... UH... I LIFT UP MY TORCH AND LEAN OVER TO GET A BETTER LOOK.
I—
APPROACHING THE EDGE, YOU SEE COINS AT THE BOTTOM, AS WELL AS WHAT LOOKS TO BE A TWO-HANDED SWORD.
BEFORE YOU CAN DO ANYTHING, THE SURFACE OF THE POOL SHIFTS UNNATURALLY. SAVE VS PARALYZATION...
WATER WEIRD.
UM... EIGHT?
YUP.
OOF. THAT'S NOT A ROLL YOU WANTED TO MISS, MORTY.
TOC TOC
MIX
A SHIMMERING TENDRIL OF WATER EMERGES FROM THE POOL, WRAPPING ITSELF AROUND YOU AND LIFTING YOU INTO THE AIR. YOU ARE GRAPPLED AND PULLED INTO THE WATER...
TAKE 14 DAMAGE.
UM... I THINK I ONLY HAVE FOUR HIT POINTS?
HERE'S A FRESH SHEET. START ROLLING UP ANOTHER CHARACTER.

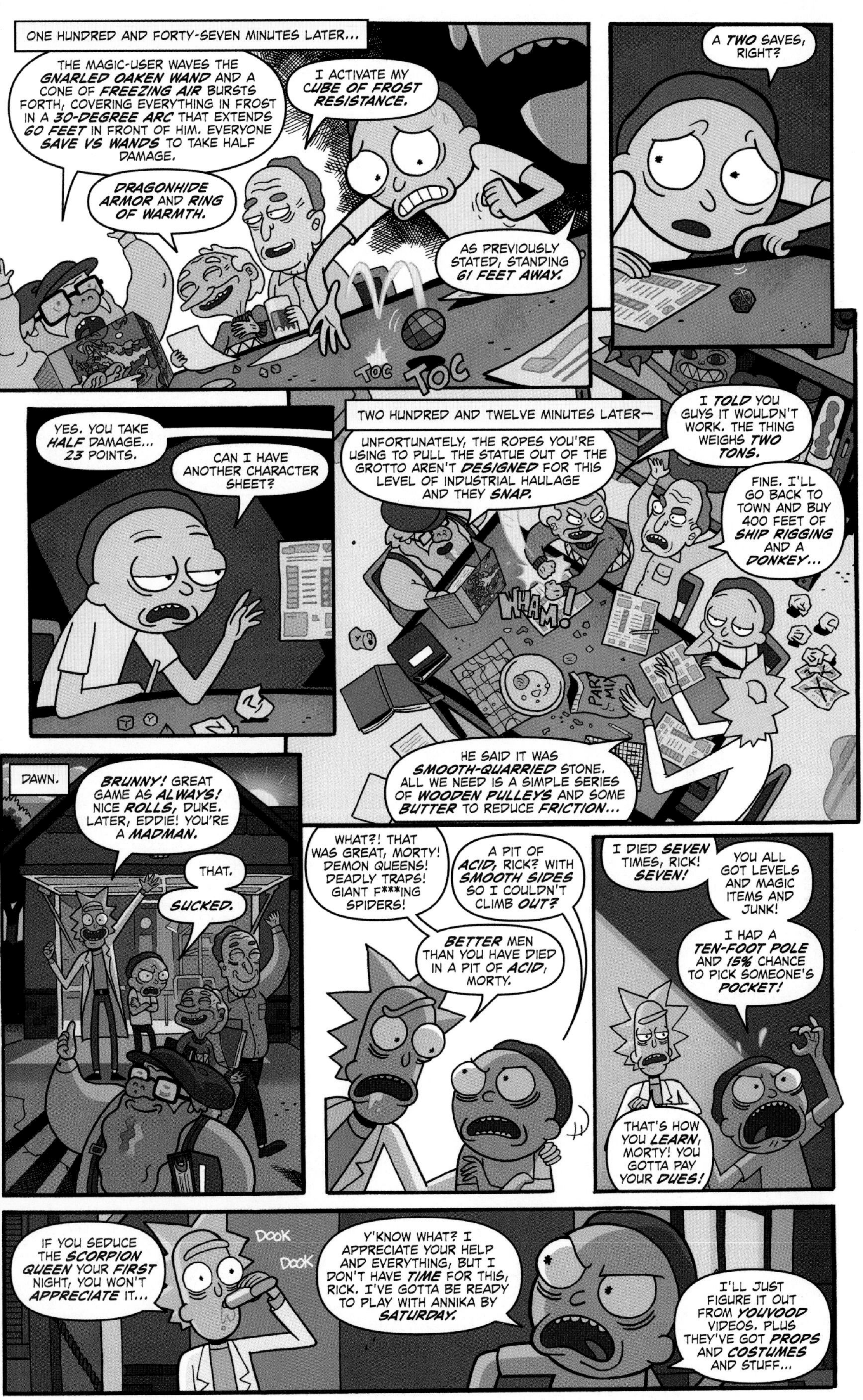

ONE HUNDRED AND FORTY-SEVEN MINUTES LATER...
THE MAGIC-USER WAVES THE GNARLED OAKEN WAND AND A CONE OF FREEZING AIR BURSTS FORTH, COVERING EVERYTHING IN FROST IN A 30-DEGREE ARC THAT EXTENDS 60 FEET IN FRONT OF HIM. EVERYONE SAVE VS WANDS TO TAKE HALF DAMAGE.
I ACTIVATE MY CUBE OF FROST RESISTANCE.
DRAGONHIDE ARMOR AND RING OF WARMTH.
AS PREVIOUSLY STATED, STANDING 61 FEET AWAY.
TOC
TOC
A TWO SAVES, RIGHT?
YES. YOU TAKE HALF DAMAGE... 23 POINTS.
CAN I HAVE ANOTHER CHARACTER SHEET?
TWO HUNDRED AND TWELVE MINUTES LATER—
UNFORTUNATELY, THE ROPES YOU'RE USING TO PULL THE STATUE OUT OF THE GROTTO AREN'T DESIGNED FOR THIS LEVEL OF INDUSTRIAL HAULAGE AND THEY SNAP.
I TOLD YOU GUYS IT WOULDN'T WORK. THE THING WEIGHS TWO TONS.
FINE. I'LL GO BACK TO TOWN AND BUY 400 FEET OF SHIP RIGGING AND A DONKEY...
WHAM!
HE SAID IT WAS SMOOTH-QUARRIED STONE. ALL WE NEED IS A SIMPLE SERIES OF WOODEN PULLEYS AND SOME BUTTER TO REDUCE FRICTION...
DAWN.
BRUNNY! GREAT GAME AS ALWAYS! NICE ROLLS, DUKE. LATER, EDDIE! YOU'RE A MADMAN.
THAT.
SUCKED.
WHAT?! THAT WAS GREAT, MORTY! DEMON QUEENS! DEADLY TRAPS! GIANT F***ING SPIDERS!
A PIT OF ACID, RICK? WITH SMOOTH SIDES SO I COULDN'T CLIMB OUT?
BETTER MEN THAN YOU HAVE DIED IN A PIT OF ACID, MORTY.
I DIED SEVEN TIMES, RICK! SEVEN!
YOU ALL GOT LEVELS AND MAGIC ITEMS AND JUNK!
I HAD A TEN-FOOT POLE AND 15% CHANCE TO PICK SOMEONE'S POCKET!
THAT'S HOW YOU LEARN, MORTY! YOU GOTTA PAY YOUR DUES!
IF YOU SEDUCE THE SCORPION QUEEN YOUR FIRST NIGHT, YOU WON'T APPRECIATE IT...
DOOK
DOOK
Y'KNOW WHAT? I APPRECIATE YOUR HELP AND EVERYTHING, BUT I DON'T HAVE TIME FOR THIS, RICK. I'VE GOTTA BE READY TO PLAY WITH ANNIKA BY SATURDAY.
I'LL JUST FIGURE IT OUT FROM YOUVOOD VIDEOS. PLUS THEY'VE GOT PROPS AND COSTUMES AND STUFF...

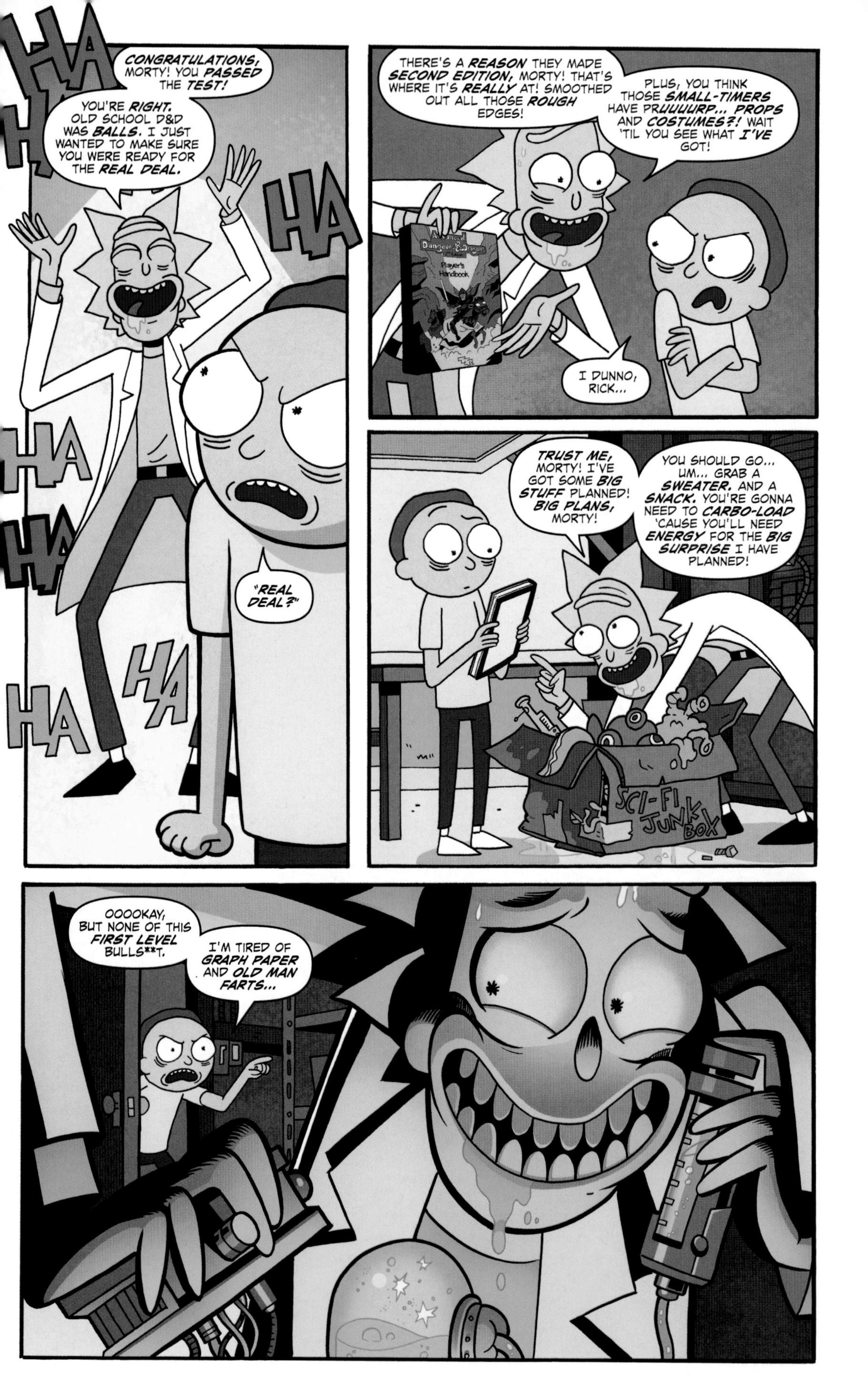

HA HA
CONGRATULATIONS, MORTY! YOU PASSED THE TEST!
YOU'RE RIGHT. OLD SCHOOL D&D WAS BALLS. I JUST WANTED TO MAKE SURE YOU WERE READY FOR THE REAL DEAL.
HA
HA
HA
"REAL DEAL?"
HA HA
THERE'S A REASON THEY MADE SECOND EDITION, MORTY! THAT'S WHERE IT'S REALLY AT! SMOOTHED OUT ALL THOSE ROUGH EDGES!
PLUS, YOU THINK THOSE SMALL-TIMERS HAVE PRUUUURP... PROPS AND COSTUMES?! WAIT 'TIL YOU SEE WHAT I'VE GOT!
Player's Handbook
I DUNNO, RICK...
TRUST ME, MORTY! I'VE GOT SOME BIG STUFF PLANNED! BIG PLANS, MORTY!
YOU SHOULD GO... UM... GRAB A SWEATER. AND A SNACK. YOU'RE GONNA NEED TO CARBO-LOAD 'CAUSE YOU'LL NEED ENERGY FOR THE BIG SURPRISE I HAVE PLANNED!
SCI-FI JUNK BOX
OOOOKAY, BUT NONE OF THIS FIRST LEVEL BULLS**T.
I'M TIRED OF GRAPH PAPER AND OLD MAN FARTS...

12 MINUTES LATER.

YOU *READY*, MORTY? YOU ALL *SANDWICHED* UP?

WHATEVER, RICK.

YOU'RE TAKING US TO *BLIPS AND CHITZ?*

NO MORTY, I'M TAKING YOU TO THE *MAGICAL LAND* OF *GREYHAWK.*

ARE WE GOING TO PLAY A GAME *INSIDE* A GAME? THAT'S A LITTLE META EVEN FOR US, ISN'T IT?

YOU WANTED *PROPS*, MORTY? *COSTUMES?* I'M GONNA GIVE YOU AN *ENTIRE WORLD!*

REALER THAN *REAL!*

ROY
A LIFE WELL LIVED

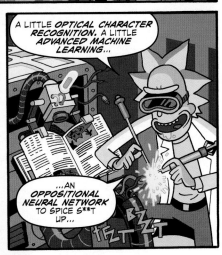

A LITTLE *OPTICAL CHARACTER RECOGNITION.* A LITTLE *ADVANCED MACHINE LEARNING...*

...AN *OPPOSITIONAL NEURAL NETWORK* TO SPICE S**T UP...

SHOULD WE BE DOING THIS, RICK?

MORTY, ONCE YOU ACCEPT THE EVENTUAL AND UNAVOIDABLE *HEAT-DEATH* OF THE *UNIVERSE...*

...YOU'D BE SURPRISED HOW *UNIMPORTANT* THE CONCEPT OF *"SHOULD"* BECOMES—

IT'S TIME TO *ROLL!*

AW GEEEE—

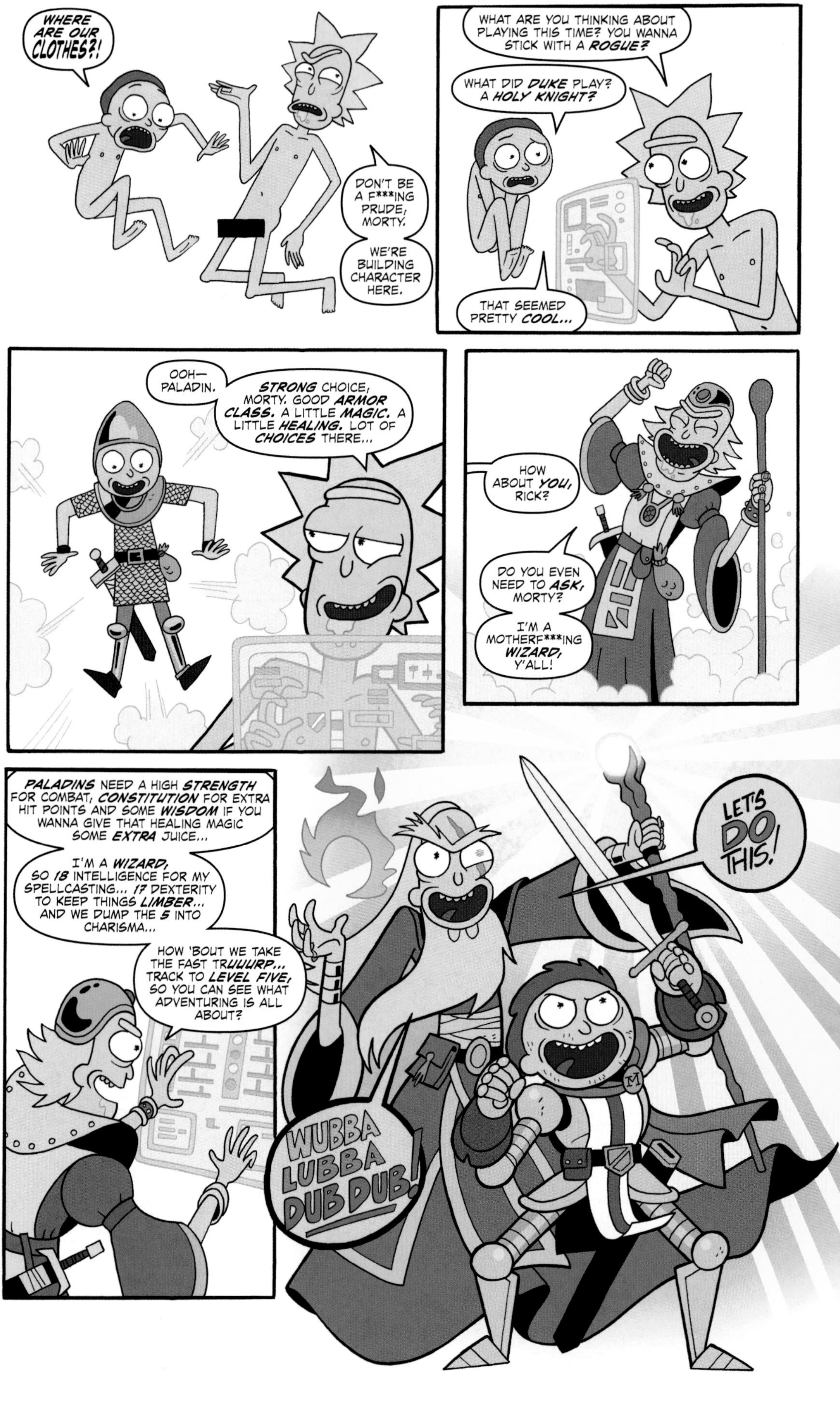
WHERE ARE OUR CLOTHES?!
DON'T BE A F***ING PRUDE, MORTY.
WE'RE BUILDING CHARACTER HERE.
WHAT ARE YOU THINKING ABOUT PLAYING THIS TIME? YOU WANNA STICK WITH A ROGUE?
WHAT DID DUKE PLAY? A HOLY KNIGHT?
THAT SEEMED PRETTY COOL...
OOH— PALADIN.
STRONG CHOICE, MORTY. GOOD ARMOR CLASS. A LITTLE MAGIC. A LITTLE HEALING. LOT OF CHOICES THERE...
HOW ABOUT YOU, RICK?
DO YOU EVEN NEED TO ASK, MORTY?
I'M A MOTHERF***ING WIZARD, Y'ALL!
PALADINS NEED A HIGH STRENGTH FOR COMBAT, CONSTITUTION FOR EXTRA HIT POINTS AND SOME WISDOM IF YOU WANNA GIVE THAT HEALING MAGIC SOME EXTRA JUICE...
I'M A WIZARD, SO 18 INTELLIGENCE FOR MY SPELLCASTING... 17 DEXTERITY TO KEEP THINGS LIMBER... AND WE DUMP THE 5 INTO CHARISMA...
HOW 'BOUT WE TAKE THE FAST TRUUURP... TRACK TO LEVEL FIVE, SO YOU CAN SEE WHAT ADVENTURING IS ALL ABOUT?
LET'S DO THIS!
WUBBA LUBBA DUB DUB!

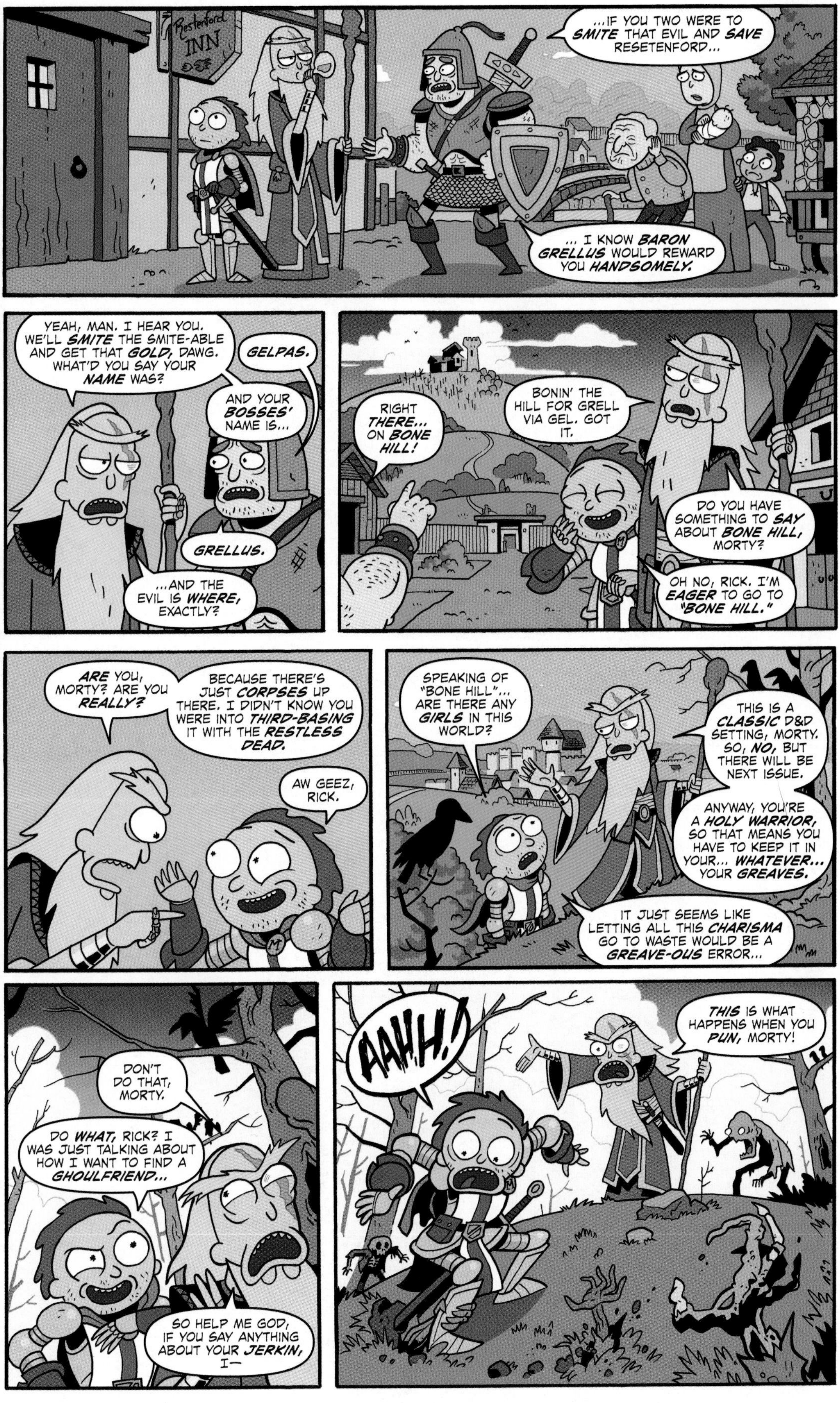

Restenford INN
...IF YOU TWO WERE TO SMITE THAT EVIL AND SAVE RESETENFORD...
... I KNOW BARON GRELLUS WOULD REWARD YOU HANDSOMELY.
YEAH, MAN. I HEAR YOU. WE'LL SMITE THE SMITE-ABLE AND GET THAT GOLD, DAWG. WHAT'D YOU SAY YOUR NAME WAS?
GELPAS.
AND YOUR BOSSES' NAME IS...
GRELLUS.
...AND THE EVIL IS WHERE, EXACTLY?
RIGHT THERE... ON BONE HILL!
BONIN' THE HILL FOR GRELL VIA GEL. GOT IT.
DO YOU HAVE SOMETHING TO SAY ABOUT BONE HILL, MORTY?
OH NO, RICK. I'M EAGER TO GO TO "BONE HILL."
ARE YOU, MORTY? ARE YOU REALLY?
BECAUSE THERE'S JUST CORPSES UP THERE. I DIDN'T KNOW YOU WERE INTO THIRD-BASING IT WITH THE RESTLESS DEAD.
AW GEEZ, RICK.
SPEAKING OF "BONE HILL"... ARE THERE ANY GIRLS IN THIS WORLD?
THIS IS A CLASSIC D&D SETTING, MORTY. SO, NO, BUT THERE WILL BE NEXT ISSUE.
ANYWAY, YOU'RE A HOLY WARRIOR, SO THAT MEANS YOU HAVE TO KEEP IT IN YOUR... WHATEVER... YOUR GREAVES.
IT JUST SEEMS LIKE LETTING ALL THIS CHARISMA GO TO WASTE WOULD BE A GREAVE-OUS ERROR...
DON'T DO THAT, MORTY.
DO WHAT, RICK? I WAS JUST TALKING ABOUT HOW I WANT TO FIND A GHOULFRIEND...
SO HELP ME GOD, IF YOU SAY ANYTHING ABOUT YOUR JERKIN, I—
AAHH!
THIS IS WHAT HAPPENS WHEN YOU PUN, MORTY!

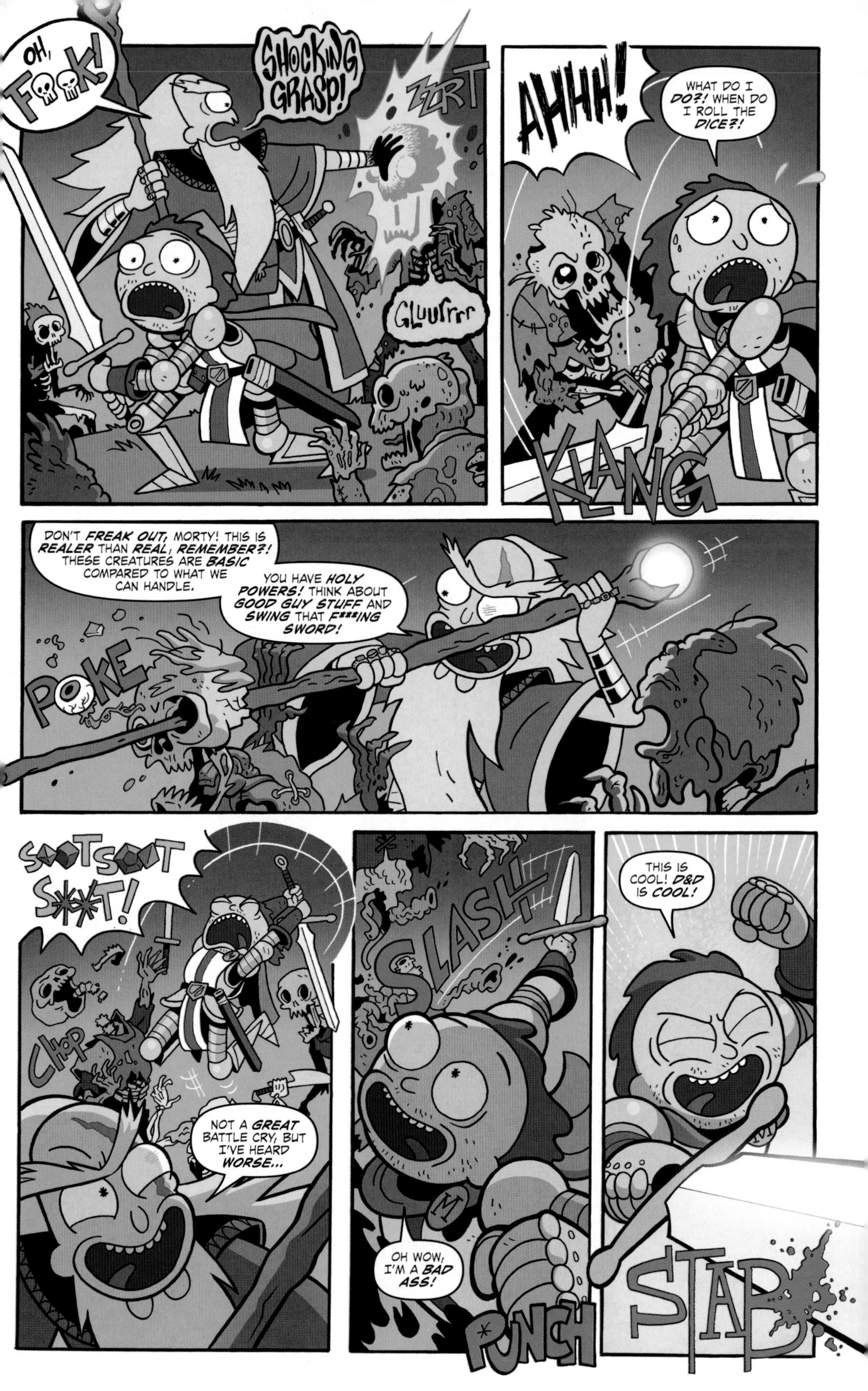
OH,
SHOCKING GRASP!
ZZRT
GLUURRRR
AHHH!
WHAT DO I DO?! WHEN DO I ROLL THE DICE?!
KLANG
DON'T FREAK OUT, MORTY! THIS IS REALER THAN REAL, REMEMBER?! THESE CREATURES ARE BASIC COMPARED TO WHAT WE CAN HANDLE.
YOU HAVE HOLY POWERS! THINK ABOUT GOOD GUY STUFF AND SWING THAT F***ING SWORD!
POKE
CHOP
NOT A GREAT BATTLE CRY, BUT I'VE HEARD WORSE...
SLASH!
OH WOW, I'M A BAD ASS!
PUNCH
THIS IS COOL! D&D IS COOL!
STAB

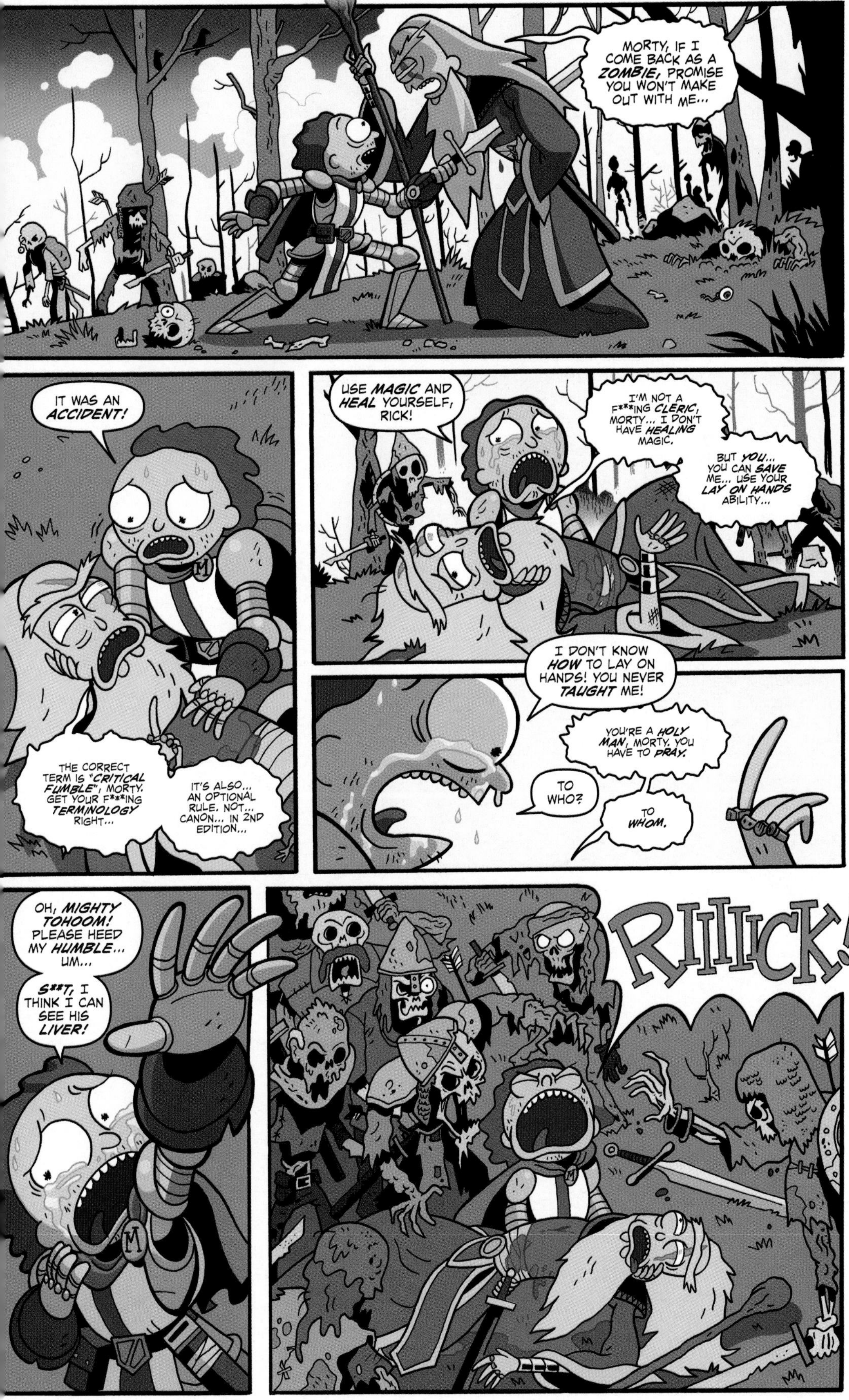
MORTY, IF I COME BACK AS A ZOMBIE, PROMISE YOU WON'T MAKE OUT WITH ME...
IT WAS AN ACCIDENT!
THE CORRECT TERM IS "CRITICAL FUMBLE", MORTY. GET YOUR F***ING TERMINOLOGY RIGHT...
IT'S ALSO... AN OPTIONAL RULE. NOT... CANON... IN 2ND EDITION...
USE MAGIC AND HEAL YOURSELF, RICK!
I'M NOT A F***ING CLERIC, MORTY... I DON'T HAVE HEALING MAGIC.
BUT YOU... YOU CAN SAVE ME... USE YOUR LAY ON HANDS ABILITY...
I DON'T KNOW HOW TO LAY ON HANDS! YOU NEVER TAUGHT ME!
YOU'RE A HOLY MAN, MORTY. YOU HAVE TO PRAY.
TO WHO?
TO WHOM.
OH, MIGHTY TOHOOM! PLEASE HEED MY HUMBLE... UM...
S**T, I THINK I CAN SEE HIS LIVER!
RIIICK!

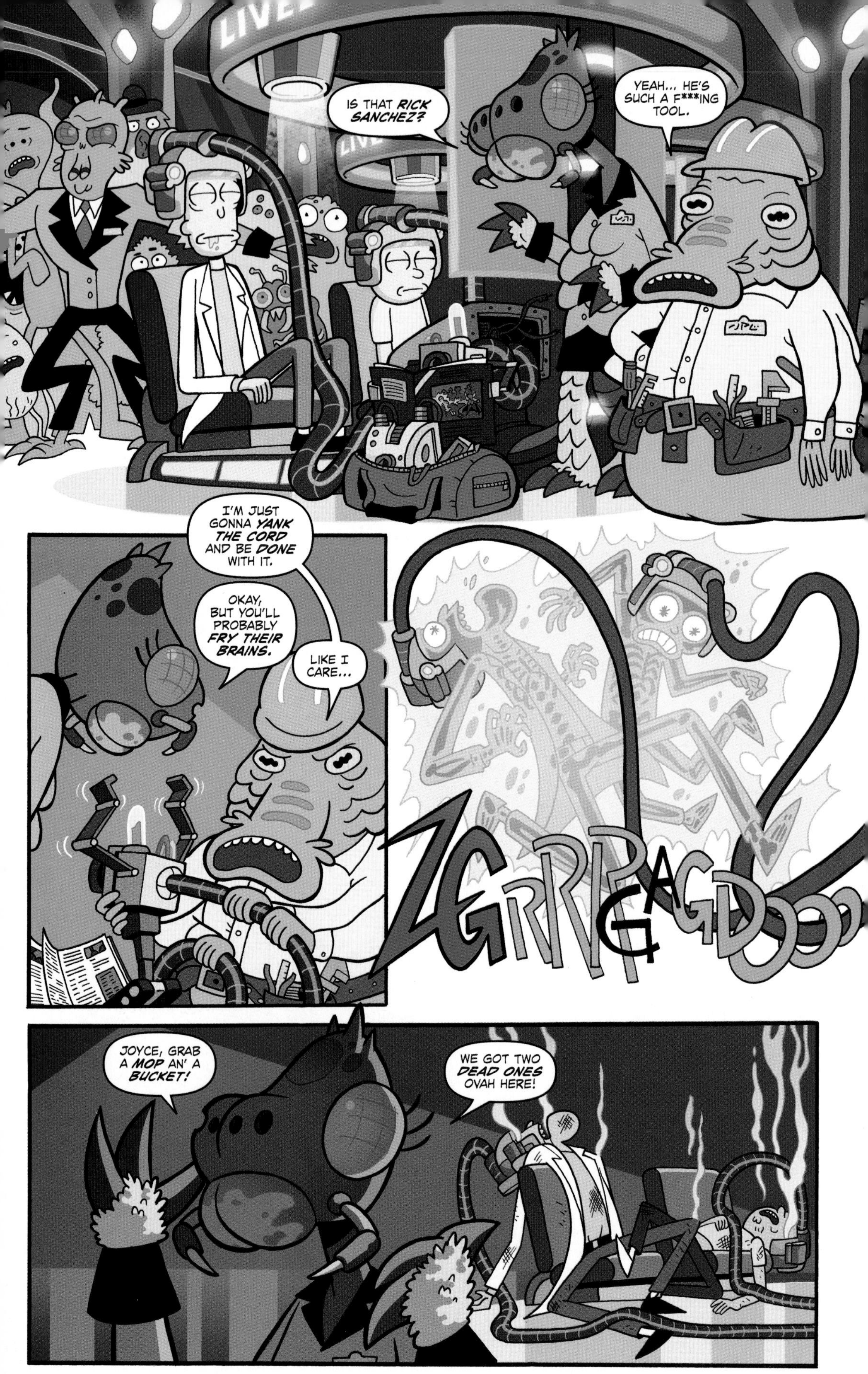
LIVE
IS THAT RICK SANCHEZ?
YEAH... HE'S SUCH A F***ING TOOL.
I'M JUST GONNA YANK THE CORD AND BE DONE WITH IT.
OKAY, BUT YOU'LL PROBABLY FRY THEIR BRAINS.
LIKE I CARE...
ZGRRPGPAGDOOOO
JOYCE, GRAB A MOP AN' A BUCKET!
WE GOT TWO DEAD ONES OVAH HERE!

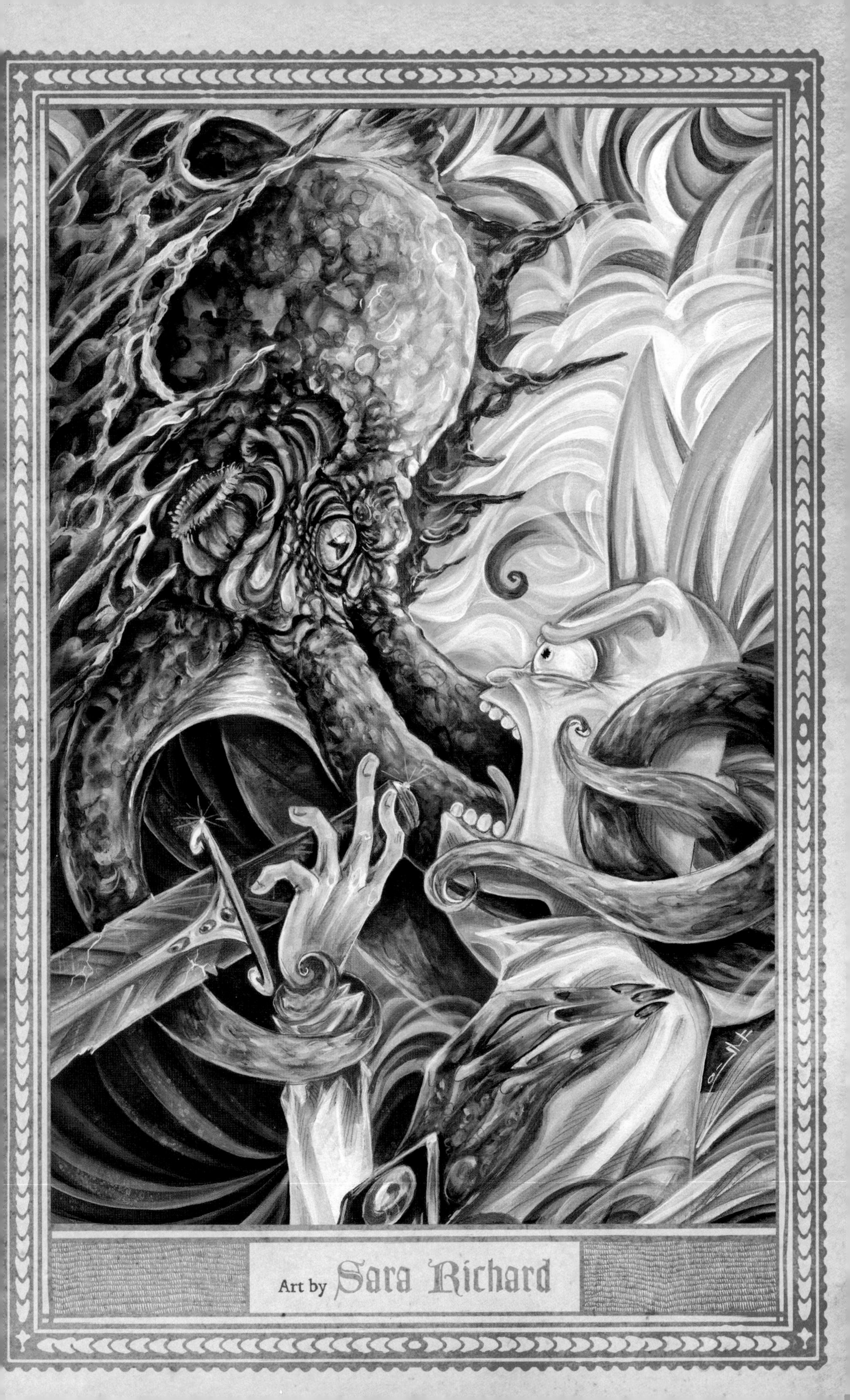

Art by Sara Richard

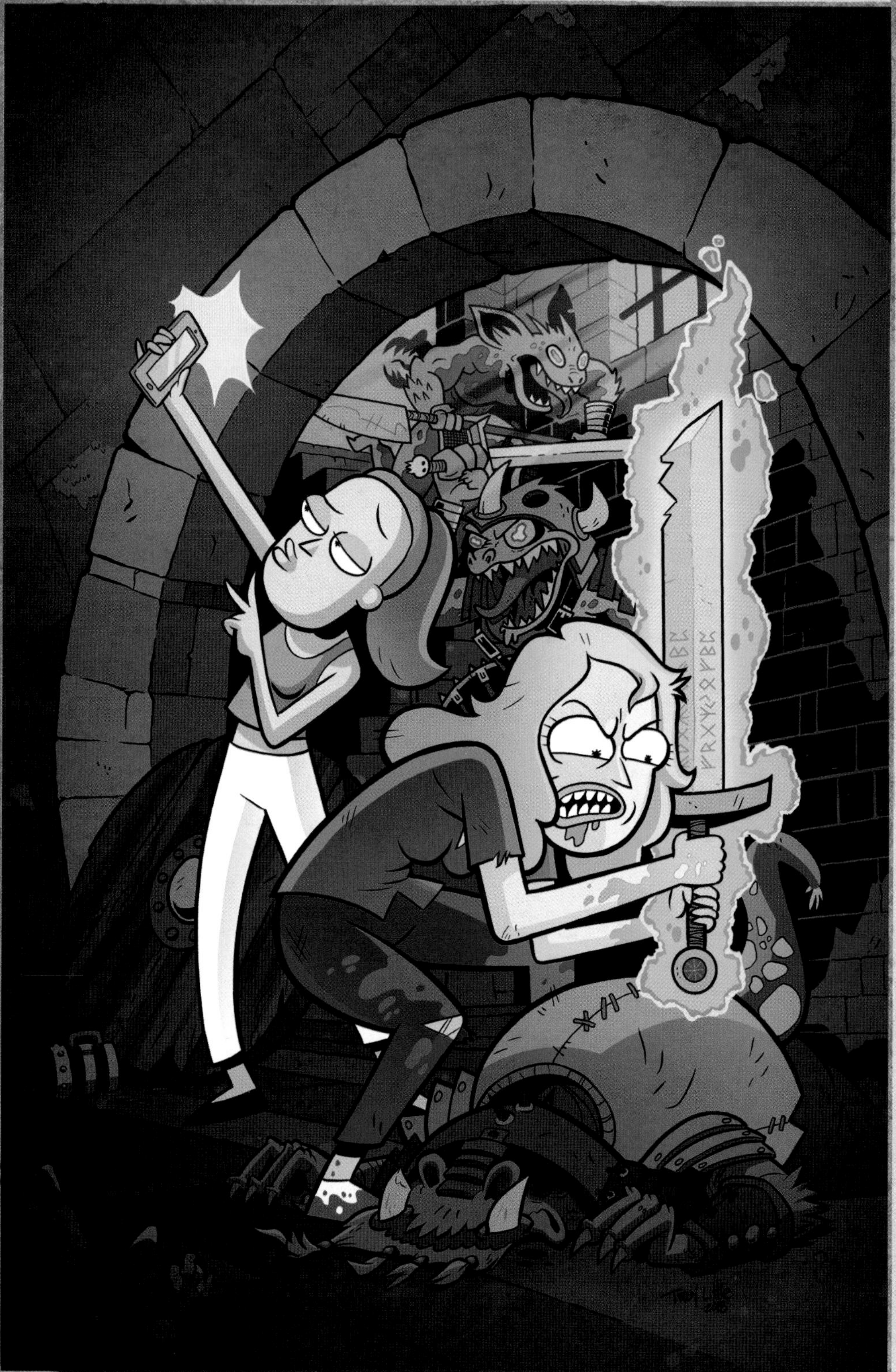

Art by Troy Little

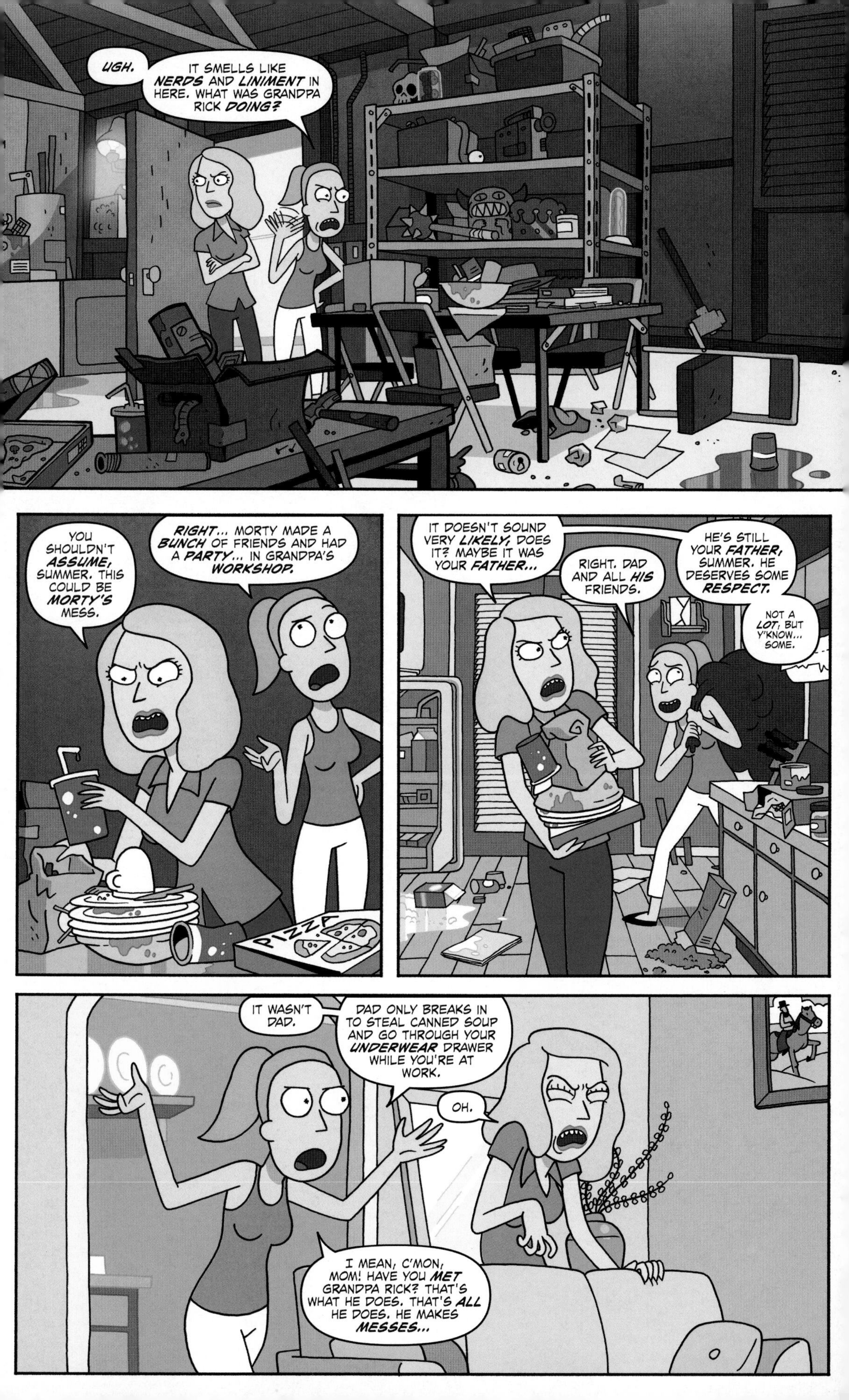
UGH.
IT SMELLS LIKE NERDS AND LINIMENT IN HERE. WHAT WAS GRANDPA RICK DOING?
YOU SHOULDN'T ASSUME, SUMMER. THIS COULD BE MORTY'S MESS.
RIGHT... MORTY MADE A BUNCH OF FRIENDS AND HAD A PARTY... IN GRANDPA'S WORKSHOP.
PIZZA
IT DOESN'T SOUND VERY LIKELY, DOES IT? MAYBE IT WAS YOUR FATHER...
RIGHT. DAD AND ALL HIS FRIENDS.
HE'S STILL YOUR FATHER, SUMMER. HE DESERVES SOME RESPECT.
NOT A LOT, BUT Y'KNOW... SOME.
IT WASN'T DAD.
DAD ONLY BREAKS IN TO STEAL CANNED SOUP AND GO THROUGH YOUR UNDERWEAR DRAWER WHILE YOU'RE AT WORK.
OH.
I MEAN, C'MON, MOM! HAVE YOU MET GRANDPA RICK? THAT'S WHAT HE DOES. THAT'S ALL HE DOES. HE MAKES MESSES...

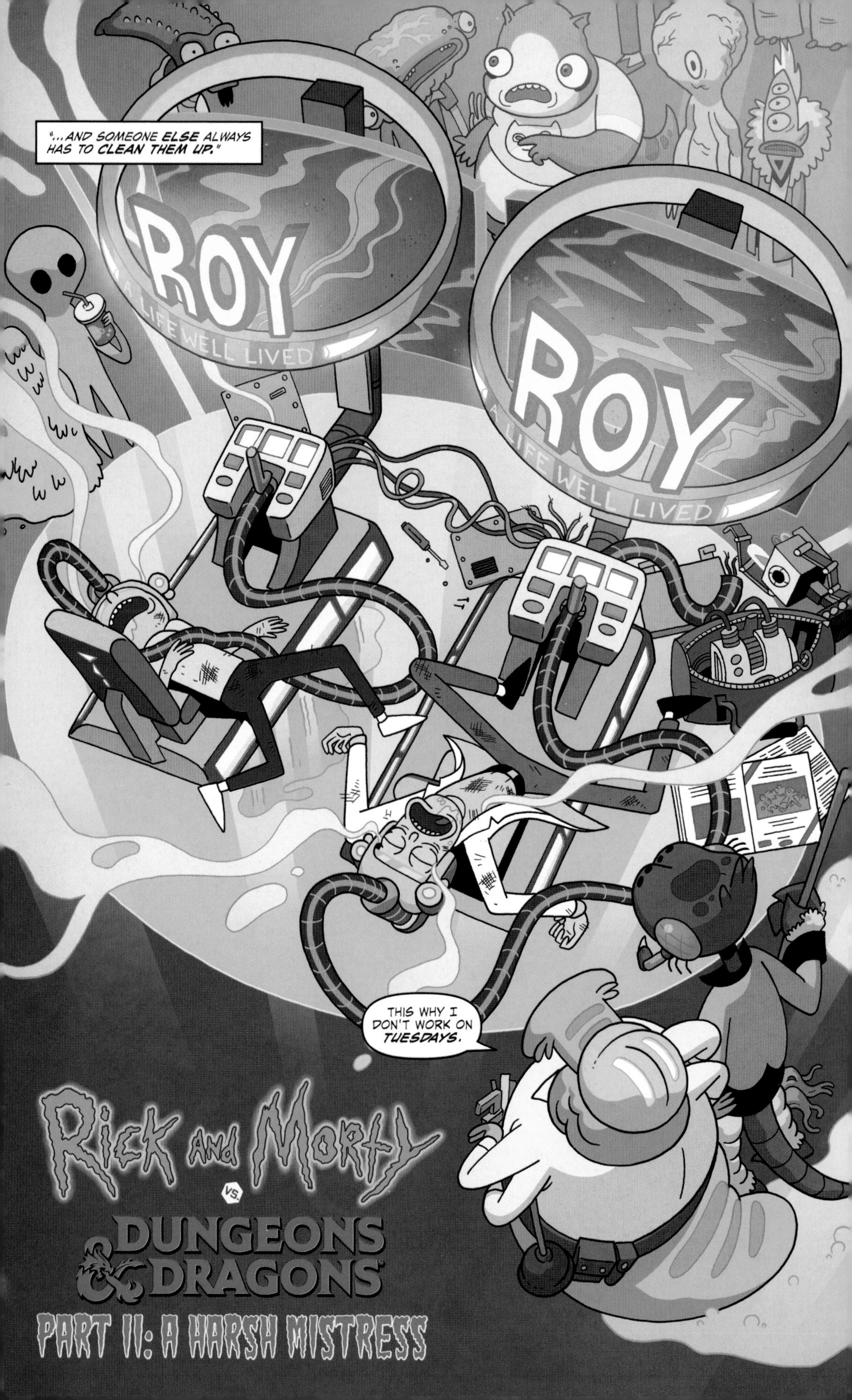
"...AND SOMEONE ELSE ALWAYS HAS TO CLEAN THEM UP."
ROY
A LIFE WELL LIVED
ROY
A LIFE WELL LIVED
THIS WHY I DON'T WORK ON TUESDAYS.
RICK AND MORTY
VS.
DUNGEONS & DRAGONS
PART II: A HARSH MISTRESS

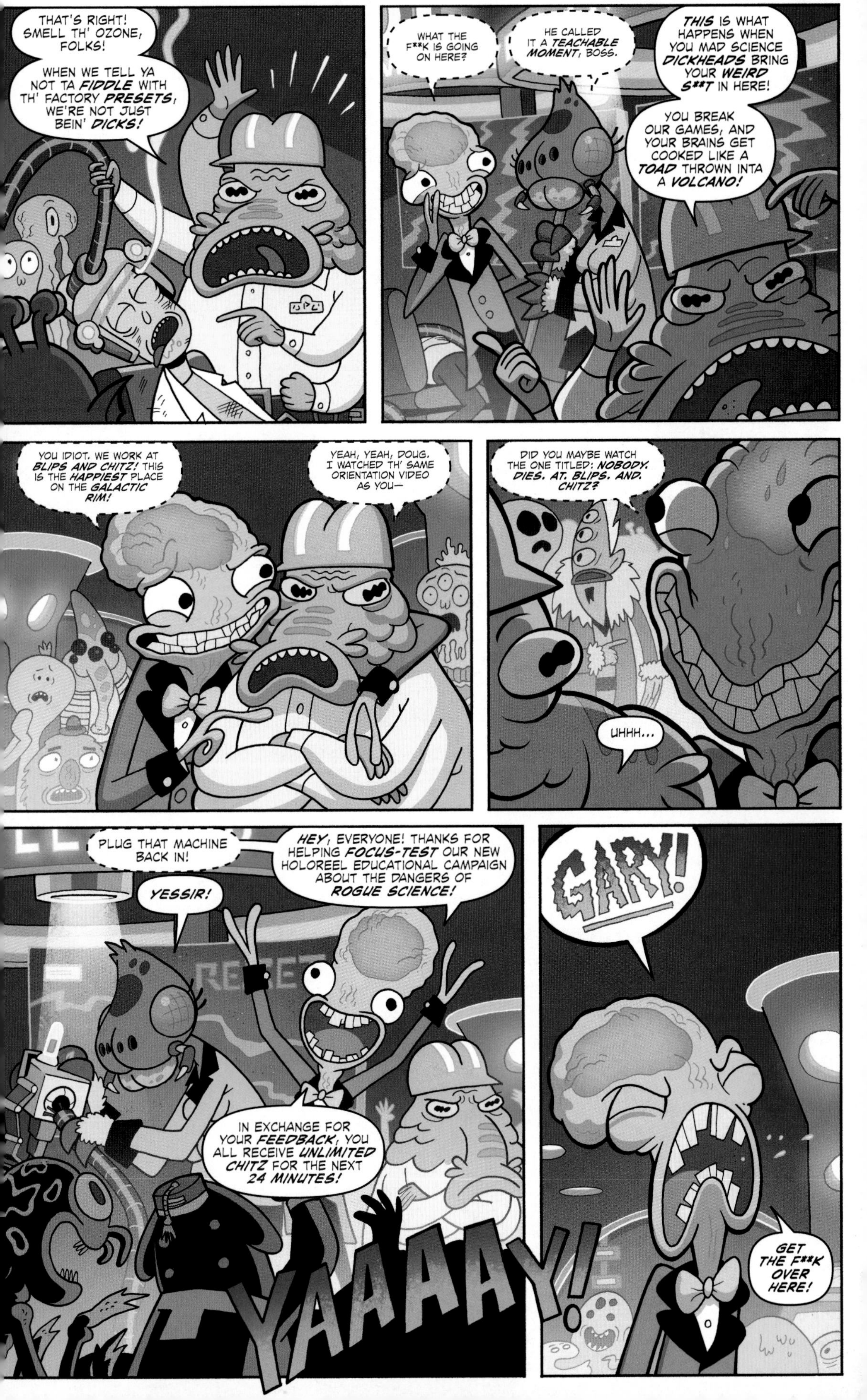
THAT'S RIGHT! SMELL TH' OZONE, FOLKS!
WHEN WE TELL YA NOT TA FIDDLE WITH TH' FACTORY PRESETS, WE'RE NOT JUST BEIN' DICKS!
WHAT THE F**K IS GOING ON HERE?
HE CALLED IT A TEACHABLE MOMENT, BOSS.
THIS IS WHAT HAPPENS WHEN YOU MAD SCIENCE DICKHEADS BRING YOUR WEIRD S**T IN HERE!
YOU BREAK OUR GAMES, AND YOUR BRAINS GET COOKED LIKE A TOAD THROWN INTA A VOLCANO!
YOU IDIOT. WE WORK AT BLIPS AND CHITZ! THIS IS THE HAPPIEST PLACE ON THE GALACTIC RIM!
YEAH, YEAH, DOUG. I WATCHED TH' SAME ORIENTATION VIDEO AS YOU—
DID YOU MAYBE WATCH THE ONE TITLED: NOBODY. DIES. AT. BLIPS. AND. CHITZ?
UHHH...
PLUG THAT MACHINE BACK IN!
YESSIR!
HEY, EVERYONE! THANKS FOR HELPING FOCUS-TEST OUR NEW HOLOREEL EDUCATIONAL CAMPAIGN ABOUT THE DANGERS OF ROGUE SCIENCE!
IN EXCHANGE FOR YOUR FEEDBACK, YOU ALL RECEIVE UNLIMITED CHITZ FOR THE NEXT 24 MINUTES!
YAAAAY!
GARY!
GET THE F**K OVER HERE!

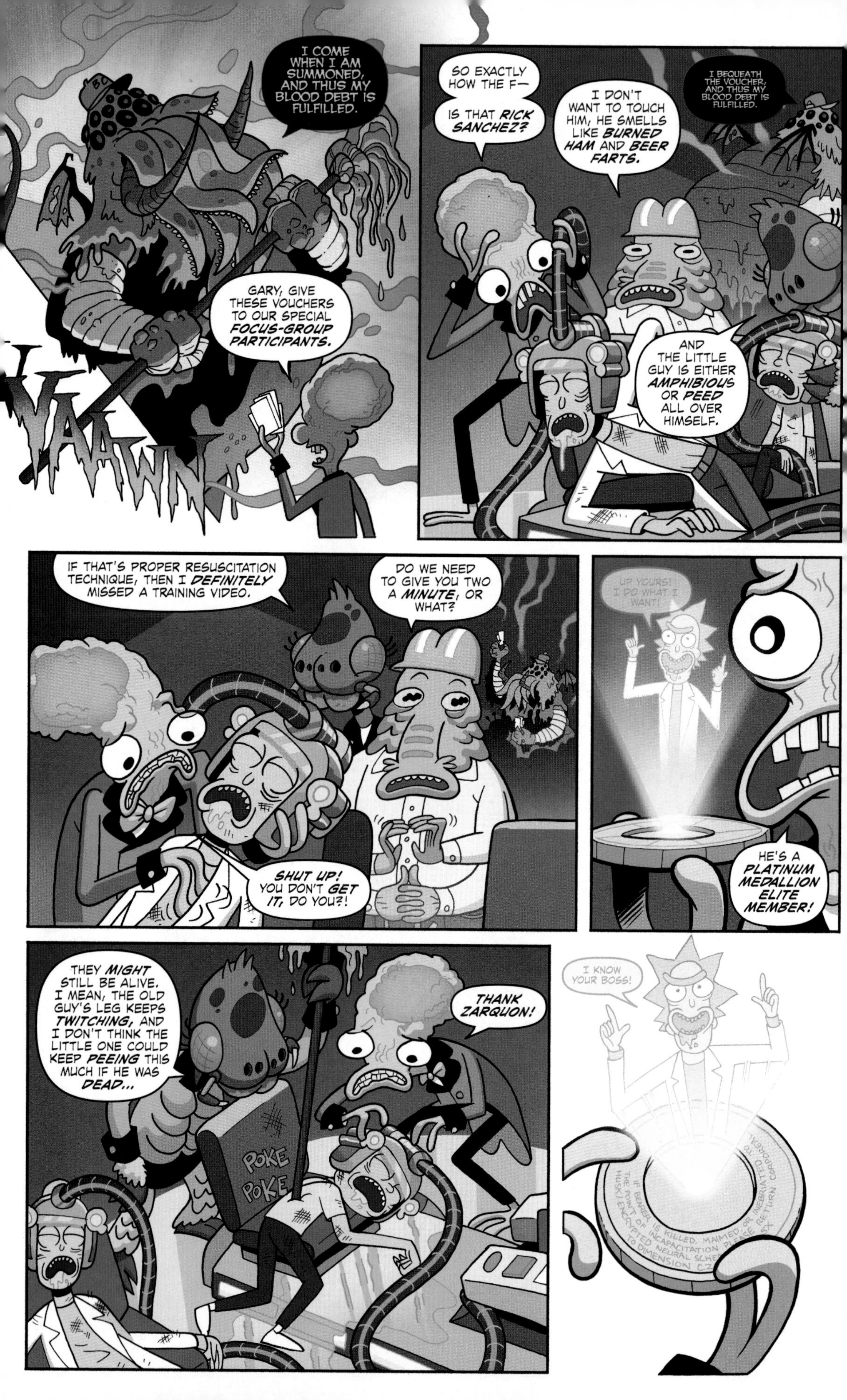

I COME WHEN I AM SUMMONED, AND THUS MY BLOOD DEBT IS FULFILLED.
GARY, GIVE THESE VOUCHERS TO OUR SPECIAL FOCUS-GROUP PARTICIPANTS.
VAAWN
SO EXACTLY HOW THE F—
IS THAT RICK SANCHEZ?
I DON'T WANT TO TOUCH HIM, HE SMELLS LIKE BURNED HAM AND BEER FARTS.
I BEQUEATH THE VOUCHER, AND THUS MY BLOOD DEBT IS FULFILLED.
AND THE LITTLE GUY IS EITHER AMPHIBIOUS OR PEED ALL OVER HIMSELF.
IF THAT'S PROPER RESUSCITATION TECHNIQUE, THEN I DEFINITELY MISSED A TRAINING VIDEO.
DO WE NEED TO GIVE YOU TWO A MINUTE, OR WHAT?
SHUT UP! YOU DON'T GET IT, DO YOU?!
UP YOURS! I DO WHAT I WANT!
HE'S A PLATINUM MEDALLION ELITE MEMBER!
THEY MIGHT STILL BE ALIVE. I MEAN, THE OLD GUY'S LEG KEEPS TWITCHING, AND I DON'T THINK THE LITTLE ONE COULD KEEP PEEING THIS MUCH IF HE WAS DEAD...
THANK ZARQUON!
POKE POKE
I KNOW YOUR BOSS!

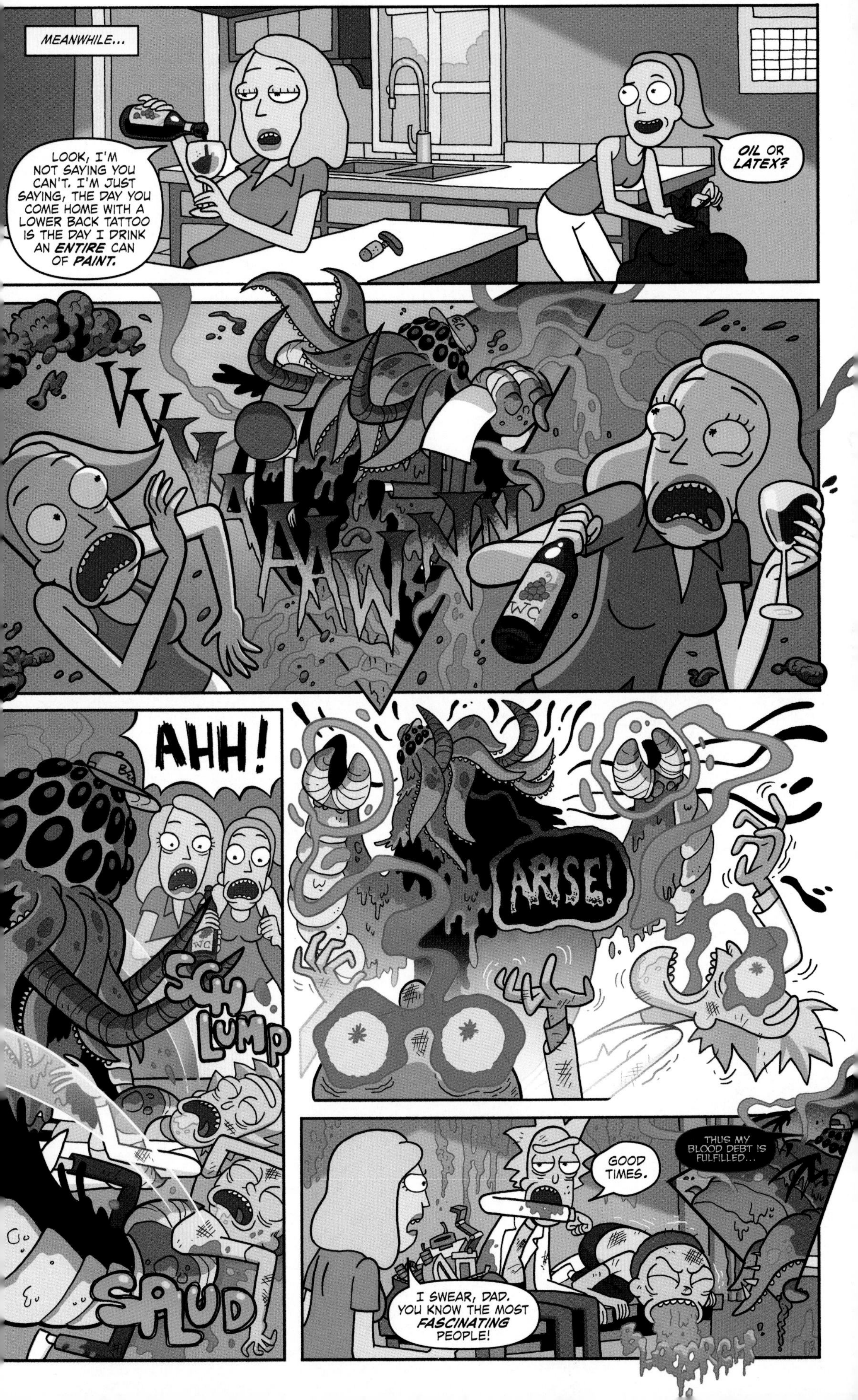
MEANWHILE...
LOOK, I'M NOT SAYING YOU CAN'T. I'M JUST SAYING, THE DAY YOU COME HOME WITH A LOWER BACK TATTOO IS THE DAY I DRINK AN ENTIRE CAN OF PAINT.
OIL OR LATEX?
VVAAWNN
AHH!
SCHLUMP
SPLUD
ARISE!
GOOD TIMES.
THUS MY BLOOD DEBT IS FULFILLED...
I SWEAR, DAD. YOU KNOW THE MOST FASCINATING PEOPLE!
BLOORCH

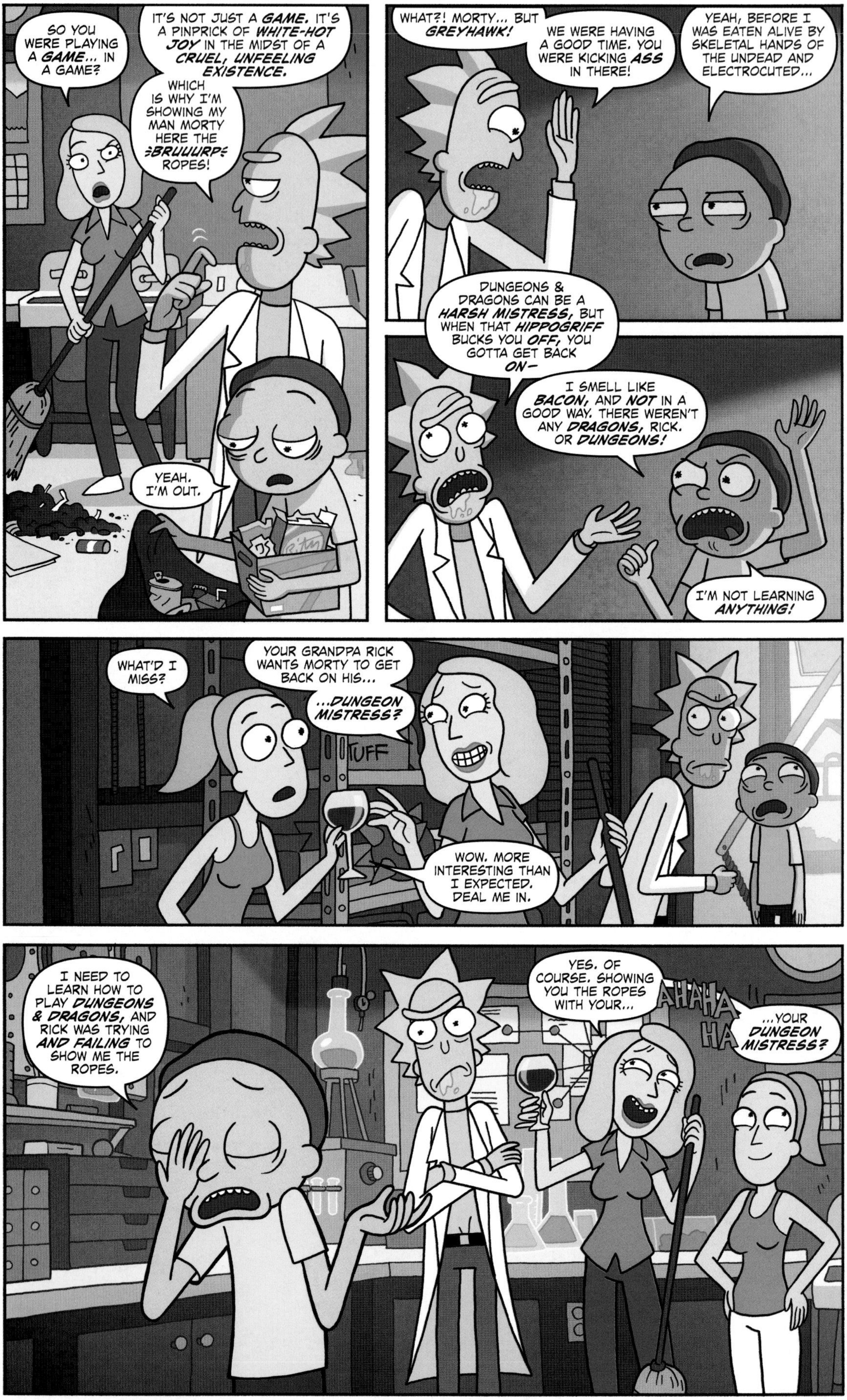
SO YOU WERE PLAYING A GAME... IN A GAME?
IT'S NOT JUST A GAME. IT'S A PINPRICK OF WHITE-HOT JOY IN THE MIDST OF A CRUEL, UNFEELING EXISTENCE.
WHICH IS WHY I'M SHOWING MY MAN MORTY HERE THE BRUUURP ROPES!
YEAH. I'M OUT.
WHAT?! MORTY... BUT GREYHAWK!
WE WERE HAVING A GOOD TIME. YOU WERE KICKING ASS IN THERE!
YEAH, BEFORE I WAS EATEN ALIVE BY SKELETAL HANDS OF THE UNDEAD AND ELECTROCUTED...
DUNGEONS & DRAGONS CAN BE A HARSH MISTRESS, BUT WHEN THAT HIPPOGRIFF BUCKS YOU OFF, YOU GOTTA GET BACK ON—
I SMELL LIKE BACON, AND NOT IN A GOOD WAY. THERE WEREN'T ANY DRAGONS, RICK. OR DUNGEONS!
I'M NOT LEARNING ANYTHING!
WHAT'D I MISS?
YOUR GRANDPA RICK WANTS MORTY TO GET BACK ON HIS...
...DUNGEON MISTRESS?
TUFF
WOW. MORE INTERESTING THAN I EXPECTED. DEAL ME IN.
I NEED TO LEARN HOW TO PLAY DUNGEONS & DRAGONS, AND RICK WAS TRYING AND FAILING TO SHOW ME THE ROPES.
YES. OF COURSE. SHOWING YOU THE ROPES WITH YOUR...
AHAHA HA
...YOUR DUNGEON MISTRESS?

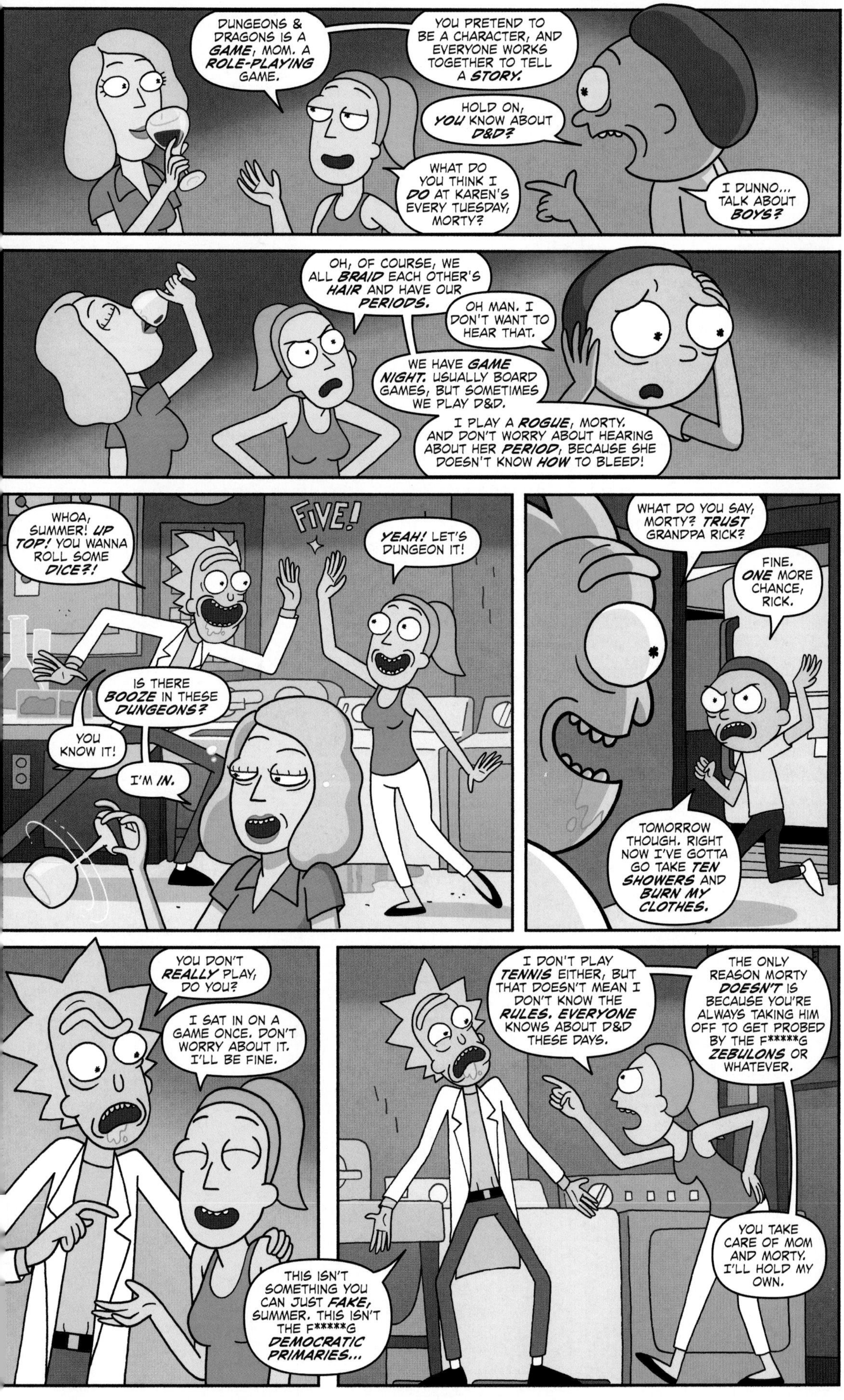
DUNGEONS & DRAGONS IS A GAME, MOM. A ROLE-PLAYING GAME.
YOU PRETEND TO BE A CHARACTER, AND EVERYONE WORKS TOGETHER TO TELL A STORY.
HOLD ON, YOU KNOW ABOUT D&D?
WHAT DO YOU THINK I DO AT KAREN'S EVERY TUESDAY, MORTY?
I DUNNO... TALK ABOUT BOYS?
OH, OF COURSE, WE ALL BRAID EACH OTHER'S HAIR AND HAVE OUR PERIODS.
OH MAN. I DON'T WANT TO HEAR THAT.
WE HAVE GAME NIGHT. USUALLY BOARD GAMES, BUT SOMETIMES WE PLAY D&D.
I PLAY A ROGUE, MORTY. AND DON'T WORRY ABOUT HEARING ABOUT HER PERIOD, BECAUSE SHE DOESN'T KNOW HOW TO BLEED!
WHOA, SUMMER! UP TOP! YOU WANNA ROLL SOME DICE?!
FIVE!
YEAH! LET'S DUNGEON IT!
IS THERE BOOZE IN THESE DUNGEONS?
YOU KNOW IT!
I'M IN.
WHAT DO YOU SAY, MORTY? TRUST GRANDPA RICK?
FINE. ONE MORE CHANCE, RICK.
TOMORROW THOUGH. RIGHT NOW I'VE GOTTA GO TAKE TEN SHOWERS AND BURN MY CLOTHES.
YOU DON'T REALLY PLAY, DO YOU?
I SAT IN ON A GAME ONCE. DON'T WORRY ABOUT IT. I'LL BE FINE.
THIS ISN'T SOMETHING YOU CAN JUST FAKE, SUMMER. THIS ISN'T THE F*****G DEMOCRATIC PRIMARIES...
I DON'T PLAY TENNIS EITHER, BUT THAT DOESN'T MEAN I DON'T KNOW THE RULES. EVERYONE KNOWS ABOUT D&D THESE DAYS.
THE ONLY REASON MORTY DOESN'T IS BECAUSE YOU'RE ALWAYS TAKING HIM OFF TO GET PROBED BY THE F*****G ZEBULONS OR WHATEVER.
YOU TAKE CARE OF MOM AND MORTY. I'LL HOLD MY OWN.

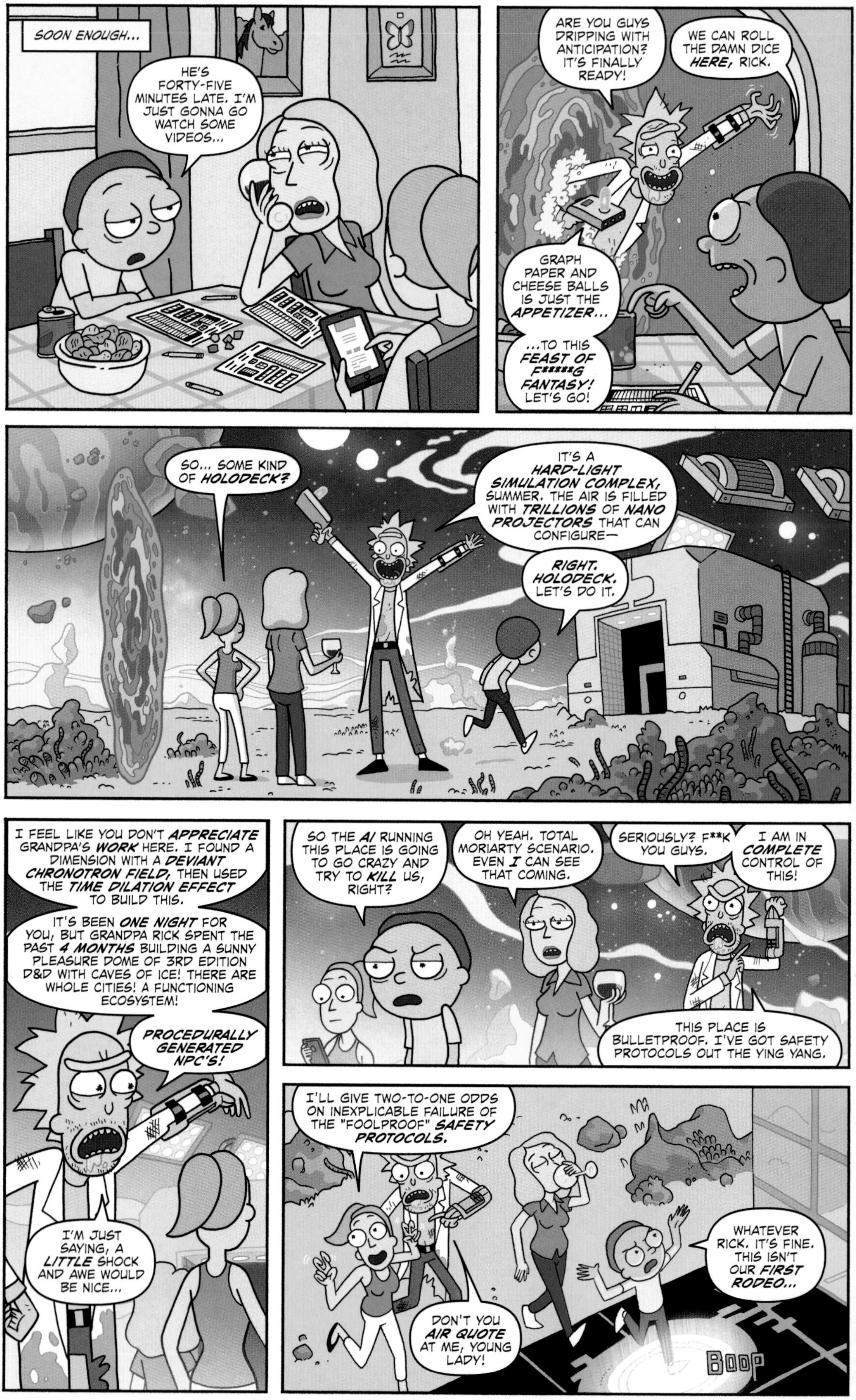
SOON ENOUGH...
HE'S FORTY-FIVE MINUTES LATE. I'M JUST GONNA GO WATCH SOME VIDEOS...
ARE YOU GUYS DRIPPING WITH ANTICIPATION? IT'S FINALLY READY!
WE CAN ROLL THE DAMN DICE HERE, RICK.
GRAPH PAPER AND CHEESE BALLS IS JUST THE APPETIZER...
...TO THIS FEAST OF F*****G FANTASY! LET'S GO!
SO... SOME KIND OF HOLODECK?
IT'S A HARD-LIGHT SIMULATION COMPLEX, SUMMER. THE AIR IS FILLED WITH TRILLIONS OF NANO PROJECTORS THAT CAN CONFIGURE—
RIGHT. HOLODECK. LET'S DO IT.
I FEEL LIKE YOU DON'T APPRECIATE GRANDPA'S WORK HERE. I FOUND A DIMENSION WITH A DEVIANT CHRONOTRON FIELD, THEN USED THE TIME DILATION EFFECT TO BUILD THIS.
IT'S BEEN ONE NIGHT FOR YOU, BUT GRANDPA RICK SPENT THE PAST 4 MONTHS BUILDING A SUNNY PLEASURE DOME OF 3RD EDITION D&D WITH CAVES OF ICE! THERE ARE WHOLE CITIES! A FUNCTIONING ECOSYSTEM!
PROCEDURALLY GENERATED NPC'S!
I'M JUST SAYING, A LITTLE SHOCK AND AWE WOULD BE NICE...
SO THE AI RUNNING THIS PLACE IS GOING TO GO CRAZY AND TRY TO KILL US, RIGHT?
OH YEAH. TOTAL MORIARTY SCENARIO. EVEN I CAN SEE THAT COMING.
SERIOUSLY? F**K YOU GUYS.
I AM IN COMPLETE CONTROL OF THIS!
THIS PLACE IS BULLETPROOF. I'VE GOT SAFETY PROTOCOLS OUT THE YING YANG.
I'LL GIVE TWO-TO-ONE ODDS ON INEXPLICABLE FAILURE OF THE "FOOLPROOF" SAFETY PROTOCOLS.
DON'T YOU AIR QUOTE AT ME, YOUNG LADY!
WHATEVER RICK. IT'S FINE. THIS ISN'T OUR FIRST RODEO...
BOOP

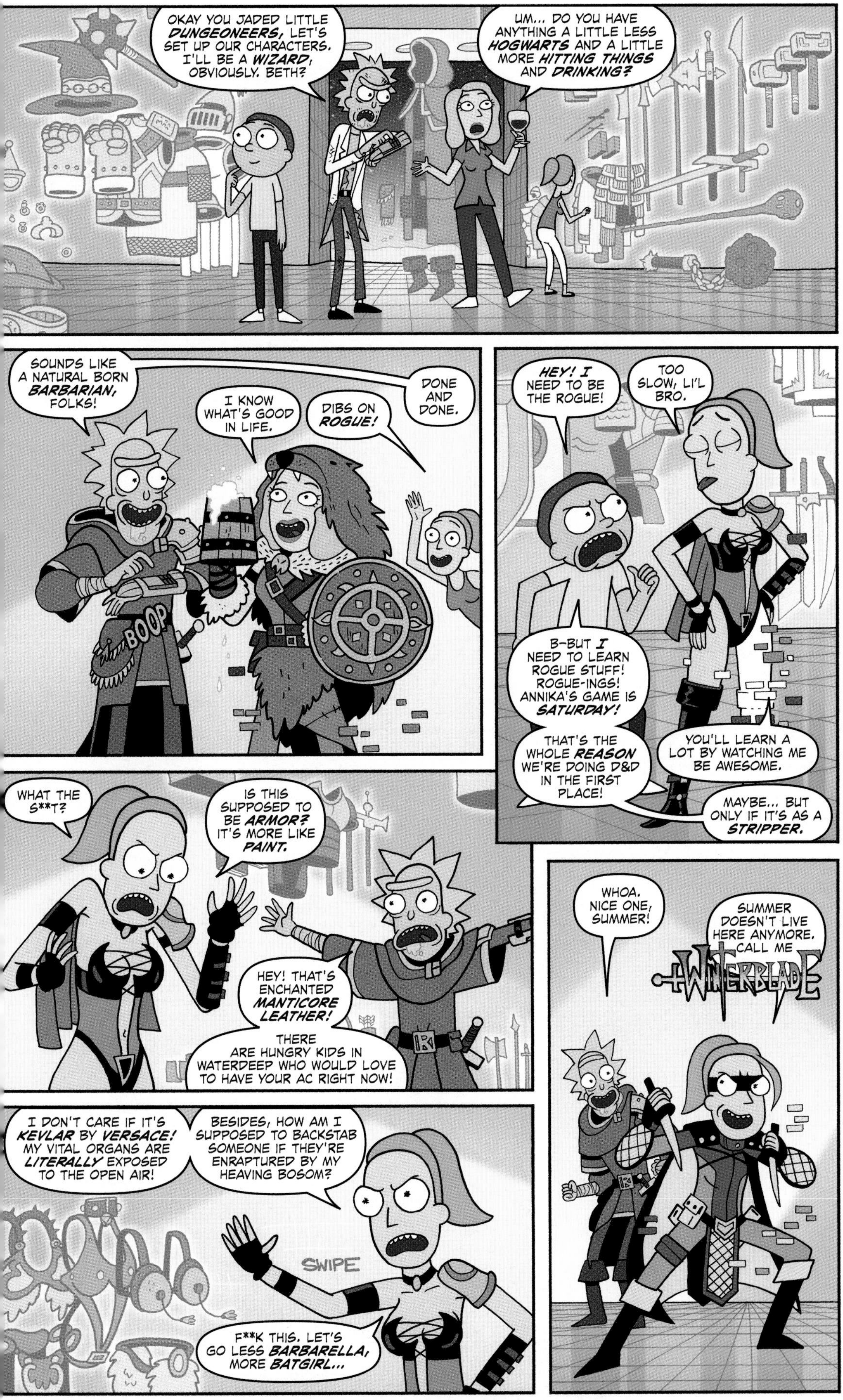
OKAY YOU JADED LITTLE DUNGEONEERS, LET'S SET UP OUR CHARACTERS. I'LL BE A WIZARD, OBVIOUSLY. BETH?
UM... DO YOU HAVE ANYTHING A LITTLE LESS HOGWARTS AND A LITTLE MORE HITTING THINGS AND DRINKING?
SOUNDS LIKE A NATURAL BORN BARBARIAN, FOLKS!
DONE AND DONE.
I KNOW WHAT'S GOOD IN LIFE.
DIBS ON ROGUE!
BOOP
HEY! I NEED TO BE THE ROGUE!
TOO SLOW, LI'L BRO.
B-BUT I NEED TO LEARN ROGUE STUFF! ROGUE-INGS! ANNIKA'S GAME IS SATURDAY!
THAT'S THE WHOLE REASON WE'RE DOING D&D IN THE FIRST PLACE!
YOU'LL LEARN A LOT BY WATCHING ME BE AWESOME.
MAYBE... BUT ONLY IF IT'S AS A STRIPPER.
WHAT THE S**T?
IS THIS SUPPOSED TO BE ARMOR? IT'S MORE LIKE PAINT.
HEY! THAT'S ENCHANTED MANTICORE LEATHER!
THERE ARE HUNGRY KIDS IN WATERDEEP WHO WOULD LOVE TO HAVE YOUR AC RIGHT NOW!
I DON'T CARE IF IT'S KEVLAR BY VERSACE! MY VITAL ORGANS ARE LITERALLY EXPOSED TO THE OPEN AIR!
BESIDES, HOW AM I SUPPOSED TO BACKSTAB SOMEONE IF THEY'RE ENRAPTURED BY MY HEAVING BOSOM?
SWIPE
F**K THIS. LET'S GO LESS BARBARELLA, MORE BATGIRL...
WHOA. NICE ONE, SUMMER!
SUMMER DOESN'T LIVE HERE ANYMORE. CALL ME
WINTERBLADE

FINE. WE CAN *BOTH* BE ROGUES!

NO DOUBLE-DIPPING ON CLASSES, MORTY. IT'S A *DICK* MOVE.

BOOP

SO WHAT THEN? I PLAY A *PALADIN* AGAIN? OR A *BARD*?

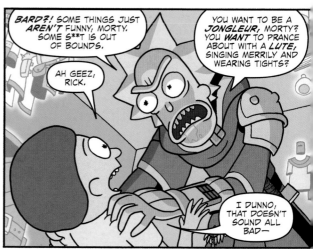

BARD?! SOME THINGS JUST *AREN'T* FUNNY, MORTY. SOME S**T IS OUT OF BOUNDS.

AH GEEZ, RICK.

YOU WANT TO BE A *JONGLEUR*, MORTY? YOU *WANT* TO PRANCE ABOUT WITH A *LUTE*, SINGING MERRILY AND WEARING TIGHTS?

I DUNNO, THAT DOESN'T SOUND ALL BAD—

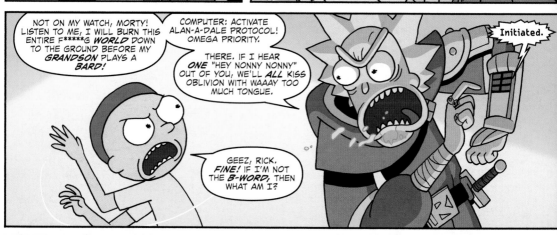

NOT ON MY WATCH, MORTY! LISTEN TO ME, I WILL BURN THIS ENTIRE F*****G *WORLD* DOWN TO THE GROUND BEFORE MY *GRANDSON* PLAYS A *BARD!*

COMPUTER: ACTIVATE ALAN-A-DALE PROTOCOL! OMEGA PRIORITY.

THERE. IF I HEAR *ONE* "HEY NONNY NONNY" OUT OF YOU, WE'LL *ALL* KISS OBLIVION WITH WAAAY TOO MUCH TONGUE.

GEEZ, RICK. *FINE!* IF I'M NOT THE *B-WORD*, THEN WHAT AM I?

Initiated.

Blip

SOMETIMES THE *OLD WAYS* ARE THE BEST, MORTY. LET ME INTRODUCE YOU TO THE *CLASSIC D&D PARTY...*

FIGHTER.

WIZARD.

THIEF.

CLERIC.

YOU'RE OUR *HEALER*, MORTY.

AW, GEEZ...

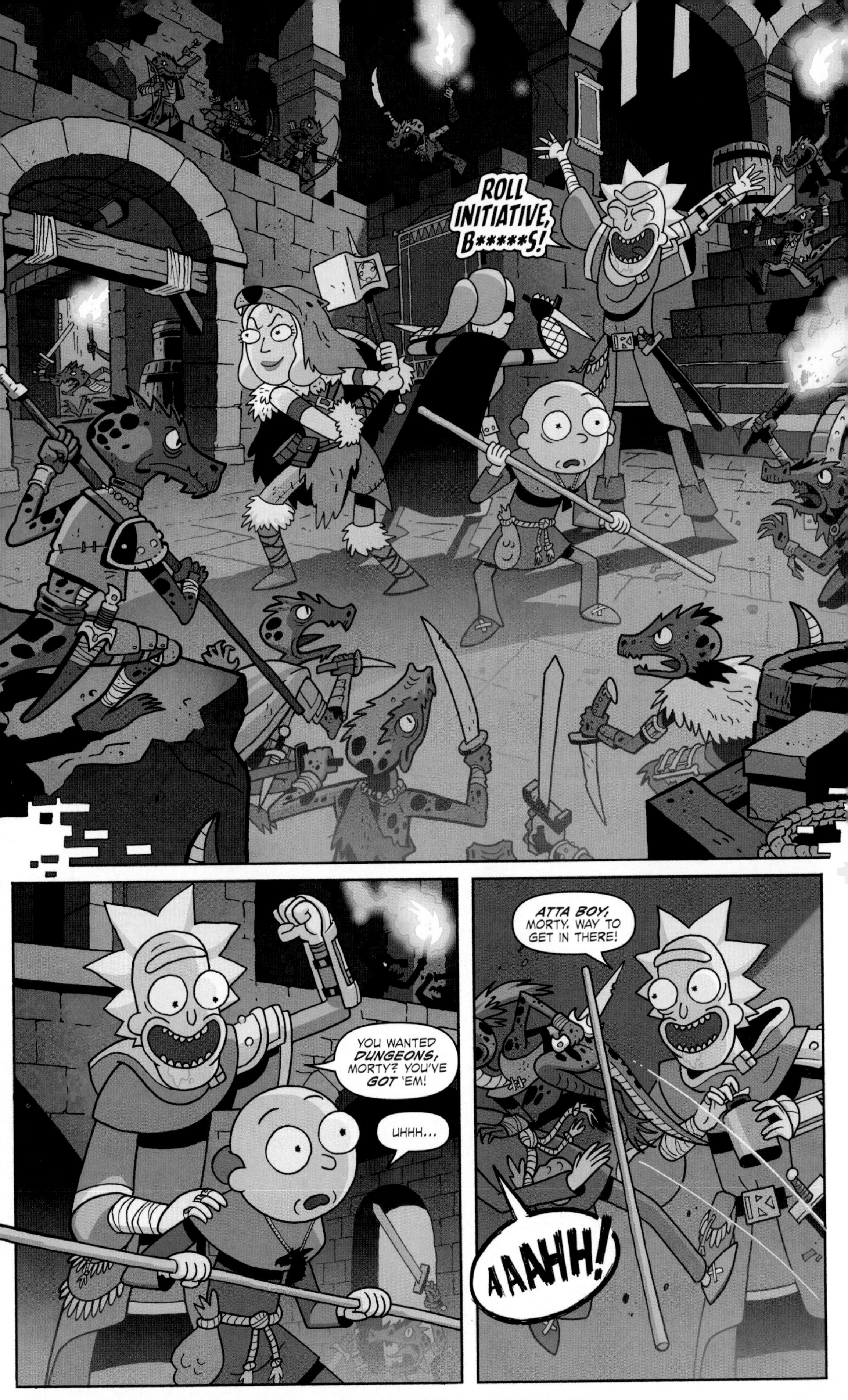
ROLL INITIATIVE, B*****S!
YOU WANTED DUNGEONS, MORTY? YOU'VE GOT 'EM!
UHHH...
ATTA BOY, MORTY. WAY TO GET IN THERE!
AAAHH!

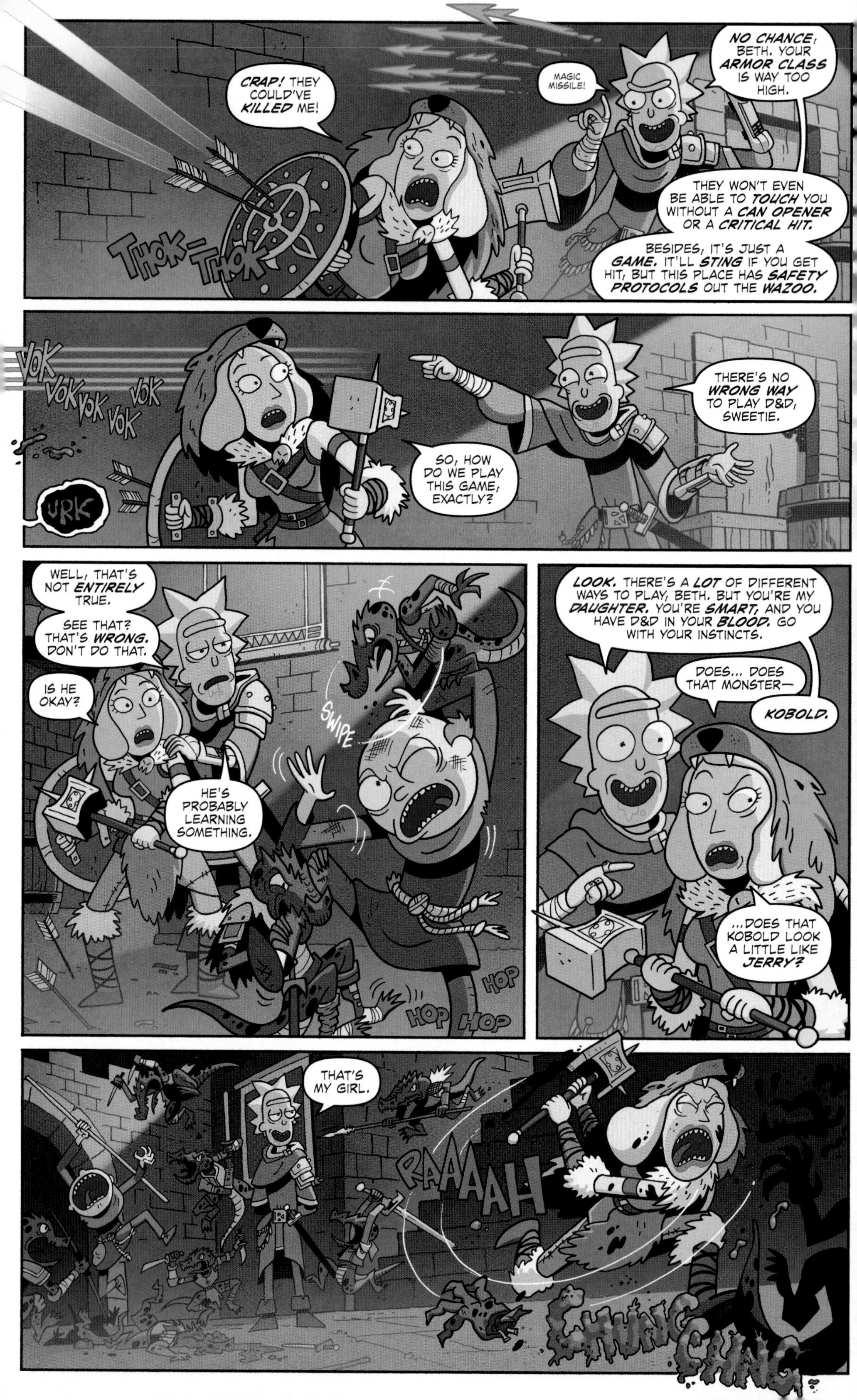
CRAP! THEY COULD'VE KILLED ME!
MAGIC MISSILE!
NO CHANCE, BETH. YOUR ARMOR CLASS IS WAY TOO HIGH.
THEY WON'T EVEN BE ABLE TO TOUCH YOU WITHOUT A CAN OPENER OR A CRITICAL HIT.
BESIDES, IT'S JUST A GAME. IT'LL STING IF YOU GET HIT, BUT THIS PLACE HAS SAFETY PROTOCOLS OUT THE WAZOO.
THOK-THOK
VOK VOK VOK VOK VOK
URK
SO, HOW DO WE PLAY THIS GAME, EXACTLY?
THERE'S NO WRONG WAY TO PLAY D&D, SWEETIE.
WELL, THAT'S NOT ENTIRELY TRUE.
SEE THAT? THAT'S WRONG. DON'T DO THAT.
IS HE OKAY?
HE'S PROBABLY LEARNING SOMETHING.
SWIPE
HOP HOP HOP
LOOK. THERE'S A LOT OF DIFFERENT WAYS TO PLAY, BETH. BUT YOU'RE MY DAUGHTER. YOU'RE SMART, AND YOU HAVE D&D IN YOUR BLOOD. GO WITH YOUR INSTINCTS.
DOES... DOES THAT MONSTER—
KOBOLD.
...DOES THAT KOBOLD LOOK A LITTLE LIKE JERRY?
THAT'S MY GIRL.
RAAAAAH
CHUNG CHUNG

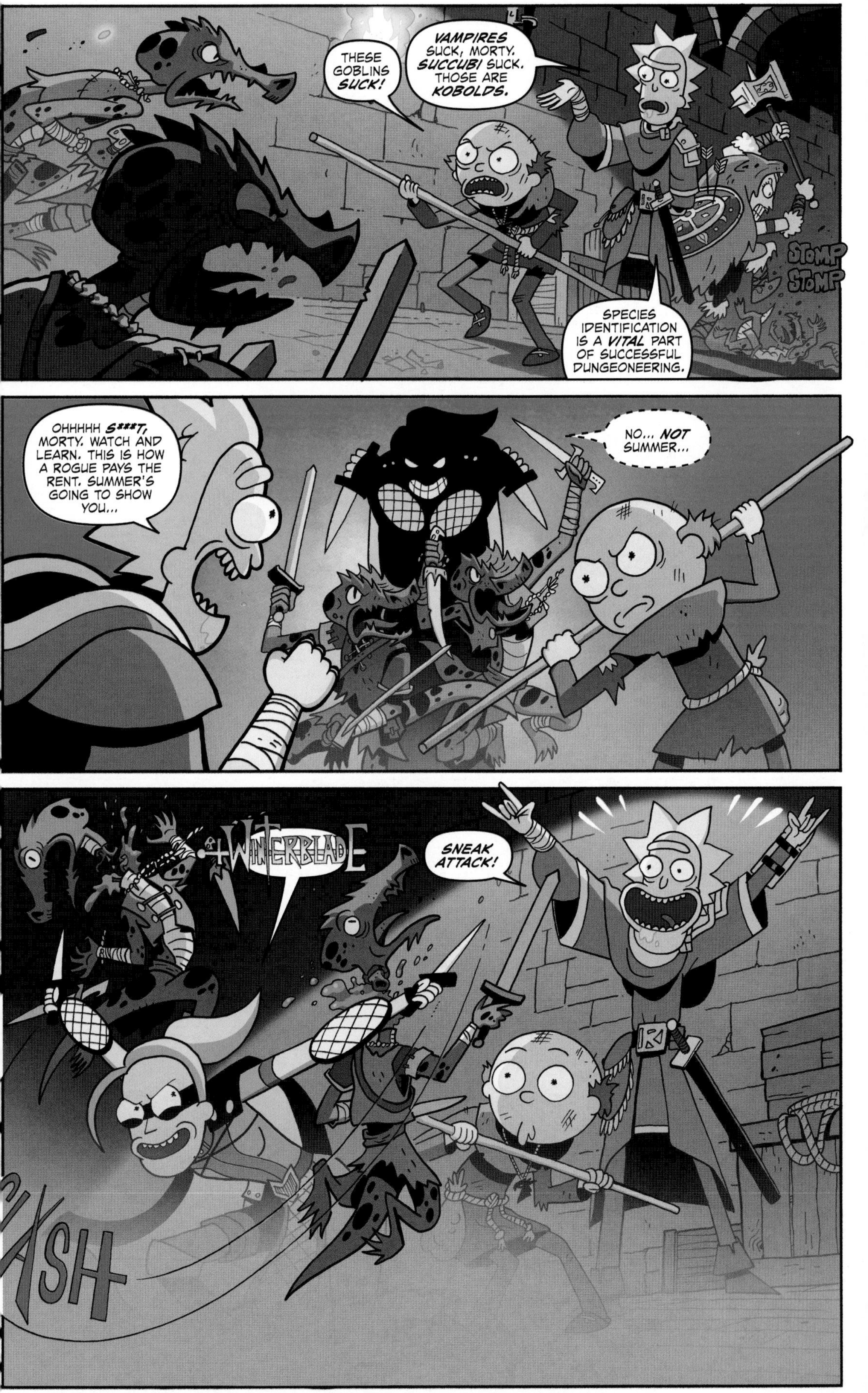
THESE GOBLINS *SUCK!*
VAMPIRES SUCK, MORTY. *SUCCUBI* SUCK. THOSE ARE *KOBOLDS.*
STOMP
STOMP
SPECIES IDENTIFICATION IS A *VITAL* PART OF SUCCESSFUL DUNGEONEERING.
OHHHHH *S***T,* MORTY. WATCH AND LEARN. THIS IS HOW A ROGUE PAYS THE RENT. SUMMER'S GOING TO SHOW YOU...
NO... *NOT* SUMMER...
WINTERBLADE
SNEAK ATTACK!

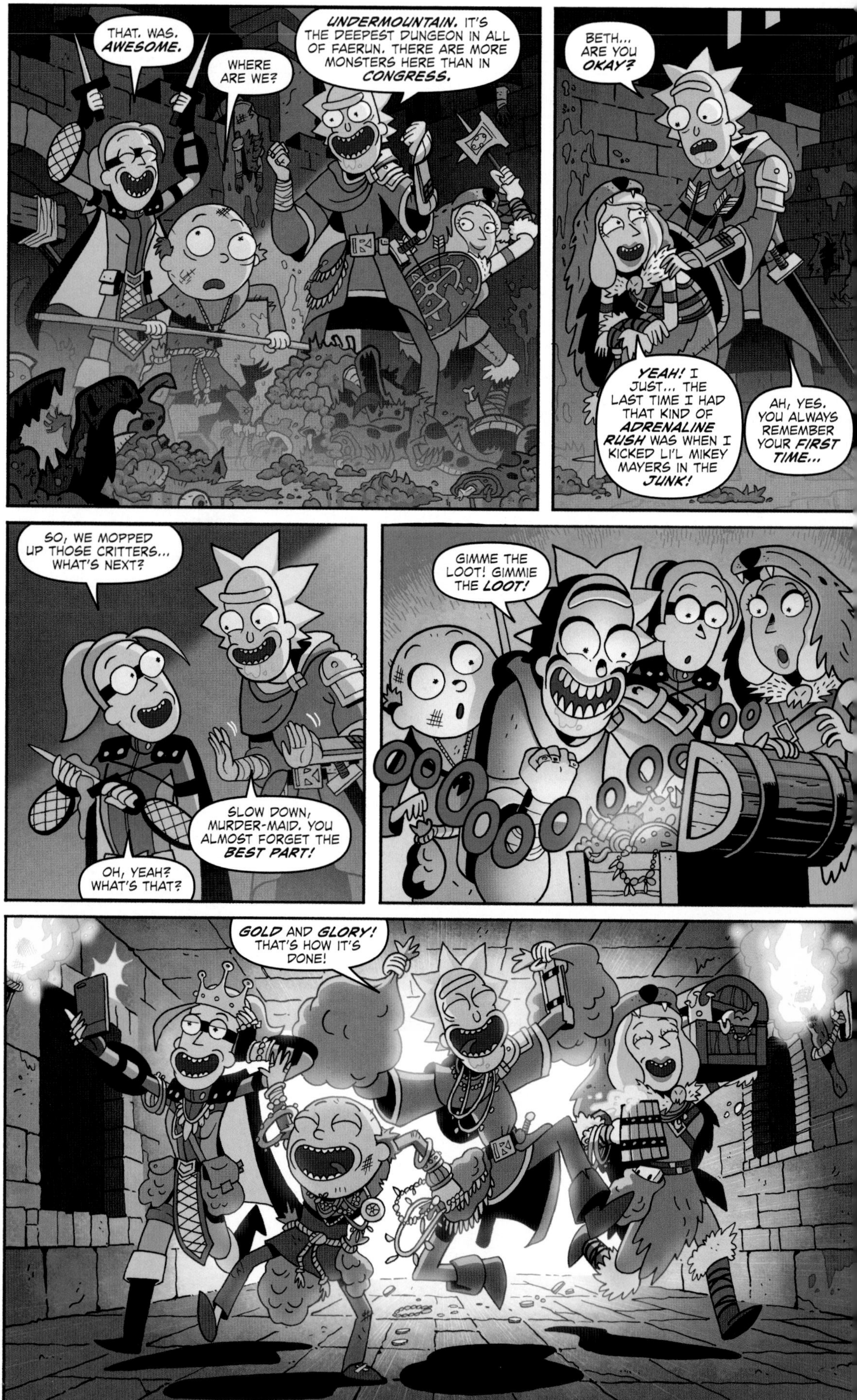
THAT. WAS. AWESOME.
WHERE ARE WE?
UNDERMOUNTAIN. IT'S THE DEEPEST DUNGEON IN ALL OF FAERUN. THERE ARE MORE MONSTERS HERE THAN IN CONGRESS.
BETH... ARE YOU OKAY?
YEAH! I JUST... THE LAST TIME I HAD THAT KIND OF ADRENALINE RUSH WAS WHEN I KICKED LI'L MIKEY MAYERS IN THE JUNK!
AH, YES. YOU ALWAYS REMEMBER YOUR FIRST TIME...
SO, WE MOPPED UP THOSE CRITTERS... WHAT'S NEXT?
SLOW DOWN, MURDER-MAID. YOU ALMOST FORGET THE BEST PART!
OH, YEAH? WHAT'S THAT?
GIMME THE LOOT! GIMMIE THE LOOT!
GOLD AND GLORY! THAT'S HOW IT'S DONE!

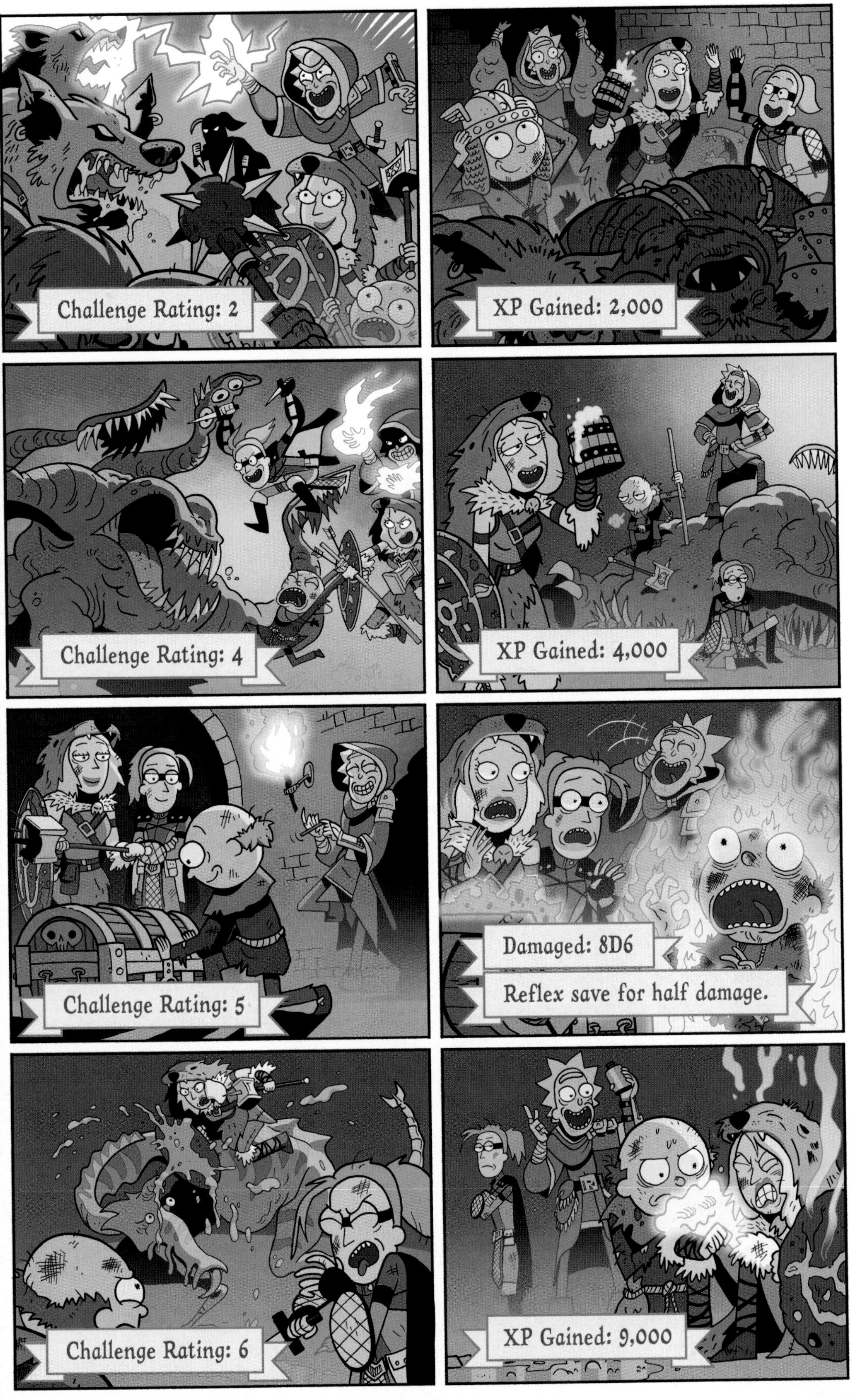
Challenge Rating: 2
XP Gained: 2,000
Challenge Rating: 4
XP Gained: 4,000
Challenge Rating: 5
Damaged: 8D6
Reflex save for half damage.
Challenge Rating: 6
XP Gained: 9,000

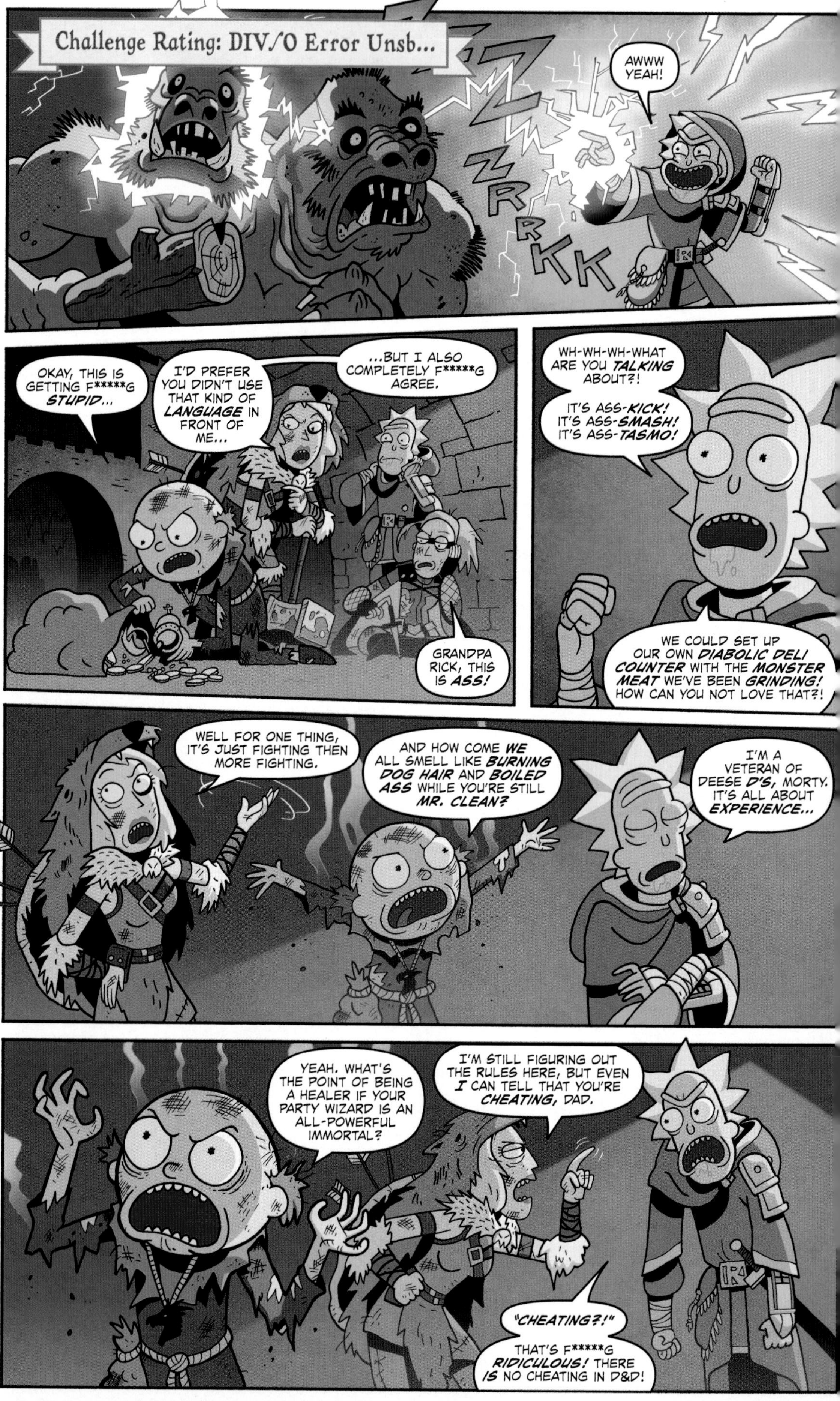
Challenge Rating: DIV/0 Error Unsb...
ZZRRKK
AWWW YEAH!
OKAY, THIS IS GETTING F*****G STUPID...
I'D PREFER YOU DIDN'T USE THAT KIND OF LANGUAGE IN FRONT OF ME...
...BUT I ALSO COMPLETELY F*****G AGREE.
GRANDPA RICK, THIS IS ASS!
WH-WH-WH-WHAT ARE YOU TALKING ABOUT?!
IT'S ASS-KICK! IT'S ASS-SMASH! IT'S ASS-TASMO!
WE COULD SET UP OUR OWN DIABOLIC DELI COUNTER WITH THE MONSTER MEAT WE'VE BEEN GRINDING! HOW CAN YOU NOT LOVE THAT?!
WELL FOR ONE THING, IT'S JUST FIGHTING THEN MORE FIGHTING.
AND HOW COME WE ALL SMELL LIKE BURNING DOG HAIR AND BOILED ASS WHILE YOU'RE STILL MR. CLEAN?
I'M A VETERAN OF DEESE D'S, MORTY. IT'S ALL ABOUT EXPERIENCE...
YEAH. WHAT'S THE POINT OF BEING A HEALER IF YOUR PARTY WIZARD IS AN ALL-POWERFUL IMMORTAL?
I'M STILL FIGURING OUT THE RULES HERE, BUT EVEN I CAN TELL THAT YOU'RE CHEATING, DAD.
"CHEATING?!"
THAT'S F*****G RIDICULOUS! THERE IS NO CHEATING IN D&D!

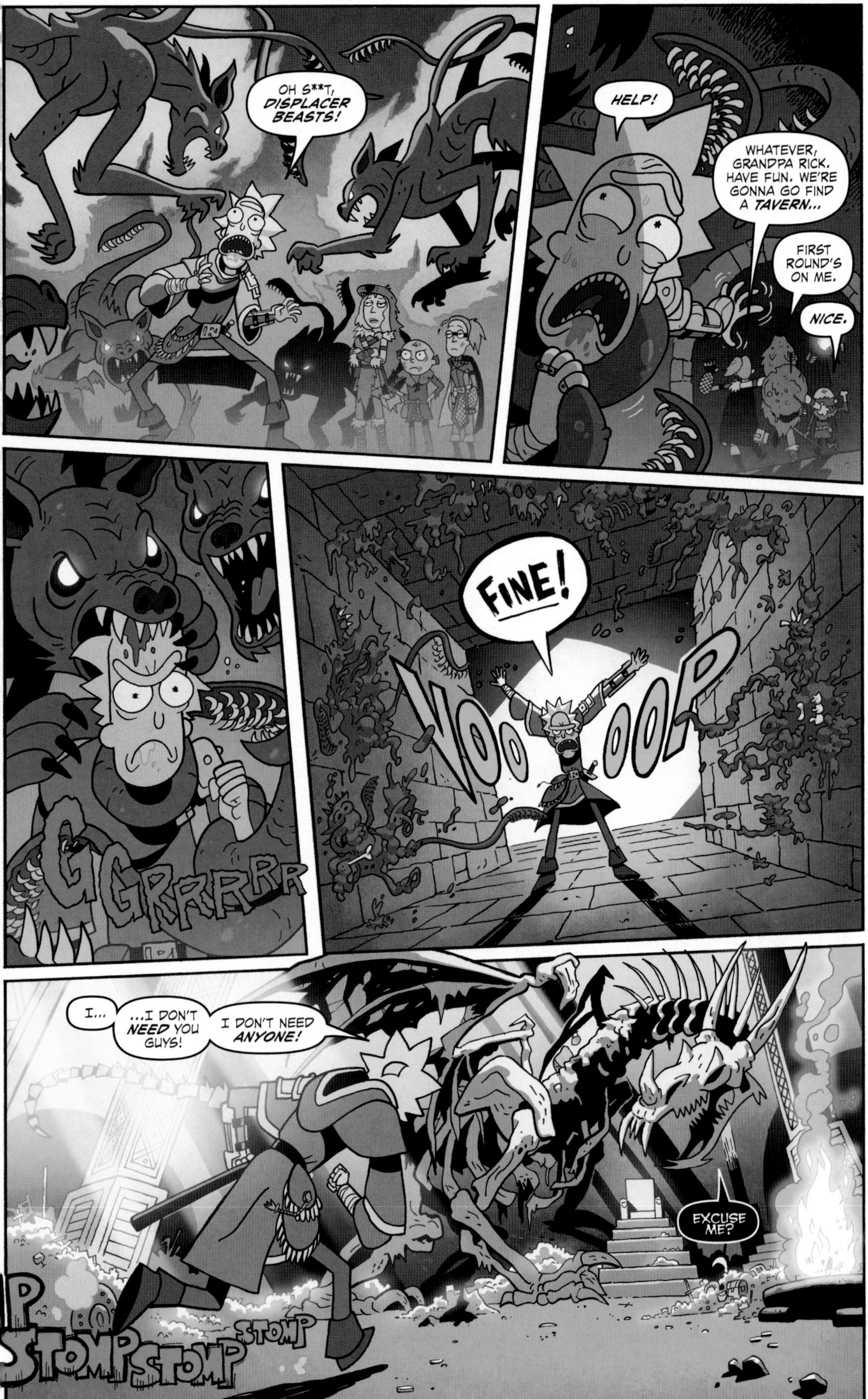
OH S**T, DISPLACER BEASTS!
HELP!
WHATEVER, GRANDPA RICK. HAVE FUN. WE'RE GONNA GO FIND A TAVERN...
FIRST ROUND'S ON ME.
NICE.
GGRRRRR
FINE!
VOO OOP
I...
...I DON'T NEED YOU GUYS!
I DON'T NEED ANYONE!
EXCUSE ME?
STOMPSTOMP
STOMP

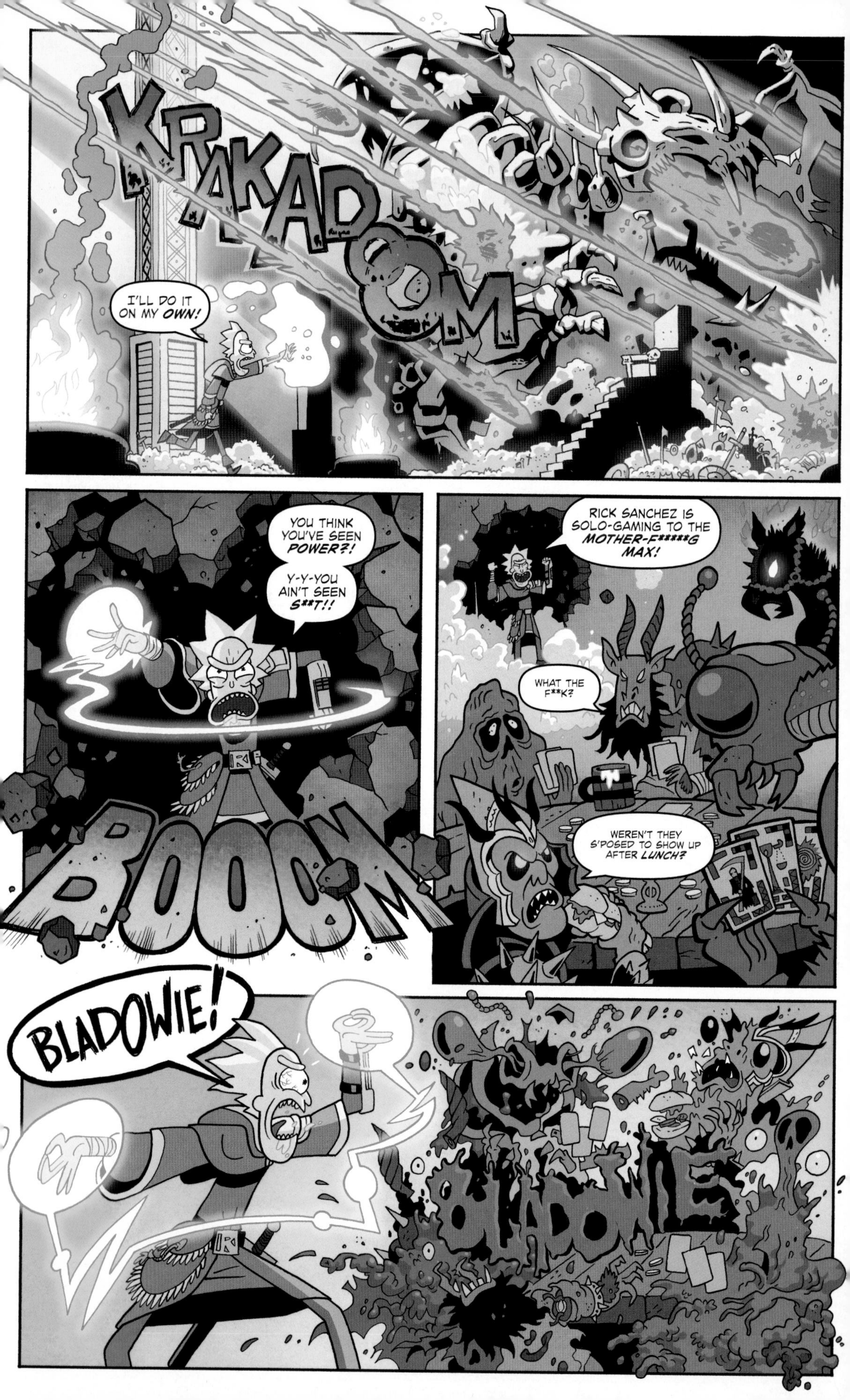
KRAKADOOM
I'LL DO IT ON MY OWN!
YOU THINK YOU'VE SEEN POWER?!
Y-Y-YOU AIN'T SEEN S**T!!
BOOOM
RICK SANCHEZ IS SOLO-GAMING TO THE MOTHER-F*****G MAX!
WHAT THE F**K?
WEREN'T THEY S'POSED TO SHOW UP AFTER LUNCH?
BLADOWIE!
BLADOWIE

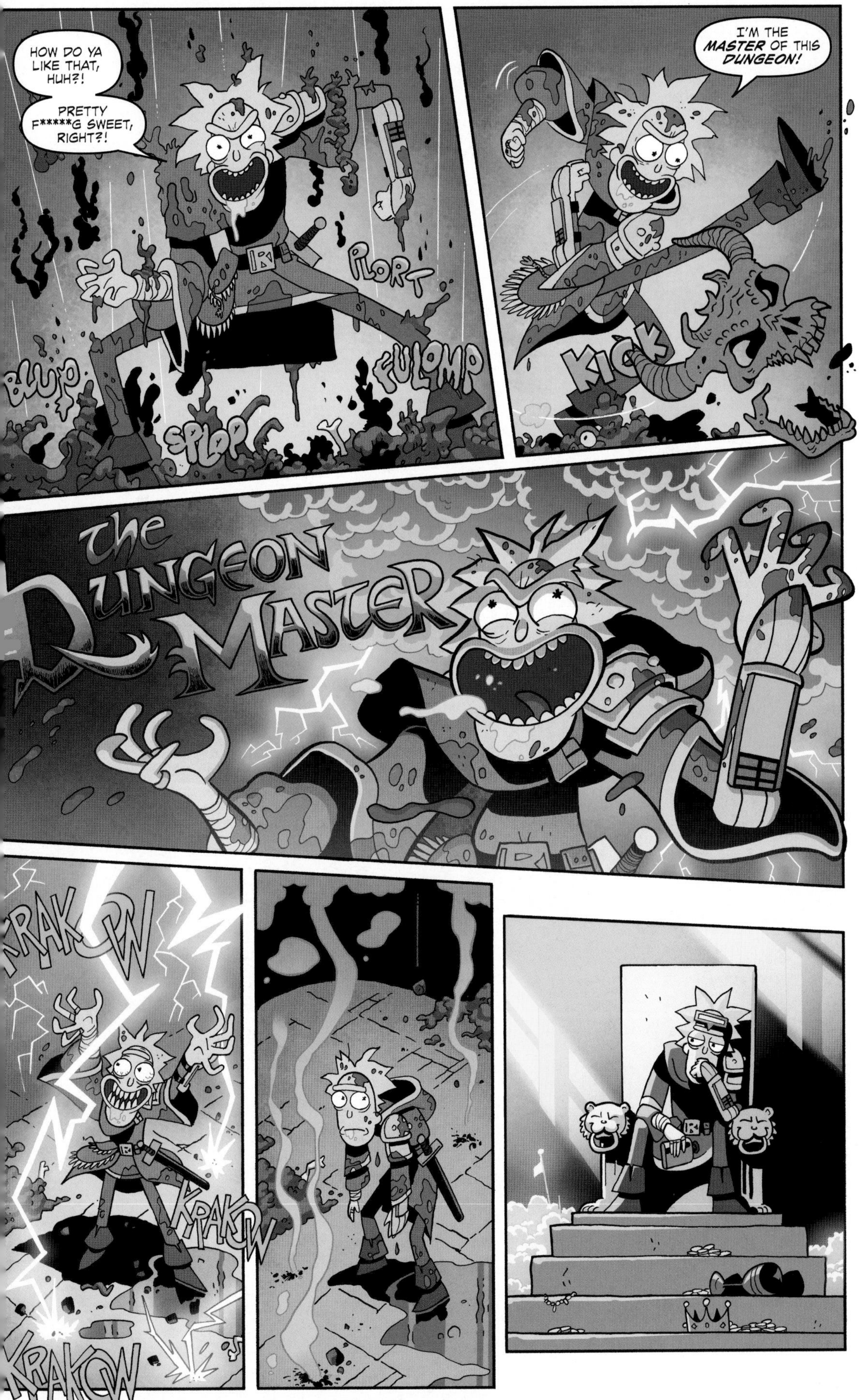
HOW DO YA LIKE THAT, HUH?!
PRETTY F*****G SWEET, RIGHT?!
PLORT
BLUP
SPLOP
FULOMP
I'M THE MASTER OF THIS DUNGEON!
KICK
The DUNGEON MASTER
KRAKOW
KRAKOW
KRAKOW

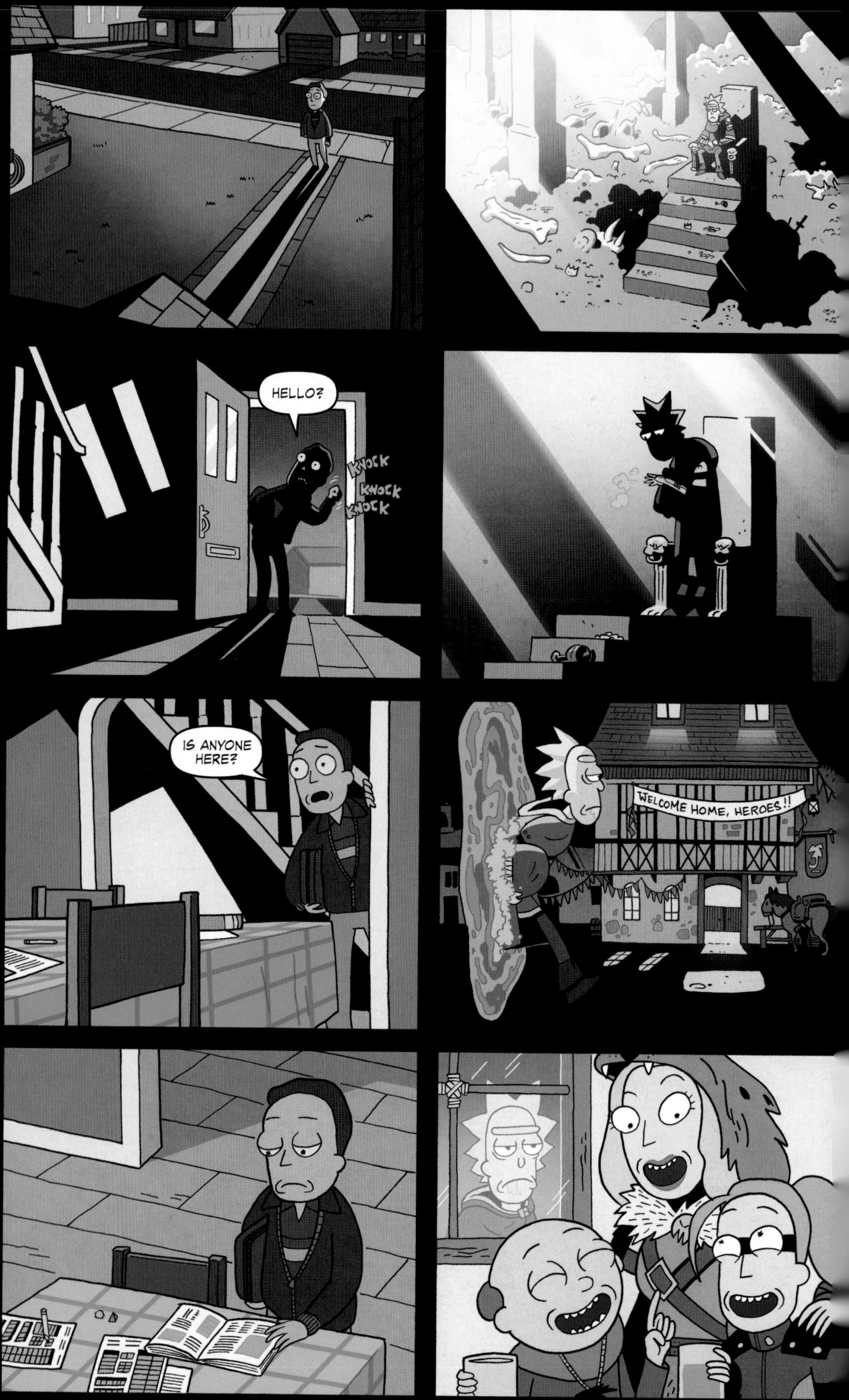
HELLO?
KNOCK
KNOCK
KNOCK
IS ANYONE HERE?
WELCOME HOME, HEROES!!

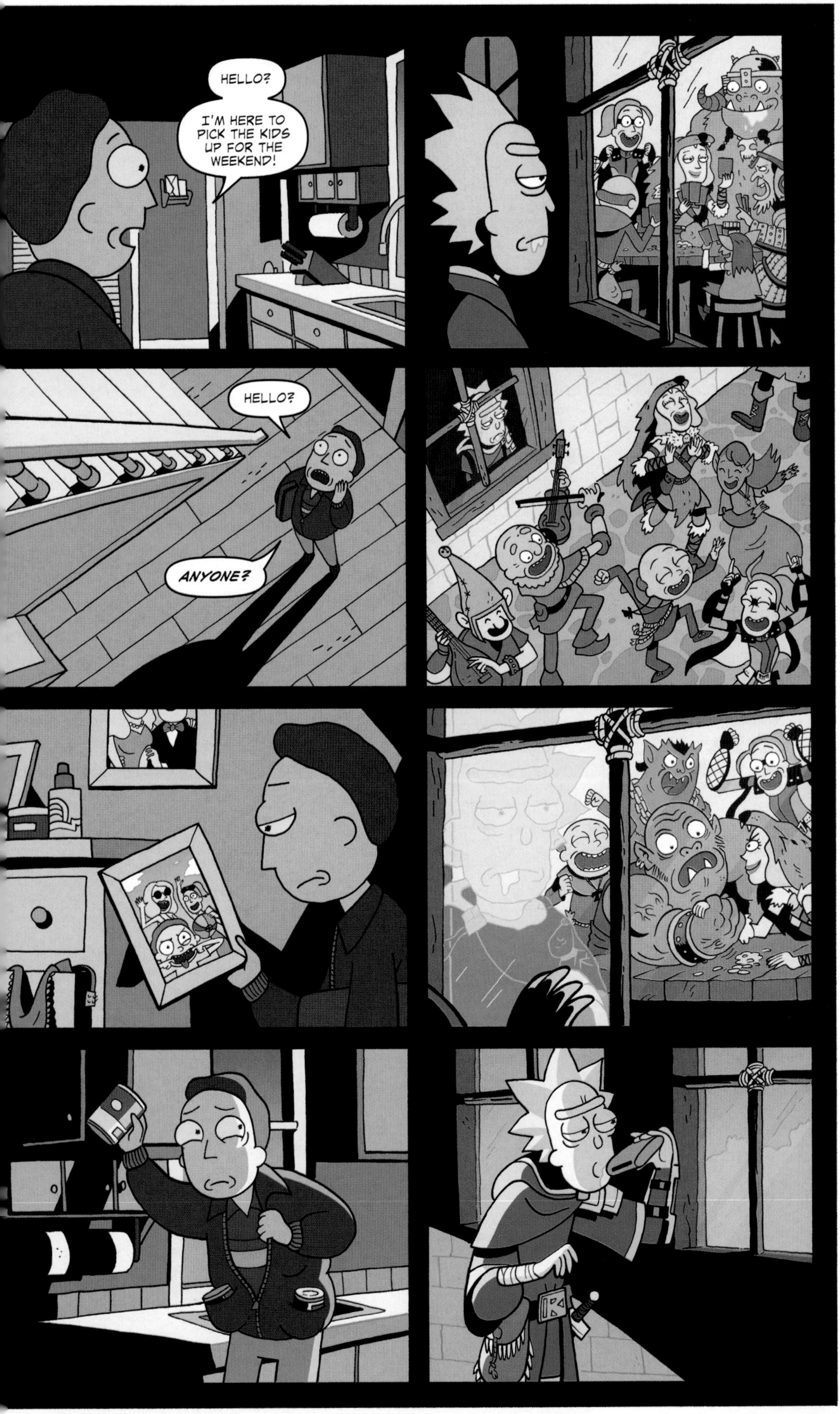
HELLO?
I'M HERE TO PICK THE KIDS UP FOR THE WEEKEND!
HELLO?
ANYONE?

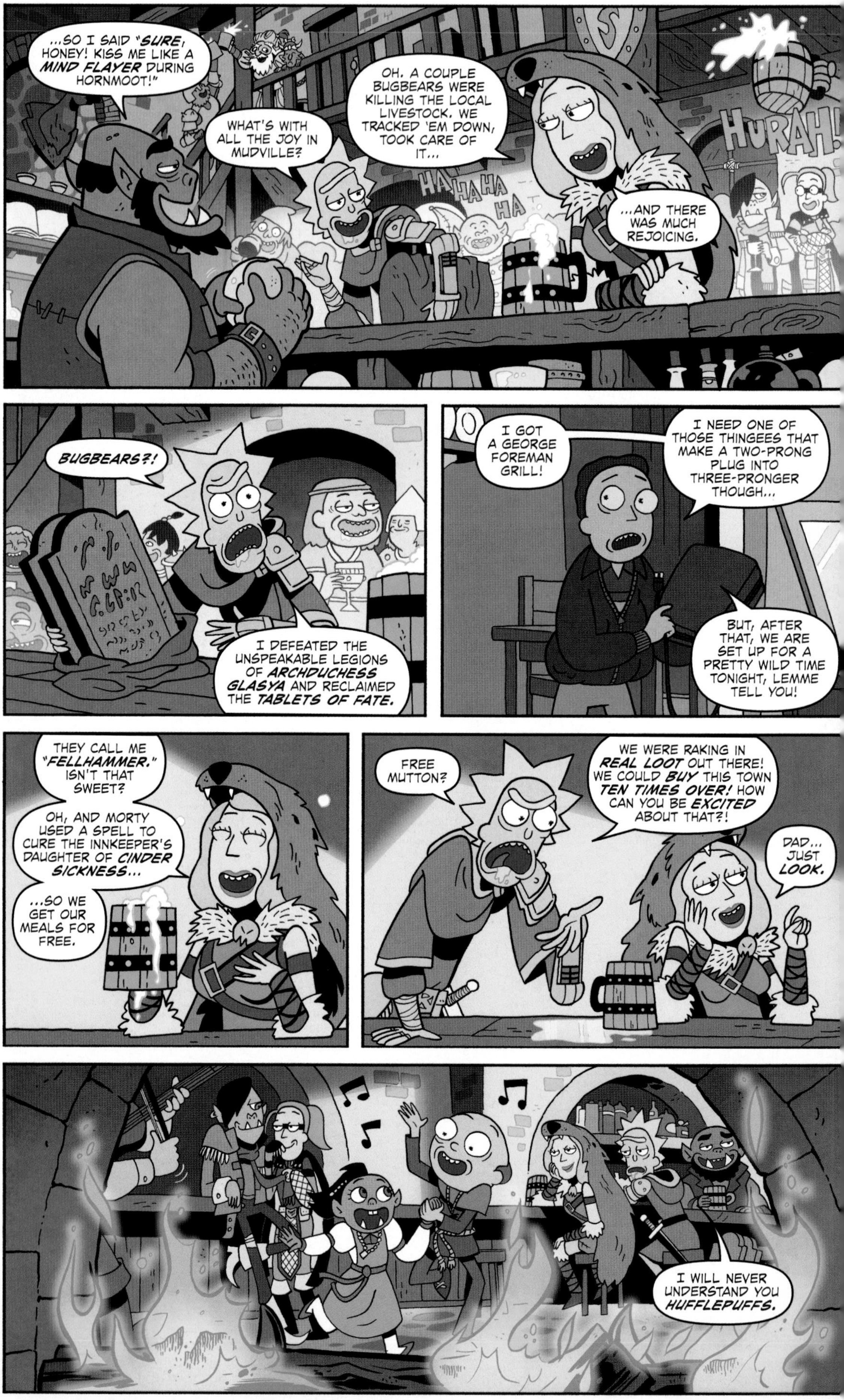
...SO I SAID "SURE, HONEY! KISS ME LIKE A MIND FLAYER DURING HORNMOOT!"
WHAT'S WITH ALL THE JOY IN MUDVILLE?
OH. A COUPLE BUGBEARS WERE KILLING THE LOCAL LIVESTOCK. WE TRACKED 'EM DOWN, TOOK CARE OF IT...
HA HA HA HA
HURAH!
...AND THERE WAS MUCH REJOICING.
BUGBEARS?!
I DEFEATED THE UNSPEAKABLE LEGIONS OF ARCHDUCHESS GLASYA AND RECLAIMED THE TABLETS OF FATE.
I GOT A GEORGE FOREMAN GRILL!
I NEED ONE OF THOSE THINGEES THAT MAKE A TWO-PRONG PLUG INTO THREE-PRONGER THOUGH...
BUT, AFTER THAT, WE ARE SET UP FOR A PRETTY WILD TIME TONIGHT, LEMME TELL YOU!
THEY CALL ME "FELLHAMMER." ISN'T THAT SWEET?
OH, AND MORTY USED A SPELL TO CURE THE INNKEEPER'S DAUGHTER OF CINDER SICKNESS...
...SO WE GET OUR MEALS FOR FREE.
FREE MUTTON?
WE WERE RAKING IN REAL LOOT OUT THERE! WE COULD BUY THIS TOWN TEN TIMES OVER! HOW CAN YOU BE EXCITED ABOUT THAT?!
DAD... JUST LOOK.
I WILL NEVER UNDERSTAND YOU HUFFLEPUFFS.

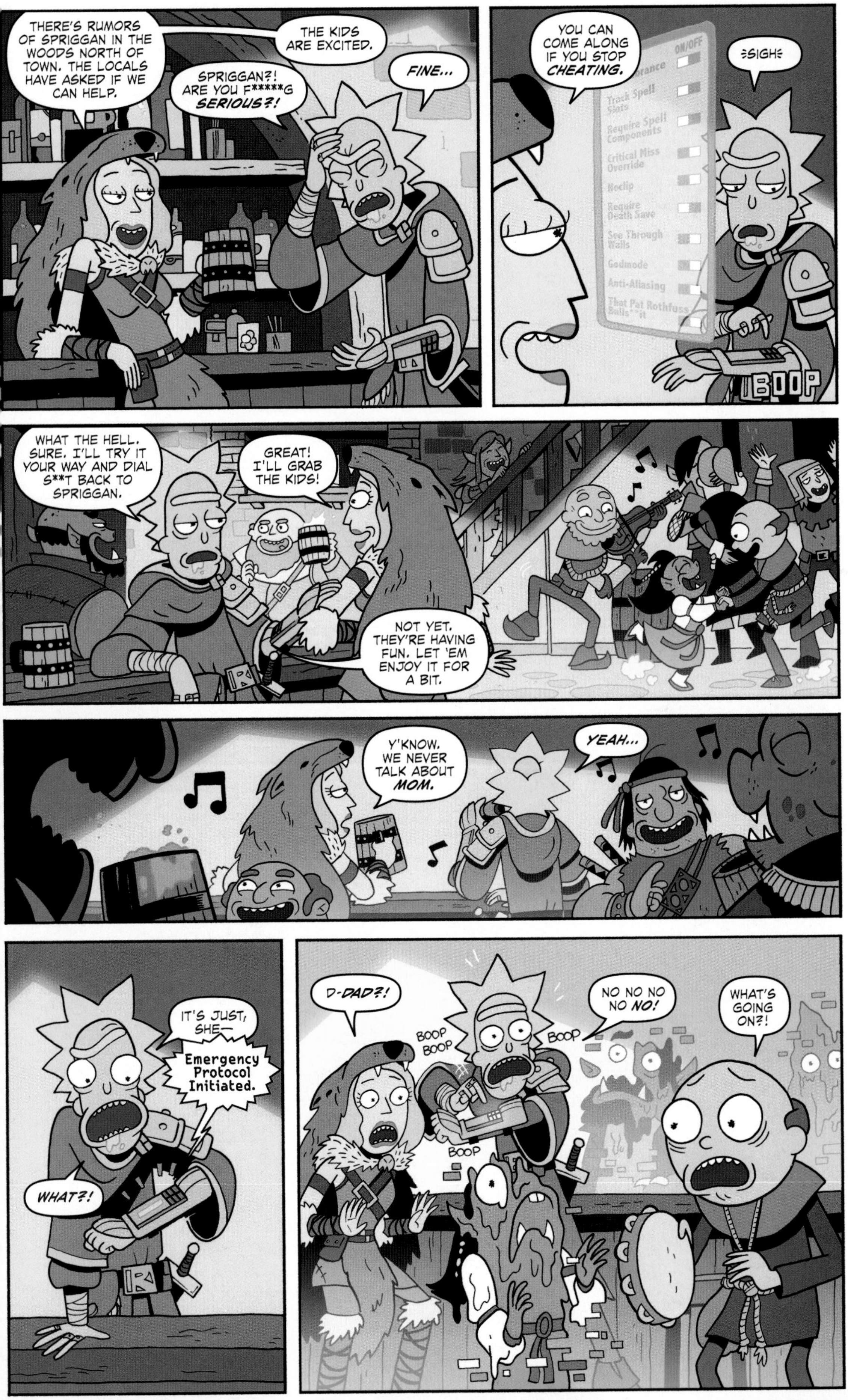
THERE'S RUMORS OF SPRIGGAN IN THE WOODS NORTH OF TOWN. THE LOCALS HAVE ASKED IF WE CAN HELP.
THE KIDS ARE EXCITED.
SPRIGGAN?! ARE YOU F*****G SERIOUS?!
FINE...
YOU CAN COME ALONG IF YOU STOP CHEATING.
≈SIGH≈
ON/OFF
...brance
Track Spell Slots
Require Spell Components
Critical Miss Override
Noclip
Require Death Save
See Through Walls
Godmode
Anti-Aliasing
That Pat Rothfuss Bulls**it
BOOP
WHAT THE HELL. SURE. I'LL TRY IT YOUR WAY AND DIAL S**T BACK TO SPRIGGAN.
GREAT! I'LL GRAB THE KIDS!
NOT YET. THEY'RE HAVING FUN. LET 'EM ENJOY IT FOR A BIT.
Y'KNOW. WE NEVER TALK ABOUT MOM.
YEAH...
IT'S JUST, SHE—
Emergency Protocol Initiated.
WHAT?!
D-DAD?!
BOOP BOOP
BOOP
BOOP
NO NO NO NO NO!
WHAT'S GOING ON?!

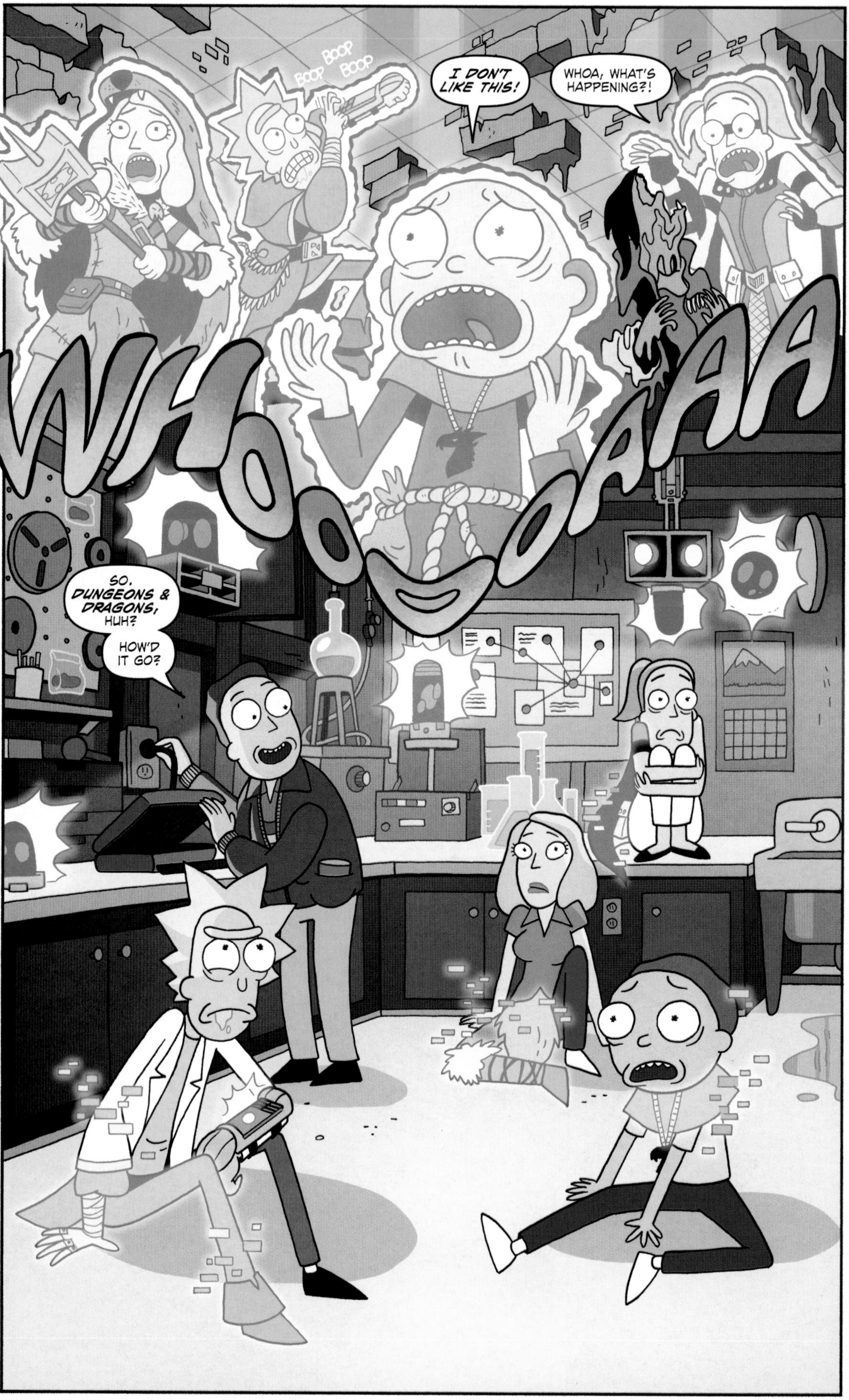

BOOP BOOP BOOP
I DON'T LIKE THIS!
WHOA, WHAT'S HAPPENING?!
WHOOOOOOAAAA
SO. DUNGEONS & DRAGONS, HUH?
HOW'D IT GO?

Art by Julia Scott

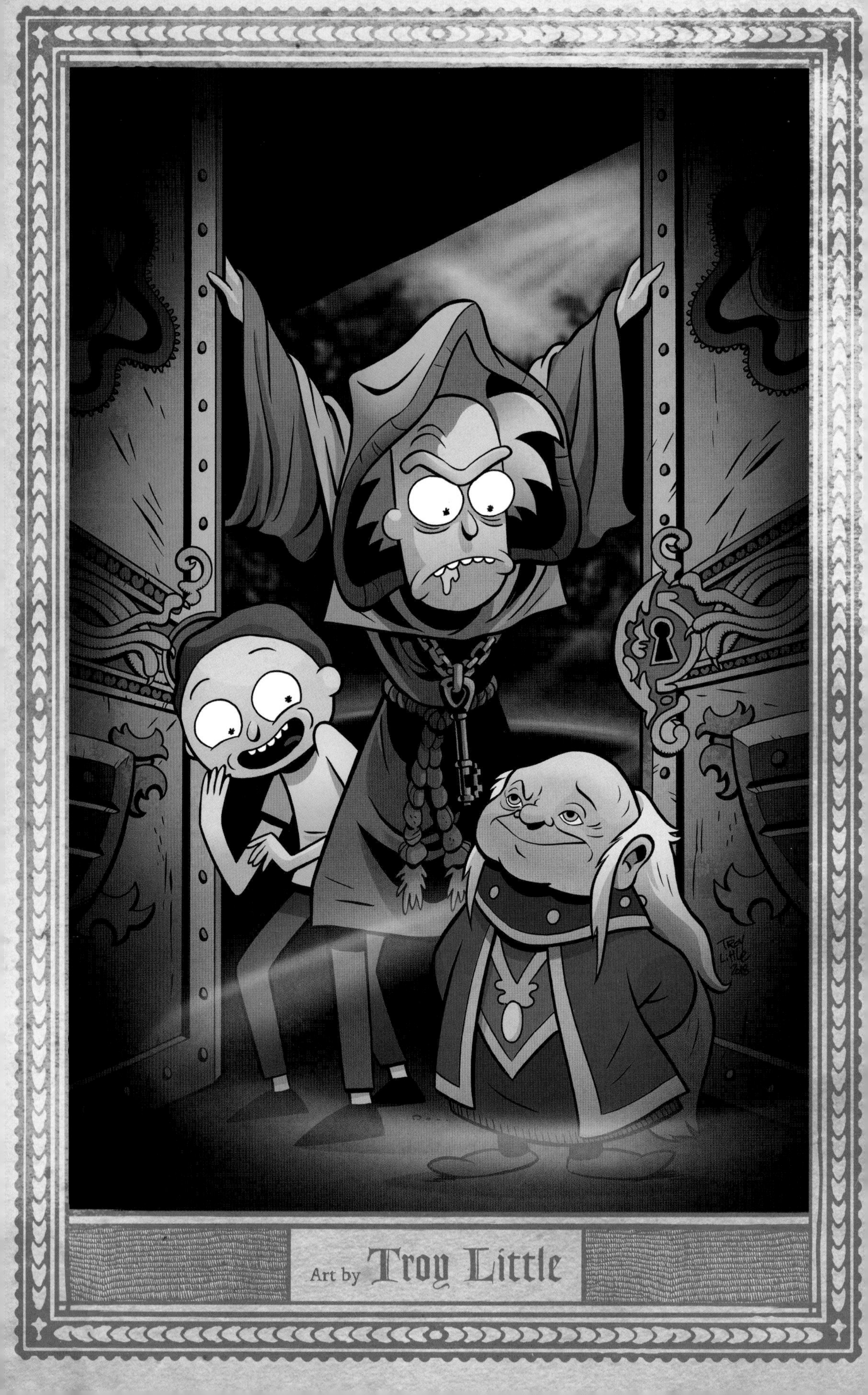

Art by Troy Little

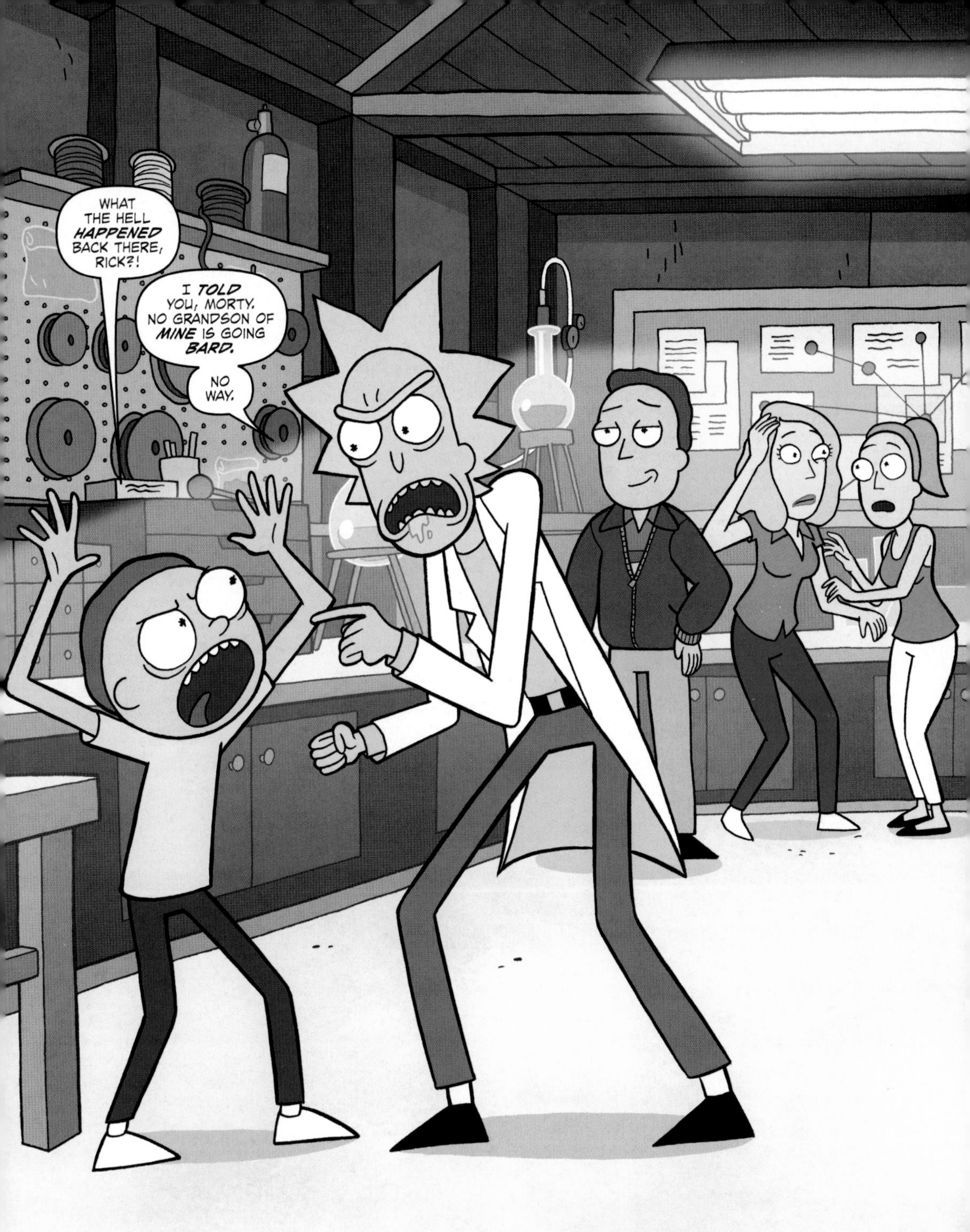
WHAT THE HELL HAPPENED BACK THERE, RICK?!
I TOLD YOU, MORTY. NO GRANDSON OF MINE IS GOING BARD.
NO WAY.

Rick and Morty vs. Dungeons & Dragons

PART III: REALITY BITES (FOR 3D6+1)

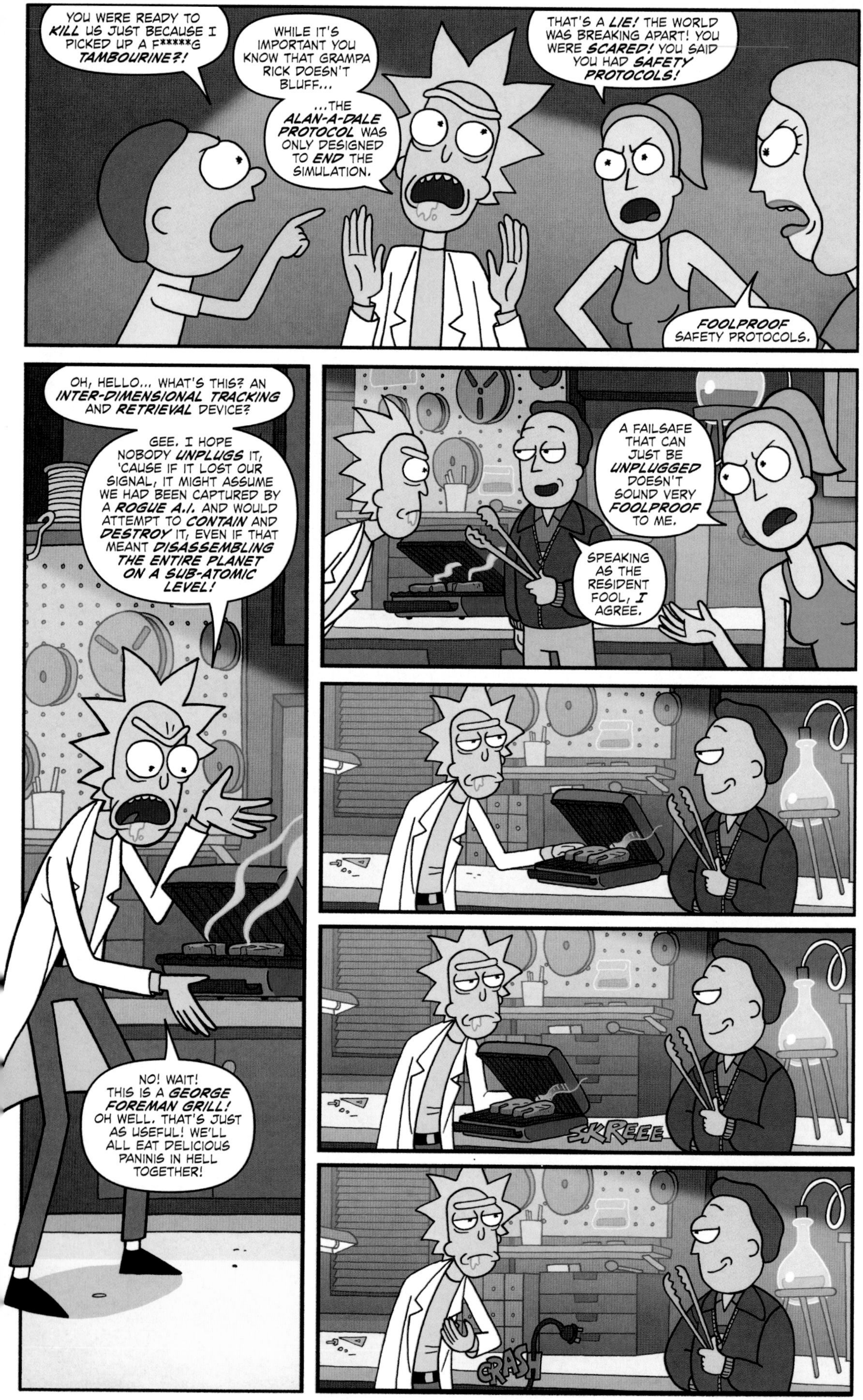
YOU WERE READY TO KILL US JUST BECAUSE I PICKED UP A F*****G TAMBOURINE?!
WHILE IT'S IMPORTANT YOU KNOW THAT GRAMPA RICK DOESN'T BLUFF...
...THE ALAN-A-DALE PROTOCOL WAS ONLY DESIGNED TO END THE SIMULATION.
THAT'S A LIE! THE WORLD WAS BREAKING APART! YOU WERE SCARED! YOU SAID YOU HAD SAFETY PROTOCOLS!
FOOLPROOF SAFETY PROTOCOLS.
OH, HELLO... WHAT'S THIS? AN INTER-DIMENSIONAL TRACKING AND RETRIEVAL DEVICE?
GEE. I HOPE NOBODY UNPLUGS IT, 'CAUSE IF IT LOST OUR SIGNAL, IT MIGHT ASSUME WE HAD BEEN CAPTURED BY A ROGUE A.I. AND WOULD ATTEMPT TO CONTAIN AND DESTROY IT, EVEN IF THAT MEANT DISASSEMBLING THE ENTIRE PLANET ON A SUB-ATOMIC LEVEL!
NO! WAIT! THIS IS A GEORGE FOREMAN GRILL! OH WELL. THAT'S JUST AS USEFUL! WE'LL ALL EAT DELICIOUS PANINIS IN HELL TOGETHER!
A FAILSAFE THAT CAN JUST BE UNPLUGGED DOESN'T SOUND VERY FOOLPROOF TO ME.
SPEAKING AS THE RESIDENT FOOL, I AGREE.
SKREEE
CRASH

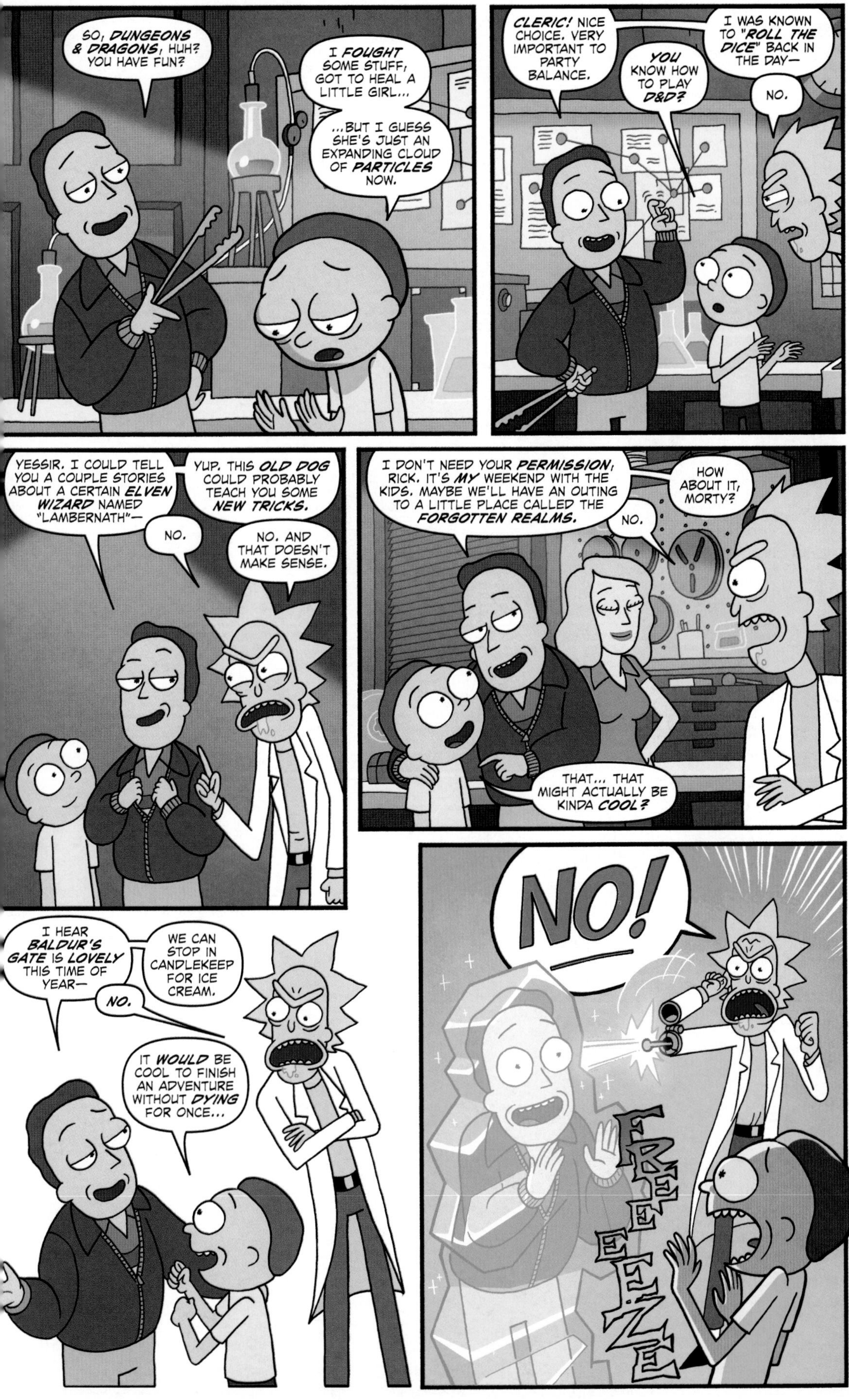
SO, DUNGEONS & DRAGONS, HUH? YOU HAVE FUN?
I FOUGHT SOME STUFF, GOT TO HEAL A LITTLE GIRL...
...BUT I GUESS SHE'S JUST AN EXPANDING CLOUD OF PARTICLES NOW.
CLERIC! NICE CHOICE. VERY IMPORTANT TO PARTY BALANCE.
YOU KNOW HOW TO PLAY D&D?
I WAS KNOWN TO "ROLL THE DICE" BACK IN THE DAY—
NO.
YESSIR. I COULD TELL YOU A COUPLE STORIES ABOUT A CERTAIN ELVEN WIZARD NAMED "LAMBERNATH"—
YUP. THIS OLD DOG COULD PROBABLY TEACH YOU SOME NEW TRICKS.
NO.
NO. AND THAT DOESN'T MAKE SENSE.
I DON'T NEED YOUR PERMISSION, RICK. IT'S MY WEEKEND WITH THE KIDS. MAYBE WE'LL HAVE AN OUTING TO A LITTLE PLACE CALLED THE FORGOTTEN REALMS.
HOW ABOUT IT, MORTY?
NO.
THAT... THAT MIGHT ACTUALLY BE KINDA COOL?
I HEAR BALDUR'S GATE IS LOVELY THIS TIME OF YEAR—
WE CAN STOP IN CANDLEKEEP FOR ICE CREAM.
NO.
IT WOULD BE COOL TO FINISH AN ADVENTURE WITHOUT DYING FOR ONCE...
NO!
FREEEEEZE

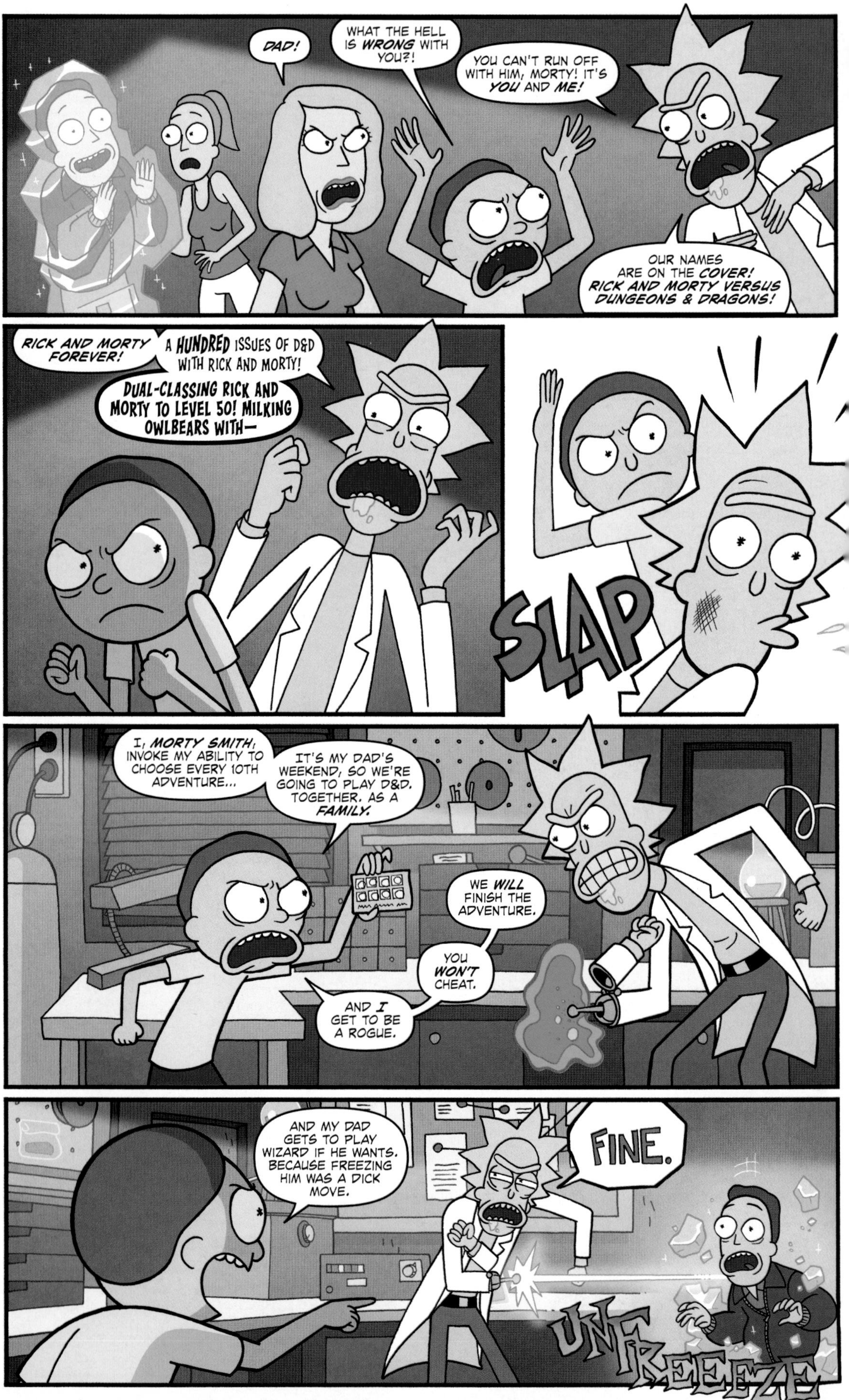
DAD!
WHAT THE HELL IS WRONG WITH YOU?!
YOU CAN'T RUN OFF WITH HIM, MORTY! IT'S YOU AND ME!
OUR NAMES ARE ON THE COVER! RICK AND MORTY VERSUS DUNGEONS & DRAGONS!
RICK AND MORTY FOREVER!
A HUNDRED ISSUES OF D&D WITH RICK AND MORTY!
DUAL-CLASSING RICK AND MORTY TO LEVEL 50! MILKING OWLBEARS WITH—
SLAP
I, MORTY SMITH, INVOKE MY ABILITY TO CHOOSE EVERY 10TH ADVENTURE...
IT'S MY DAD'S WEEKEND, SO WE'RE GOING TO PLAY D&D. TOGETHER. AS A FAMILY.
WE WILL FINISH THE ADVENTURE.
YOU WON'T CHEAT.
AND I GET TO BE A ROGUE.
AND MY DAD GETS TO PLAY WIZARD IF HE WANTS. BECAUSE FREEZING HIM WAS A DICK MOVE.
FINE.
UNFREEEZE

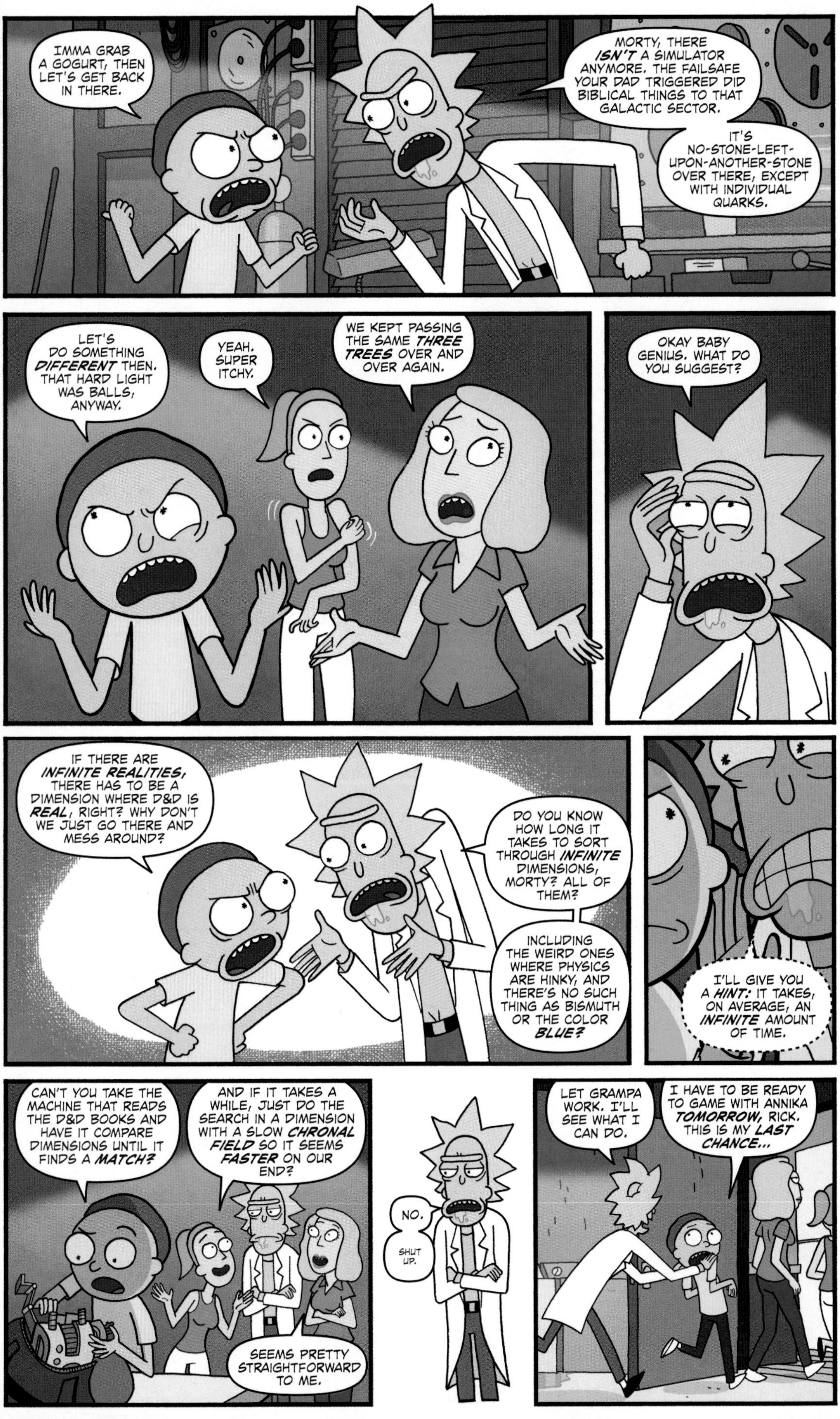
IMMA GRAB A GOGURT, THEN LET'S GET BACK IN THERE.
MORTY, THERE ISN'T A SIMULATOR ANYMORE. THE FAILSAFE YOUR DAD TRIGGERED DID BIBLICAL THINGS TO THAT GALACTIC SECTOR.
IT'S NO-STONE-LEFT-UPON-ANOTHER-STONE OVER THERE, EXCEPT WITH INDIVIDUAL QUARKS.
LET'S DO SOMETHING DIFFERENT THEN. THAT HARD LIGHT WAS BALLS, ANYWAY.
YEAH. SUPER ITCHY.
WE KEPT PASSING THE SAME THREE TREES OVER AND OVER AGAIN.
OKAY BABY GENIUS. WHAT DO YOU SUGGEST?
IF THERE ARE INFINITE REALITIES, THERE HAS TO BE A DIMENSION WHERE D&D IS REAL, RIGHT? WHY DON'T WE JUST GO THERE AND MESS AROUND?
DO YOU KNOW HOW LONG IT TAKES TO SORT THROUGH INFINITE DIMENSIONS, MORTY? ALL OF THEM?
INCLUDING THE WEIRD ONES WHERE PHYSICS ARE HINKY, AND THERE'S NO SUCH THING AS BISMUTH OR THE COLOR BLUE?
I'LL GIVE YOU A HINT: IT TAKES, ON AVERAGE, AN INFINITE AMOUNT OF TIME.
CAN'T YOU TAKE THE MACHINE THAT READS THE D&D BOOKS AND HAVE IT COMPARE DIMENSIONS UNTIL IT FINDS A MATCH?
AND IF IT TAKES A WHILE, JUST DO THE SEARCH IN A DIMENSION WITH A SLOW CHRONAL FIELD SO IT SEEMS FASTER ON OUR END?
SEEMS PRETTY STRAIGHTFORWARD TO ME.
NO.
SHUT UP.
LET GRAMPA WORK. I'LL SEE WHAT I CAN DO.
I HAVE TO BE READY TO GAME WITH ANNIKA TOMORROW, RICK. THIS IS MY LAST CHANCE...

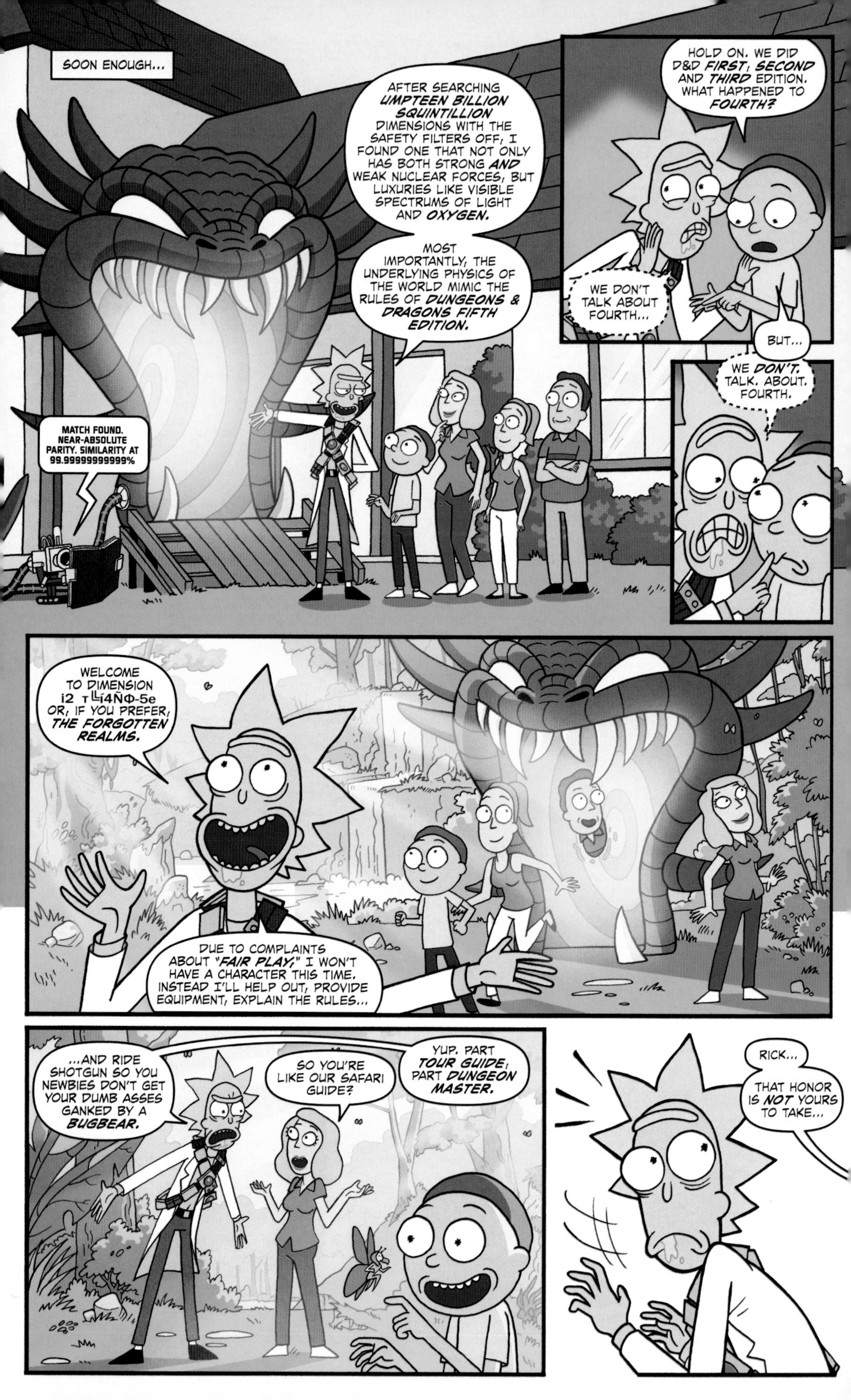
SOON ENOUGH...
AFTER SEARCHING UMPTEEN BILLION SQUINTILLION DIMENSIONS WITH THE SAFETY FILTERS OFF, I FOUND ONE THAT NOT ONLY HAS BOTH STRONG AND WEAK NUCLEAR FORCES, BUT LUXURIES LIKE VISIBLE SPECTRUMS OF LIGHT AND OXYGEN.
MOST IMPORTANTLY, THE UNDERLYING PHYSICS OF THE WORLD MIMIC THE RULES OF DUNGEONS & DRAGONS FIFTH EDITION.
MATCH FOUND. NEAR-ABSOLUTE PARITY. SIMILARITY AT 99.99999999999%
HOLD ON. WE DID D&D FIRST, SECOND AND THIRD EDITION. WHAT HAPPENED TO FOURTH?
WE DON'T TALK ABOUT FOURTH...
BUT...
WE DON'T. TALK. ABOUT. FOURTH.
WELCOME TO DIMENSION i2 τ╙í4ÑΦ-5e OR, IF YOU PREFER, THE FORGOTTEN REALMS.
DUE TO COMPLAINTS ABOUT "FAIR PLAY," I WON'T HAVE A CHARACTER THIS TIME. INSTEAD I'LL HELP OUT, PROVIDE EQUIPMENT, EXPLAIN THE RULES...
...AND RIDE SHOTGUN SO YOU NEWBIES DON'T GET YOUR DUMB ASSES GANKED BY A BUGBEAR.
SO YOU'RE LIKE OUR SAFARI GUIDE?
YUP. PART TOUR GUIDE, PART DUNGEON MASTER.
RICK...
THAT HONOR IS NOT YOURS TO TAKE...

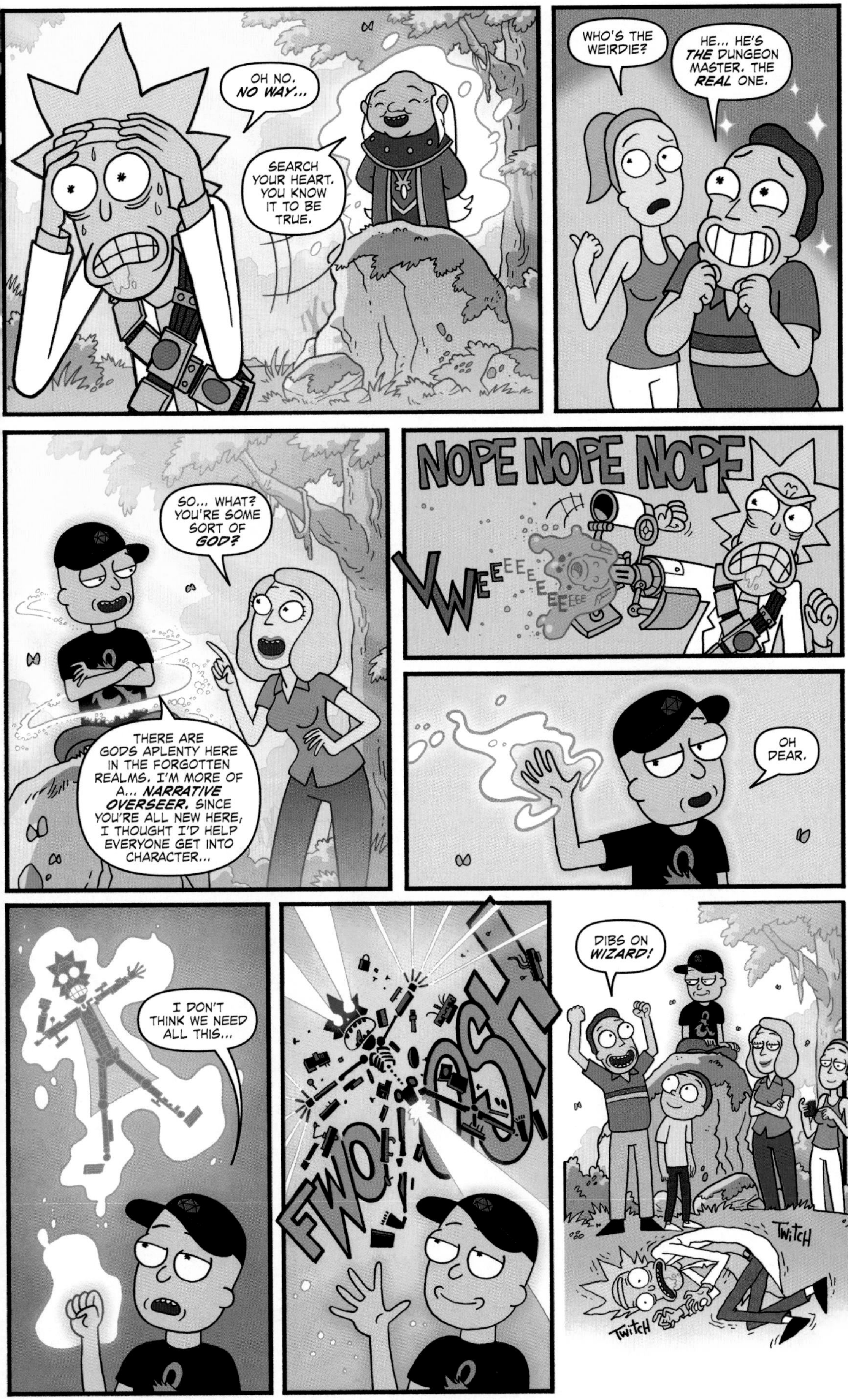

OH NO. NO WAY...
SEARCH YOUR HEART. YOU KNOW IT TO BE TRUE.
WHO'S THE WEIRDIE?
HE... HE'S THE DUNGEON MASTER. THE REAL ONE.
SO... WHAT? YOU'RE SOME SORT OF GOD?
THERE ARE GODS APLENTY HERE IN THE FORGOTTEN REALMS. I'M MORE OF A... NARRATIVE OVERSEER. SINCE YOU'RE ALL NEW HERE, I THOUGHT I'D HELP EVERYONE GET INTO CHARACTER...
NOPE NOPE NOPE
VWEEEEEEEEEE
OH DEAR.
I DON'T THINK WE NEED ALL THIS...
FWOOSH
DIBS ON WIZARD!
TWITCH
TWITCH

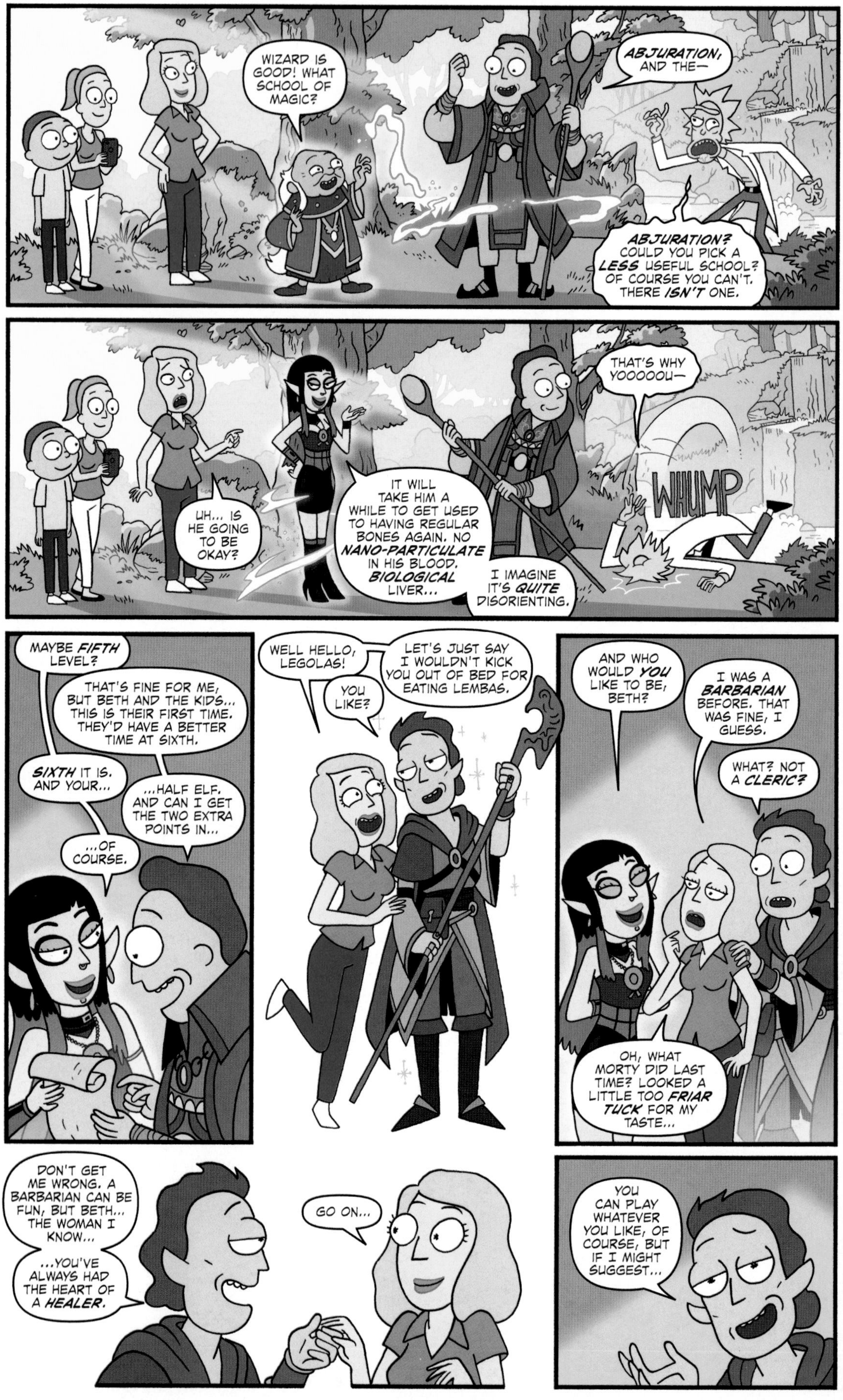
WIZARD IS GOOD! WHAT SCHOOL OF MAGIC?
ABJURATION, AND THE—
ABJURATION? COULD YOU PICK A LESS USEFUL SCHOOL? OF COURSE YOU CAN'T. THERE ISN'T ONE.
THAT'S WHY YOOOOOU—
WHUMP
UH... IS HE GOING TO BE OKAY?
IT WILL TAKE HIM A WHILE TO GET USED TO HAVING REGULAR BONES AGAIN. NO NANO-PARTICULATE IN HIS BLOOD. BIOLOGICAL LIVER...
I IMAGINE IT'S QUITE DISORIENTING.
MAYBE FIFTH LEVEL?
THAT'S FINE FOR ME, BUT BETH AND THE KIDS... THIS IS THEIR FIRST TIME. THEY'D HAVE A BETTER TIME AT SIXTH.
SIXTH IT IS. AND YOUR...
...HALF ELF. AND CAN I GET THE TWO EXTRA POINTS IN...
...OF COURSE.
WELL HELLO, LEGOLAS!
YOU LIKE?
LET'S JUST SAY I WOULDN'T KICK YOU OUT OF BED FOR EATING LEMBAS.
AND WHO WOULD YOU LIKE TO BE, BETH?
I WAS A BARBARIAN BEFORE. THAT WAS FINE, I GUESS.
WHAT? NOT A CLERIC?
OH, WHAT MORTY DID LAST TIME? LOOKED A LITTLE TOO FRIAR TUCK FOR MY TASTE...
DON'T GET ME WRONG. A BARBARIAN CAN BE FUN, BUT BETH... THE WOMAN I KNOW...
...YOU'VE ALWAYS HAD THE HEART OF A HEALER.
GO ON...
YOU CAN PLAY WHATEVER YOU LIKE, OF COURSE, BUT IF I MIGHT SUGGEST...

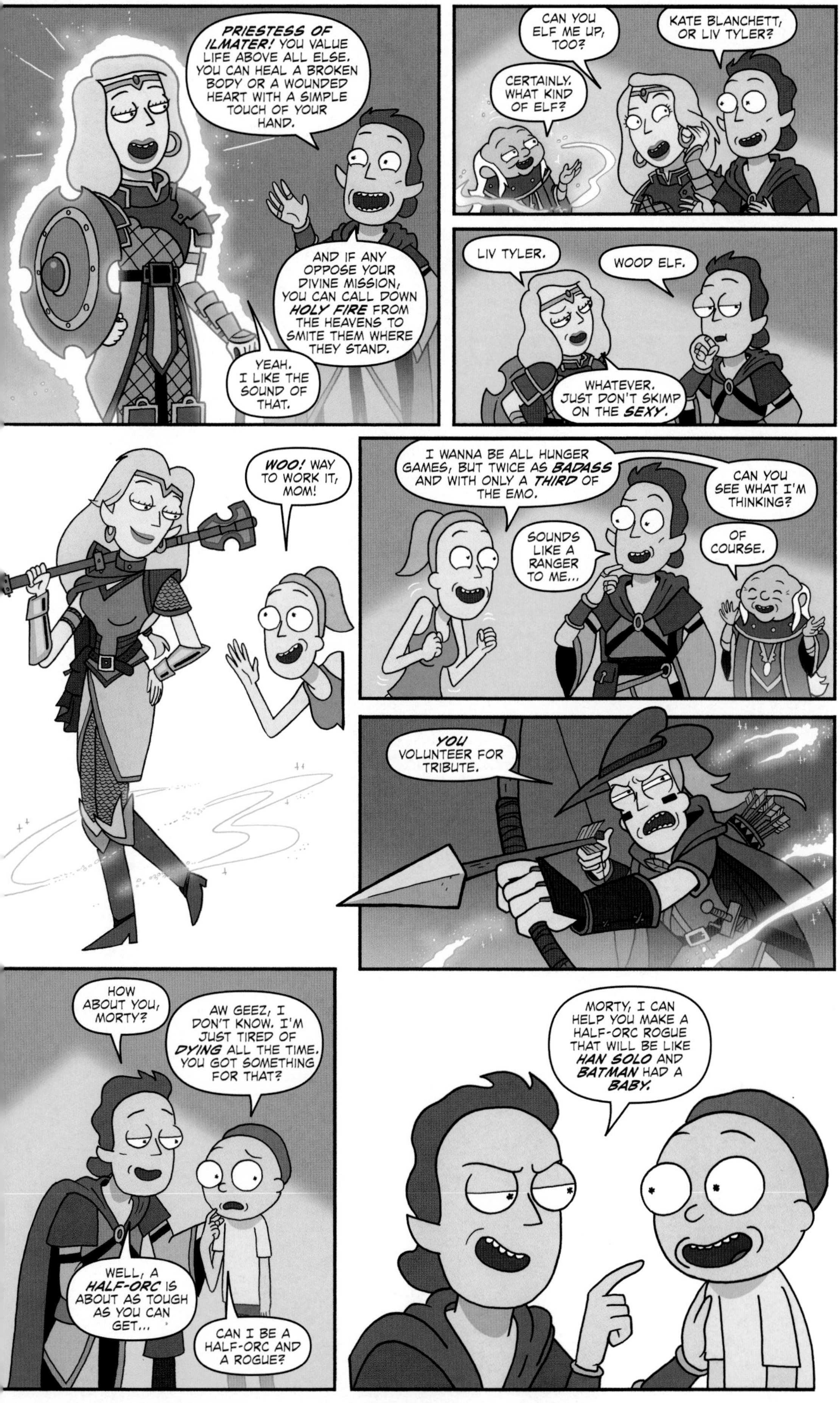

PRIESTESS OF ILMATER! YOU VALUE LIFE ABOVE ALL ELSE. YOU CAN HEAL A BROKEN BODY OR A WOUNDED HEART WITH A SIMPLE TOUCH OF YOUR HAND.
AND IF ANY OPPOSE YOUR DIVINE MISSION, YOU CAN CALL DOWN HOLY FIRE FROM THE HEAVENS TO SMITE THEM WHERE THEY STAND.
YEAH. I LIKE THE SOUND OF THAT.
CAN YOU ELF ME UP, TOO?
KATE BLANCHETT, OR LIV TYLER?
CERTAINLY. WHAT KIND OF ELF?
LIV TYLER.
WOOD ELF.
WHATEVER. JUST DON'T SKIMP ON THE SEXY.
WOO! WAY TO WORK IT, MOM!
I WANNA BE ALL HUNGER GAMES, BUT TWICE AS BADASS AND WITH ONLY A THIRD OF THE EMO.
CAN YOU SEE WHAT I'M THINKING?
SOUNDS LIKE A RANGER TO ME...
OF COURSE.
YOU VOLUNTEER FOR TRIBUTE.
HOW ABOUT YOU, MORTY?
AW GEEZ, I DON'T KNOW. I'M JUST TIRED OF DYING ALL THE TIME. YOU GOT SOMETHING FOR THAT?
WELL, A HALF-ORC IS ABOUT AS TOUGH AS YOU CAN GET...
CAN I BE A HALF-ORC AND A ROGUE?
MORTY, I CAN HELP YOU MAKE A HALF-ORC ROGUE THAT WILL BE LIKE HAN SOLO AND BATMAN HAD A BABY.

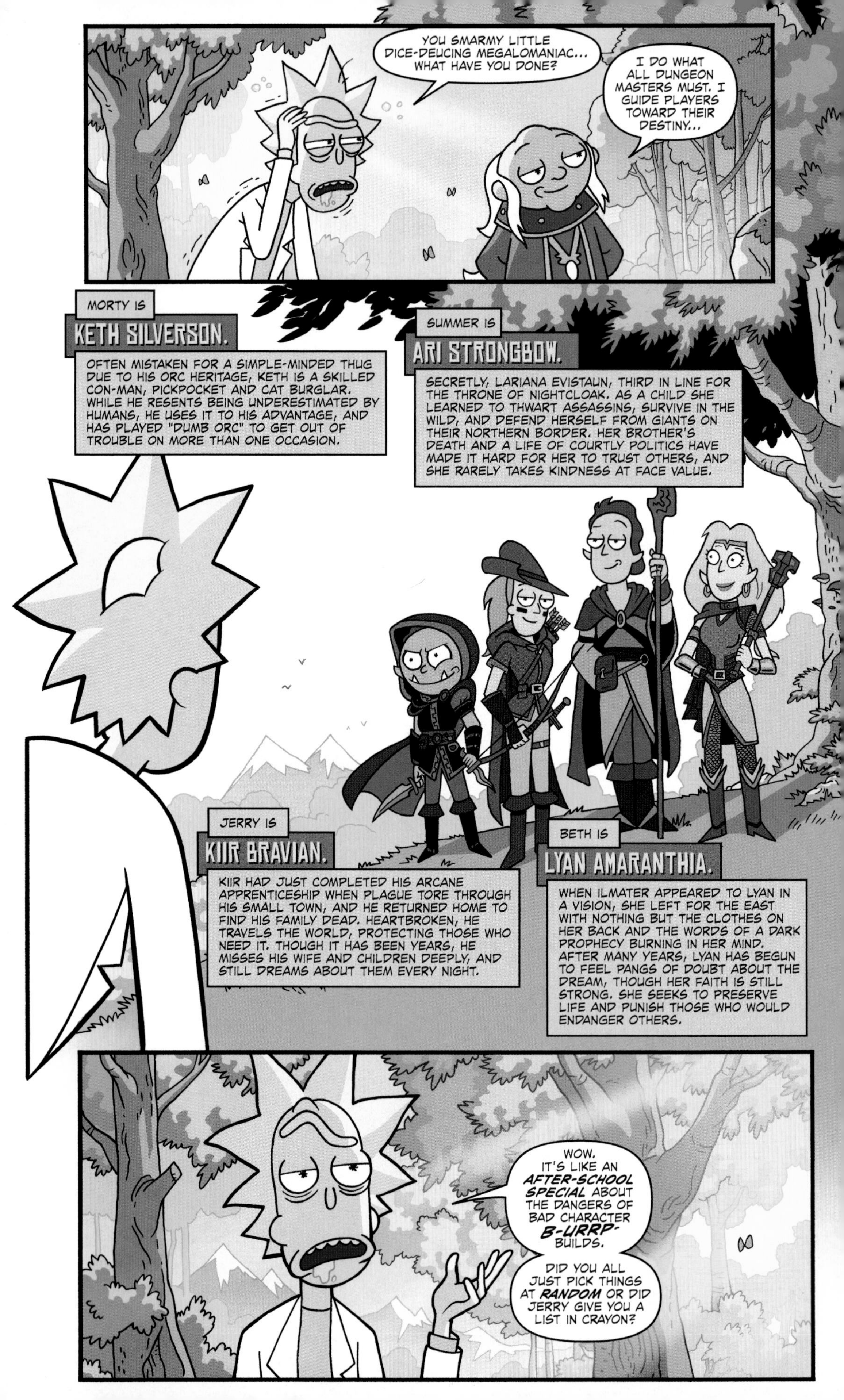
YOU SMARMY LITTLE DICE-DEUCING MEGALOMANIAC... WHAT HAVE YOU DONE?
I DO WHAT ALL DUNGEON MASTERS MUST. I GUIDE PLAYERS TOWARD THEIR DESTINY...
MORTY IS
KETH SILVERSON.
OFTEN MISTAKEN FOR A SIMPLE-MINDED THUG DUE TO HIS ORC HERITAGE, KETH IS A SKILLED CON-MAN, PICKPOCKET AND CAT BURGLAR. WHILE HE RESENTS BEING UNDERESTIMATED BY HUMANS, HE USES IT TO HIS ADVANTAGE, AND HAS PLAYED "DUMB ORC" TO GET OUT OF TROUBLE ON MORE THAN ONE OCCASION.
SUMMER IS
ARI STRONGBOW.
SECRETLY, LARIANA EVISTAUN, THIRD IN LINE FOR THE THRONE OF NIGHTCLOAK. AS A CHILD SHE LEARNED TO THWART ASSASSINS, SURVIVE IN THE WILD, AND DEFEND HERSELF FROM GIANTS ON THEIR NORTHERN BORDER. HER BROTHER'S DEATH AND A LIFE OF COURTLY POLITICS HAVE MADE IT HARD FOR HER TO TRUST OTHERS, AND SHE RARELY TAKES KINDNESS AT FACE VALUE.
JERRY IS
KIIR BRAVIAN.
KIIR HAD JUST COMPLETED HIS ARCANE APPRENTICESHIP WHEN PLAGUE TORE THROUGH HIS SMALL TOWN, AND HE RETURNED HOME TO FIND HIS FAMILY DEAD. HEARTBROKEN, HE TRAVELS THE WORLD, PROTECTING THOSE WHO NEED IT. THOUGH IT HAS BEEN YEARS, HE MISSES HIS WIFE AND CHILDREN DEEPLY, AND STILL DREAMS ABOUT THEM EVERY NIGHT.
BETH IS
LYAN AMARANTHIA.
WHEN ILMATER APPEARED TO LYAN IN A VISION, SHE LEFT FOR THE EAST WITH NOTHING BUT THE CLOTHES ON HER BACK AND THE WORDS OF A DARK PROPHECY BURNING IN HER MIND. AFTER MANY YEARS, LYAN HAS BEGUN TO FEEL PANGS OF DOUBT ABOUT THE DREAM, THOUGH HER FAITH IS STILL STRONG. SHE SEEKS TO PRESERVE LIFE AND PUNISH THOSE WHO WOULD ENDANGER OTHERS.
WOW. IT'S LIKE AN *AFTER-SCHOOL SPECIAL* ABOUT THE DANGERS OF BAD CHARACTER *B-URRP-* BUILDS.
DID YOU ALL JUST PICK THINGS AT *RANDOM* OR DID JERRY GIVE YOU A LIST IN CRAYON?

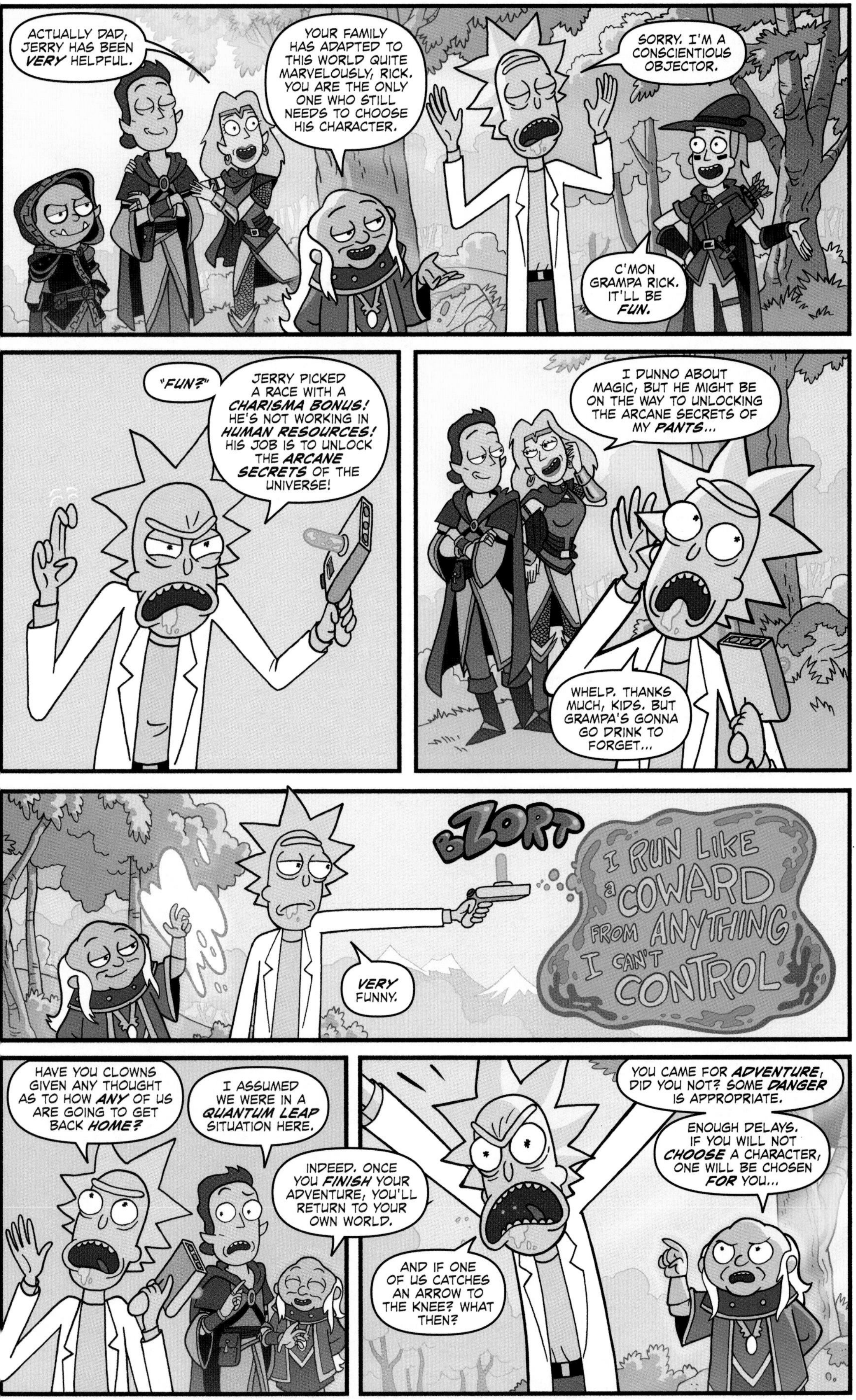

ACTUALLY DAD, JERRY HAS BEEN VERY HELPFUL.
YOUR FAMILY HAS ADAPTED TO THIS WORLD QUITE MARVELOUSLY, RICK. YOU ARE THE ONLY ONE WHO STILL NEEDS TO CHOOSE HIS CHARACTER.
SORRY. I'M A CONSCIENTIOUS OBJECTOR.
C'MON GRAMPA RICK. IT'LL BE FUN.
"FUN?"
JERRY PICKED A RACE WITH A CHARISMA BONUS! HE'S NOT WORKING IN HUMAN RESOURCES! HIS JOB IS TO UNLOCK THE ARCANE SECRETS OF THE UNIVERSE!
I DUNNO ABOUT MAGIC, BUT HE MIGHT BE ON THE WAY TO UNLOCKING THE ARCANE SECRETS OF MY PANTS...
WHELP. THANKS MUCH, KIDS. BUT GRAMPA'S GONNA GO DRINK TO FORGET...
BZORT
I RUN LIKE A COWARD FROM ANYTHING I CAN'T CONTROL
VERY FUNNY.
HAVE YOU CLOWNS GIVEN ANY THOUGHT AS TO HOW ANY OF US ARE GOING TO GET BACK HOME?
I ASSUMED WE WERE IN A QUANTUM LEAP SITUATION HERE.
INDEED. ONCE YOU FINISH YOUR ADVENTURE, YOU'LL RETURN TO YOUR OWN WORLD.
AND IF ONE OF US CATCHES AN ARROW TO THE KNEE? WHAT THEN?
YOU CAME FOR ADVENTURE, DID YOU NOT? SOME DANGER IS APPROPRIATE.
ENOUGH DELAYS. IF YOU WILL NOT CHOOSE A CHARACTER, ONE WILL BE CHOSEN FOR YOU...

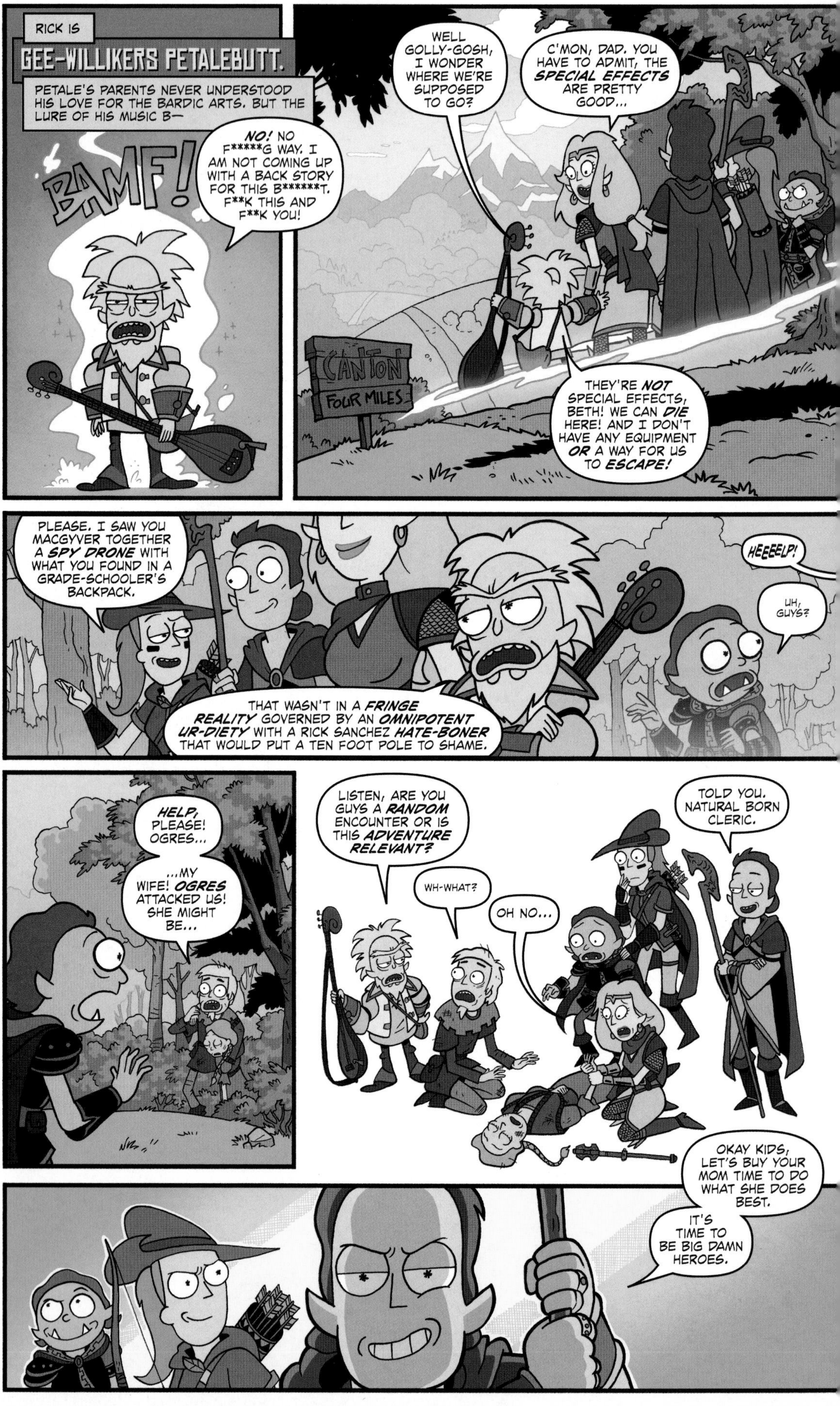
RICK IS
GEE-WILLIKERS PETALEBUTT.
PETALE'S PARENTS NEVER UNDERSTOOD HIS LOVE FOR THE BARDIC ARTS. BUT THE LURE OF HIS MUSIC B—
BAMF!
NO! NO F*****G WAY. I AM NOT COMING UP WITH A BACK STORY FOR THIS B******T. F**K THIS AND F**K YOU!
WELL GOLLY-GOSH, I WONDER WHERE WE'RE SUPPOSED TO GO?
C'MON, DAD. YOU HAVE TO ADMIT, THE SPECIAL EFFECTS ARE PRETTY GOOD...
CANTON
FOUR MILES
THEY'RE NOT SPECIAL EFFECTS, BETH! WE CAN DIE HERE! AND I DON'T HAVE ANY EQUIPMENT OR A WAY FOR US TO ESCAPE!
PLEASE. I SAW YOU MACGYVER TOGETHER A SPY DRONE WITH WHAT YOU FOUND IN A GRADE-SCHOOLER'S BACKPACK.
THAT WASN'T IN A FRINGE REALITY GOVERNED BY AN OMNIPOTENT UR-DIETY WITH A RICK SANCHEZ HATE-BONER THAT WOULD PUT A TEN FOOT POLE TO SHAME.
HEEEELP!
UH, GUYS?
HELP, PLEASE! OGRES...
...MY WIFE! OGRES ATTACKED US! SHE MIGHT BE...
LISTEN, ARE YOU GUYS A RANDOM ENCOUNTER OR IS THIS ADVENTURE RELEVANT?
WH-WHAT?
OH NO...
TOLD YOU. NATURAL BORN CLERIC.
OKAY KIDS, LET'S BUY YOUR MOM TIME TO DO WHAT SHE DOES BEST.
IT'S TIME TO BE BIG DAMN HEROES.

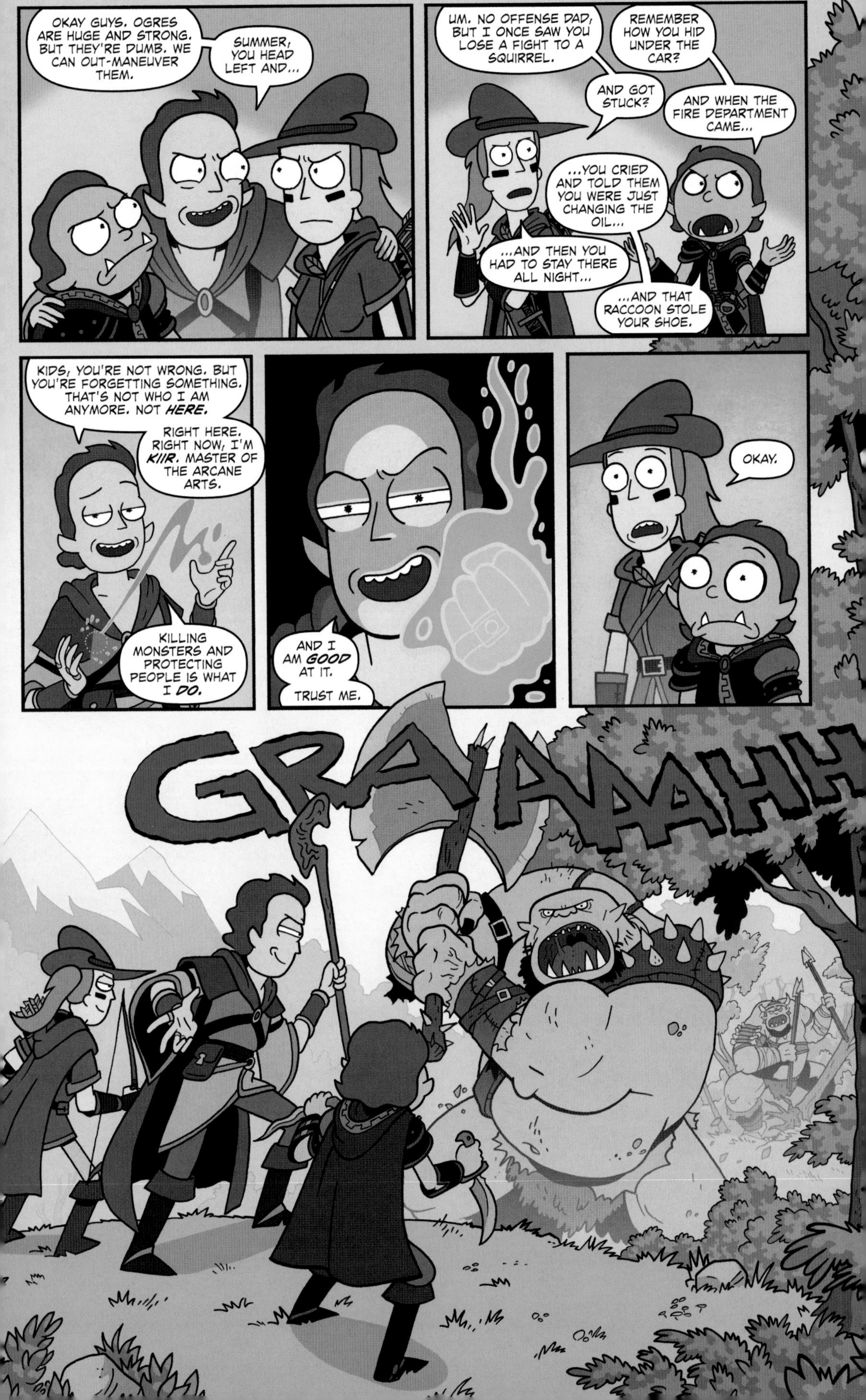
OKAY GUYS. OGRES ARE HUGE AND STRONG. BUT THEY'RE DUMB. WE CAN OUT-MANEUVER THEM.
SUMMER, YOU HEAD LEFT AND...
UM. NO OFFENSE DAD, BUT I ONCE SAW YOU LOSE A FIGHT TO A SQUIRREL.
REMEMBER HOW YOU HID UNDER THE CAR?
AND GOT STUCK?
AND WHEN THE FIRE DEPARTMENT CAME...
...YOU CRIED AND TOLD THEM YOU WERE JUST CHANGING THE OIL...
...AND THEN YOU HAD TO STAY THERE ALL NIGHT...
...AND THAT RACCOON STOLE YOUR SHOE.
KIDS, YOU'RE NOT WRONG. BUT YOU'RE FORGETTING SOMETHING. THAT'S NOT WHO I AM ANYMORE. NOT HERE.
RIGHT HERE. RIGHT NOW, I'M KIIR. MASTER OF THE ARCANE ARTS.
KILLING MONSTERS AND PROTECTING PEOPLE IS WHAT I DO.
AND I AM GOOD AT IT.
TRUST ME.
OKAY.
GRAAAHH

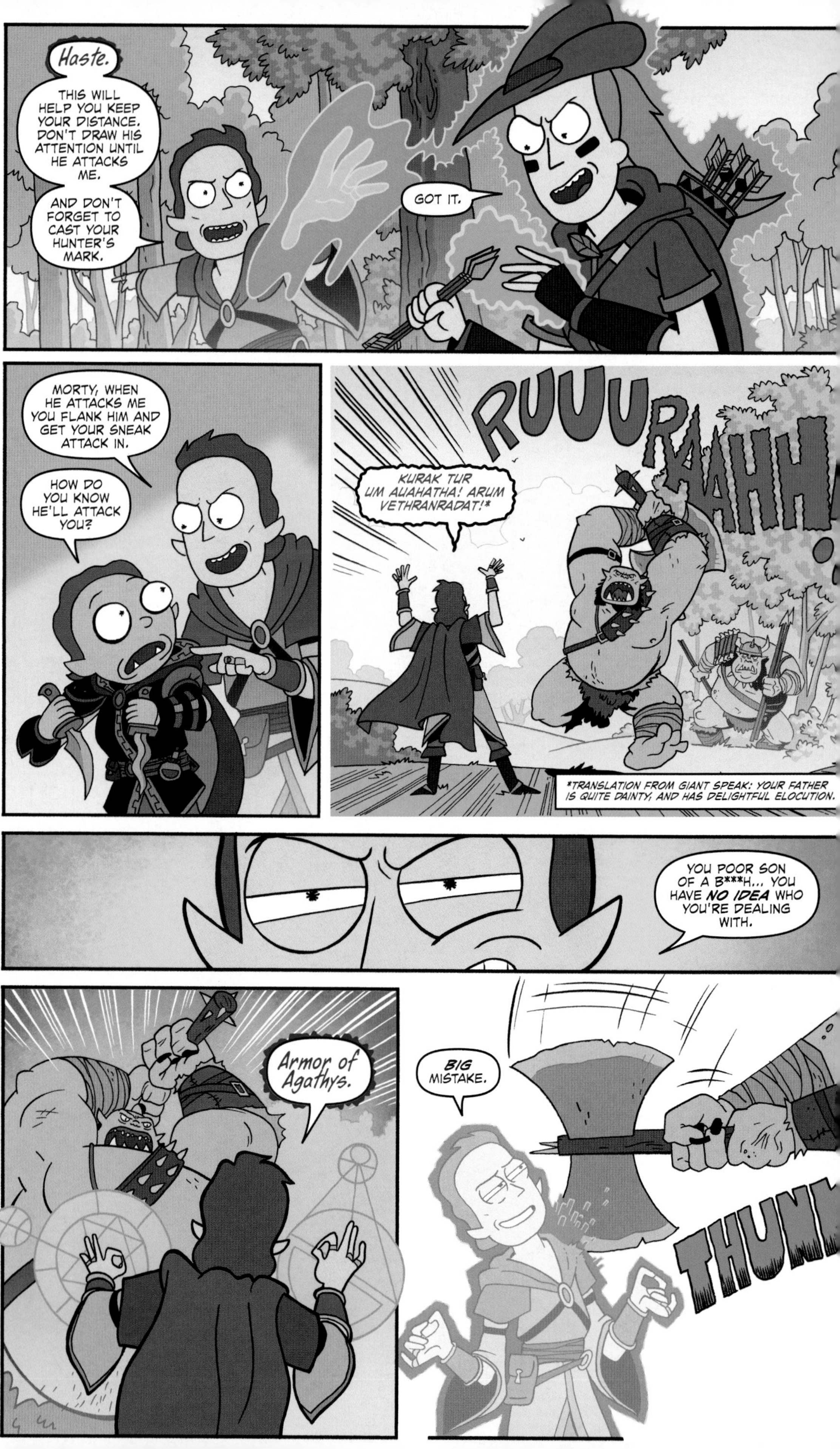

Haste.
THIS WILL HELP YOU KEEP YOUR DISTANCE. DON'T DRAW HIS ATTENTION UNTIL HE ATTACKS ME.
AND DON'T FORGET TO CAST YOUR HUNTER'S MARK.
GOT IT.
MORTY, WHEN HE ATTACKS ME YOU FLANK HIM AND GET YOUR SNEAK ATTACK IN.
HOW DO YOU KNOW HE'LL ATTACK YOU?
RUUURAAHH
KURAK TUR UM AUAHATHA! ARUM VETHRANRADAT!*
*TRANSLATION FROM GIANT SPEAK: YOUR FATHER IS QUITE DAINTY, AND HAS DELIGHTFUL ELOCUTION.
YOU POOR SON OF A B***H... YOU HAVE NO IDEA WHO YOU'RE DEALING WITH.
Armor of Agathys.
BIG MISTAKE.
THUN

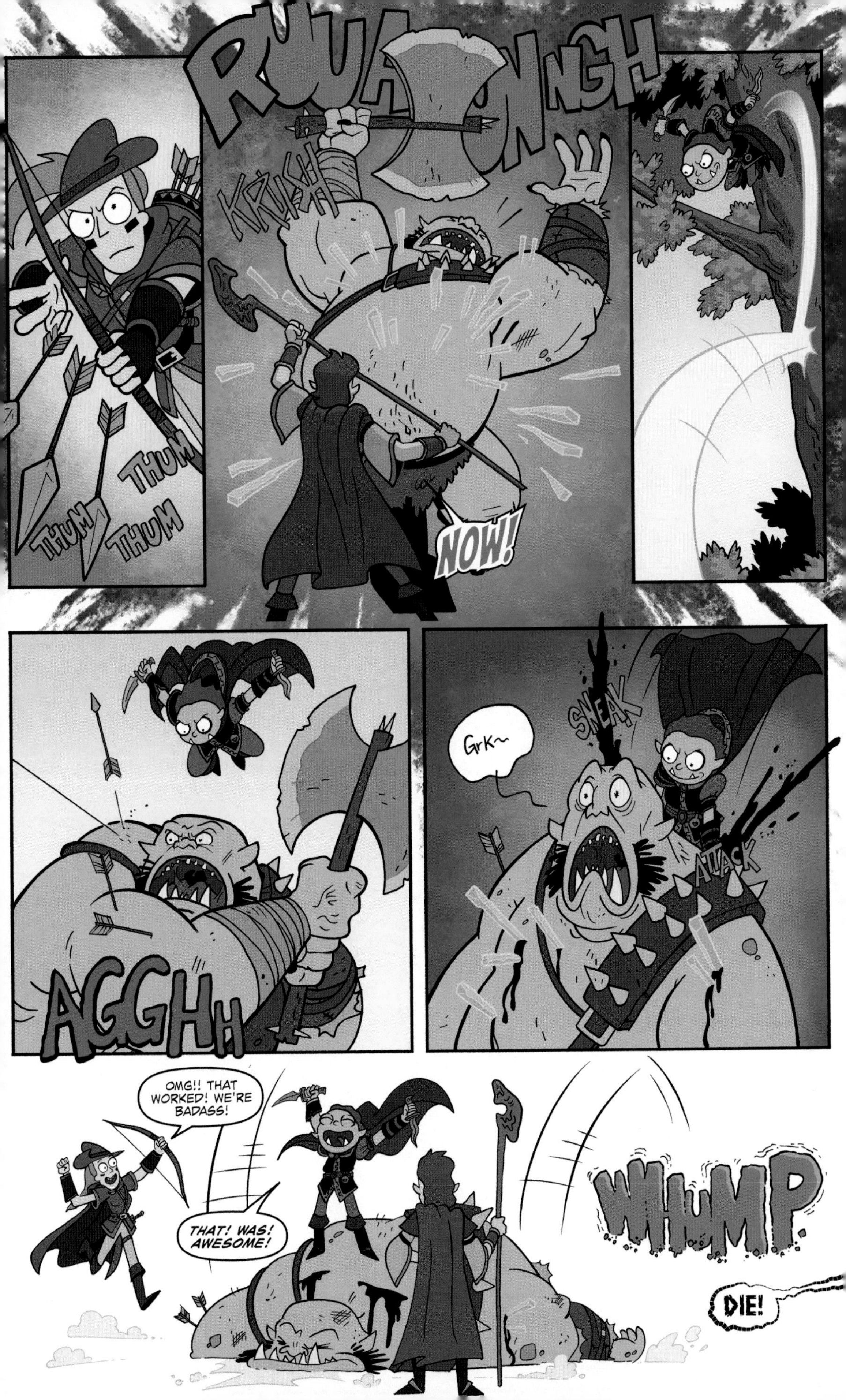
RWUAONNGH
KRUSH
THUM
THUM
THUM
NOW!
AGGHH
Grk~
SNEAK
ATTACK
OMG!! THAT WORKED! WE'RE BADASS!
THAT! WAS! AWESOME!
WHUMP
DIE!

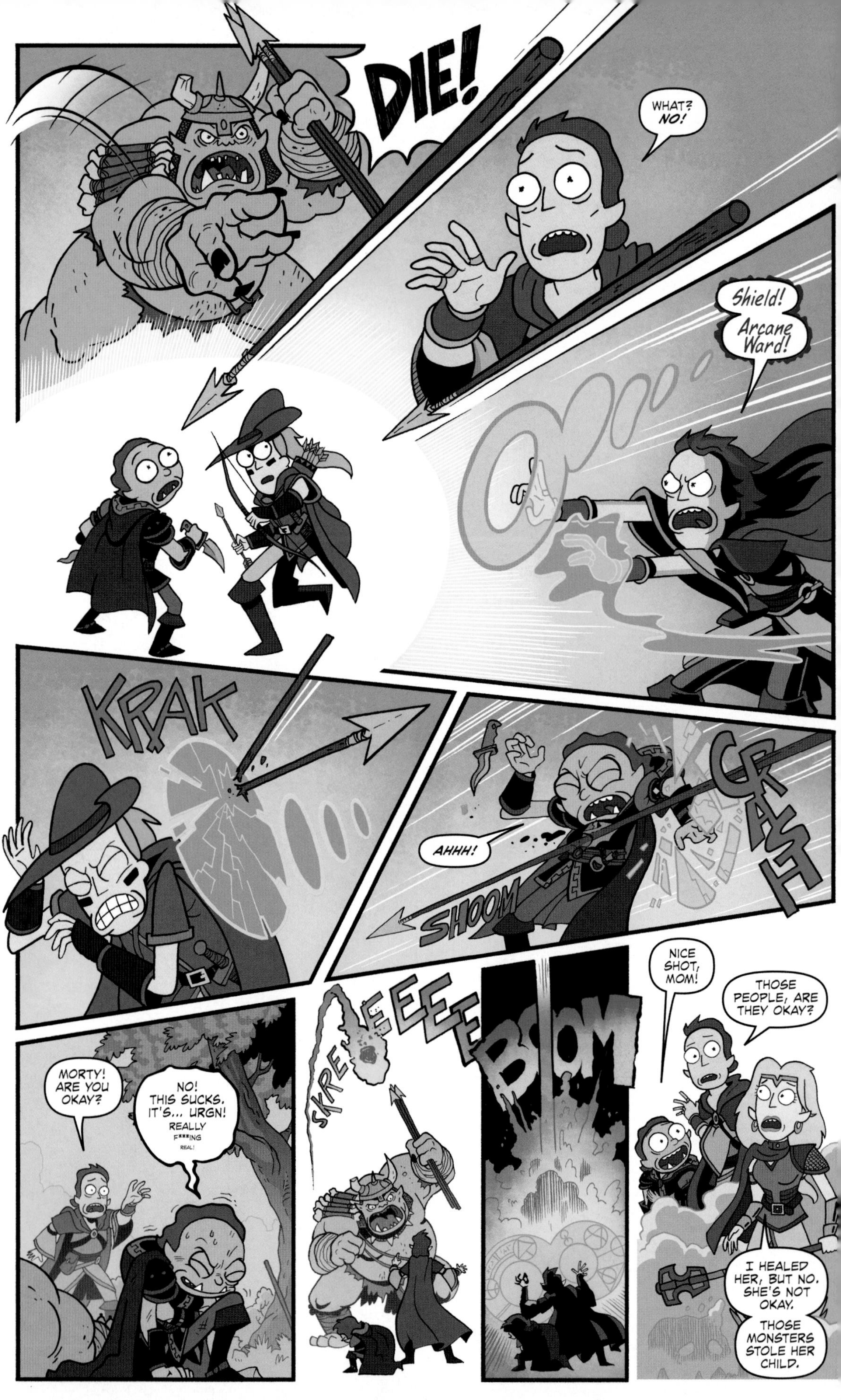
DIE!
WHAT? NO!
Shield! Arcane Ward!
KRAK
AHHH!
CRASH
SHOOM
MORTY! ARE YOU OKAY?
NO! THIS SUCKS. IT'S... URGN! REALLY F***ING REAL!
SKREEEEEE
BOOM
NICE SHOT, MOM!
THOSE PEOPLE, ARE THEY OKAY?
I HEALED HER, BUT NO. SHE'S NOT OKAY.
THOSE MONSTERS STOLE HER CHILD.

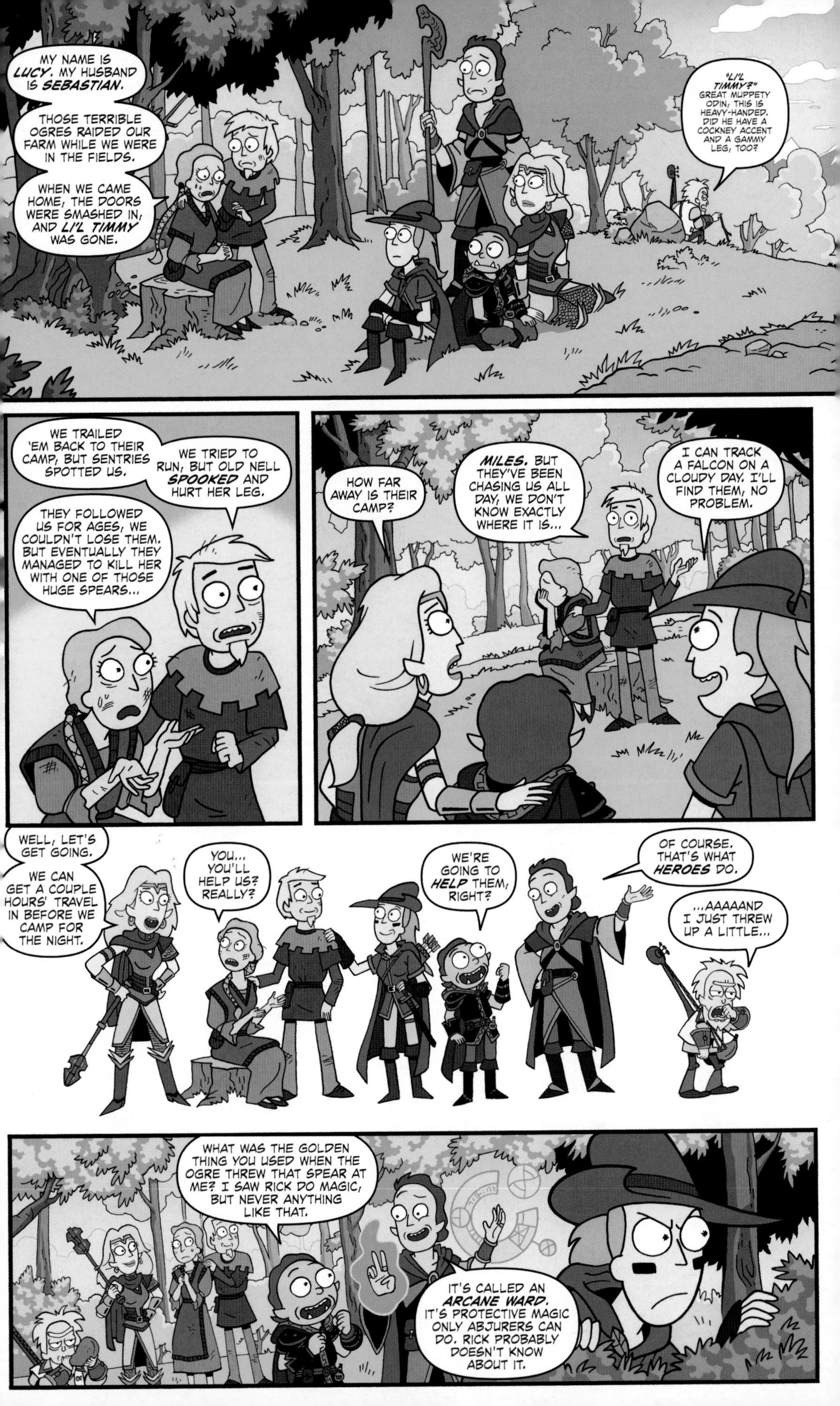
MY NAME IS LUCY. MY HUSBAND IS SEBASTIAN.
THOSE TERRIBLE OGRES RAIDED OUR FARM WHILE WE WERE IN THE FIELDS.
WHEN WE CAME HOME, THE DOORS WERE SMASHED IN, AND LI'L TIMMY WAS GONE.
"LI'L TIMMY?" GREAT MUPPETY ODIN, THIS IS HEAVY-HANDED. DID HE HAVE A COCKNEY ACCENT AND A GAMMY LEG, TOO?
WE TRAILED 'EM BACK TO THEIR CAMP, BUT SENTRIES SPOTTED US.
WE TRIED TO RUN, BUT OLD NELL SPOOKED AND HURT HER LEG.
THEY FOLLOWED US FOR AGES, WE COULDN'T LOSE THEM. BUT EVENTUALLY THEY MANAGED TO KILL HER WITH ONE OF THOSE HUGE SPEARS...
HOW FAR AWAY IS THEIR CAMP?
MILES. BUT THEY'VE BEEN CHASING US ALL DAY, WE DON'T KNOW EXACTLY WHERE IT IS...
I CAN TRACK A FALCON ON A CLOUDY DAY. I'LL FIND THEM, NO PROBLEM.
WELL, LET'S GET GOING.
WE CAN GET A COUPLE HOURS' TRAVEL IN BEFORE WE CAMP FOR THE NIGHT.
YOU... YOU'LL HELP US? REALLY?
WE'RE GOING TO HELP THEM, RIGHT?
OF COURSE. THAT'S WHAT HEROES DO.
...AAAAAND I JUST THREW UP A LITTLE...
WHAT WAS THE GOLDEN THING YOU USED WHEN THE OGRE THREW THAT SPEAR AT ME? I SAW RICK DO MAGIC, BUT NEVER ANYTHING LIKE THAT.
IT'S CALLED AN ARCANE WARD. IT'S PROTECTIVE MAGIC ONLY ABJURERS CAN DO. RICK PROBABLY DOESN'T KNOW ABOUT IT.

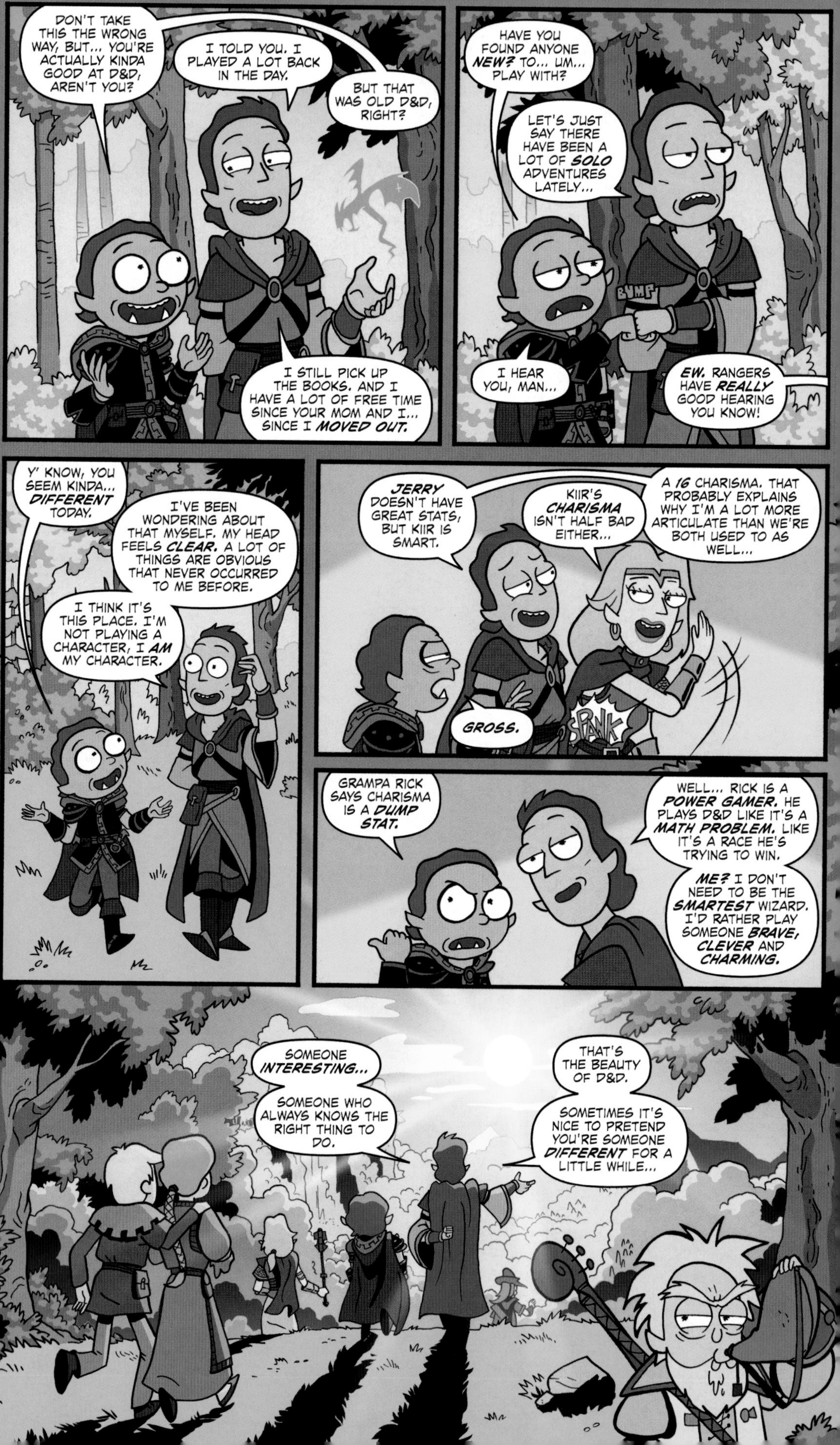

DON'T TAKE THIS THE WRONG WAY, BUT... YOU'RE ACTUALLY KINDA GOOD AT D&D, AREN'T YOU?
I TOLD YOU. I PLAYED A LOT BACK IN THE DAY.
BUT THAT WAS OLD D&D, RIGHT?
I STILL PICK UP THE BOOKS. AND I HAVE A LOT OF FREE TIME SINCE YOUR MOM AND I... SINCE I MOVED OUT.
HAVE YOU FOUND ANYONE NEW? TO... UM... PLAY WITH?
LET'S JUST SAY THERE HAVE BEEN A LOT OF SOLO ADVENTURES LATELY...
BUMF
I HEAR YOU, MAN...
EW. RANGERS HAVE REALLY GOOD HEARING YOU KNOW!
Y' KNOW, YOU SEEM KINDA... DIFFERENT TODAY.
I'VE BEEN WONDERING ABOUT THAT MYSELF. MY HEAD FEELS CLEAR. A LOT OF THINGS ARE OBVIOUS THAT NEVER OCCURRED TO ME BEFORE.
I THINK IT'S THIS PLACE. I'M NOT PLAYING A CHARACTER, I AM MY CHARACTER.
JERRY DOESN'T HAVE GREAT STATS, BUT KIIR IS SMART.
KIIR'S CHARISMA ISN'T HALF BAD EITHER...
A 16 CHARISMA. THAT PROBABLY EXPLAINS WHY I'M A LOT MORE ARTICULATE THAN WE'RE BOTH USED TO AS WELL...
GROSS.
SPANK
GRAMPA RICK SAYS CHARISMA IS A DUMP STAT.
WELL... RICK IS A POWER GAMER. HE PLAYS D&D LIKE IT'S A MATH PROBLEM. LIKE IT'S A RACE HE'S TRYING TO WIN.
ME? I DON'T NEED TO BE THE SMARTEST WIZARD. I'D RATHER PLAY SOMEONE BRAVE, CLEVER AND CHARMING.
SOMEONE INTERESTING...
SOMEONE WHO ALWAYS KNOWS THE RIGHT THING TO DO.
THAT'S THE BEAUTY OF D&D.
SOMETIMES IT'S NICE TO PRETEND YOU'RE SOMEONE DIFFERENT FOR A LITTLE WHILE...

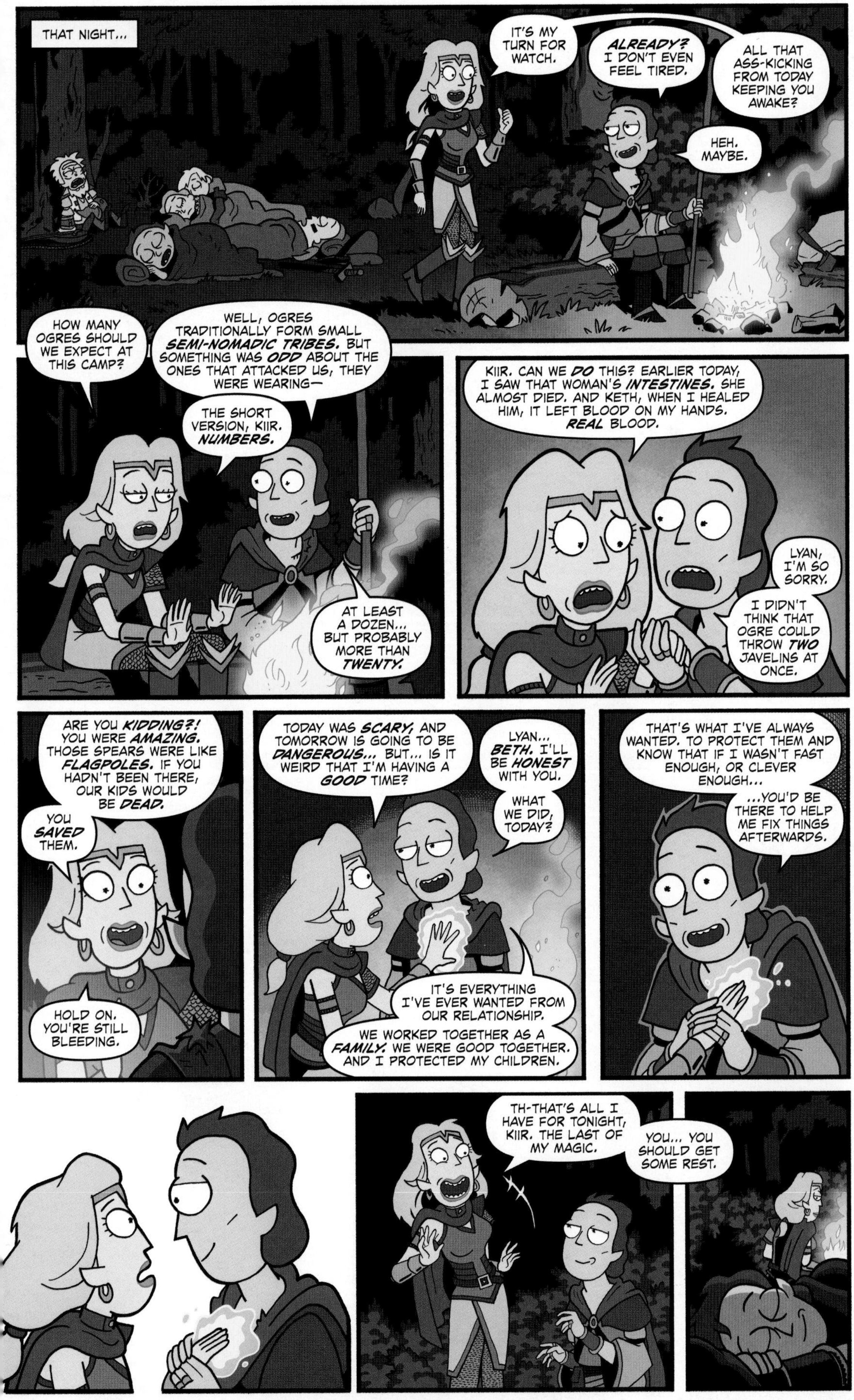

THAT NIGHT...
IT'S MY TURN FOR WATCH.
ALREADY? I DON'T EVEN FEEL TIRED.
ALL THAT ASS-KICKING FROM TODAY KEEPING YOU AWAKE?
HEH. MAYBE.
HOW MANY OGRES SHOULD WE EXPECT AT THIS CAMP?
WELL, OGRES TRADITIONALLY FORM SMALL SEMI-NOMADIC TRIBES. BUT SOMETHING WAS ODD ABOUT THE ONES THAT ATTACKED US, THEY WERE WEARING—
THE SHORT VERSION, KIIR. NUMBERS.
AT LEAST A DOZEN... BUT PROBABLY MORE THAN TWENTY.
KIIR. CAN WE DO THIS? EARLIER TODAY, I SAW THAT WOMAN'S INTESTINES. SHE ALMOST DIED. AND KETH, WHEN I HEALED HIM, IT LEFT BLOOD ON MY HANDS. REAL BLOOD.
LYAN, I'M SO SORRY.
I DIDN'T THINK THAT OGRE COULD THROW TWO JAVELINS AT ONCE.
ARE YOU KIDDING?! YOU WERE AMAZING. THOSE SPEARS WERE LIKE FLAGPOLES. IF YOU HADN'T BEEN THERE, OUR KIDS WOULD BE DEAD.
YOU SAVED THEM.
HOLD ON. YOU'RE STILL BLEEDING.
TODAY WAS SCARY, AND TOMORROW IS GOING TO BE DANGEROUS... BUT... IS IT WEIRD THAT I'M HAVING A GOOD TIME?
LYAN... BETH. I'LL BE HONEST WITH YOU.
WHAT WE DID, TODAY?
IT'S EVERYTHING I'VE EVER WANTED FROM OUR RELATIONSHIP.
WE WORKED TOGETHER AS A FAMILY. WE WERE GOOD TOGETHER. AND I PROTECTED MY CHILDREN.
THAT'S WHAT I'VE ALWAYS WANTED. TO PROTECT THEM AND KNOW THAT IF I WASN'T FAST ENOUGH, OR CLEVER ENOUGH...
...YOU'D BE THERE TO HELP ME FIX THINGS AFTERWARDS.
TH-THAT'S ALL I HAVE FOR TONIGHT, KIIR. THE LAST OF MY MAGIC.
YOU... YOU SHOULD GET SOME REST.

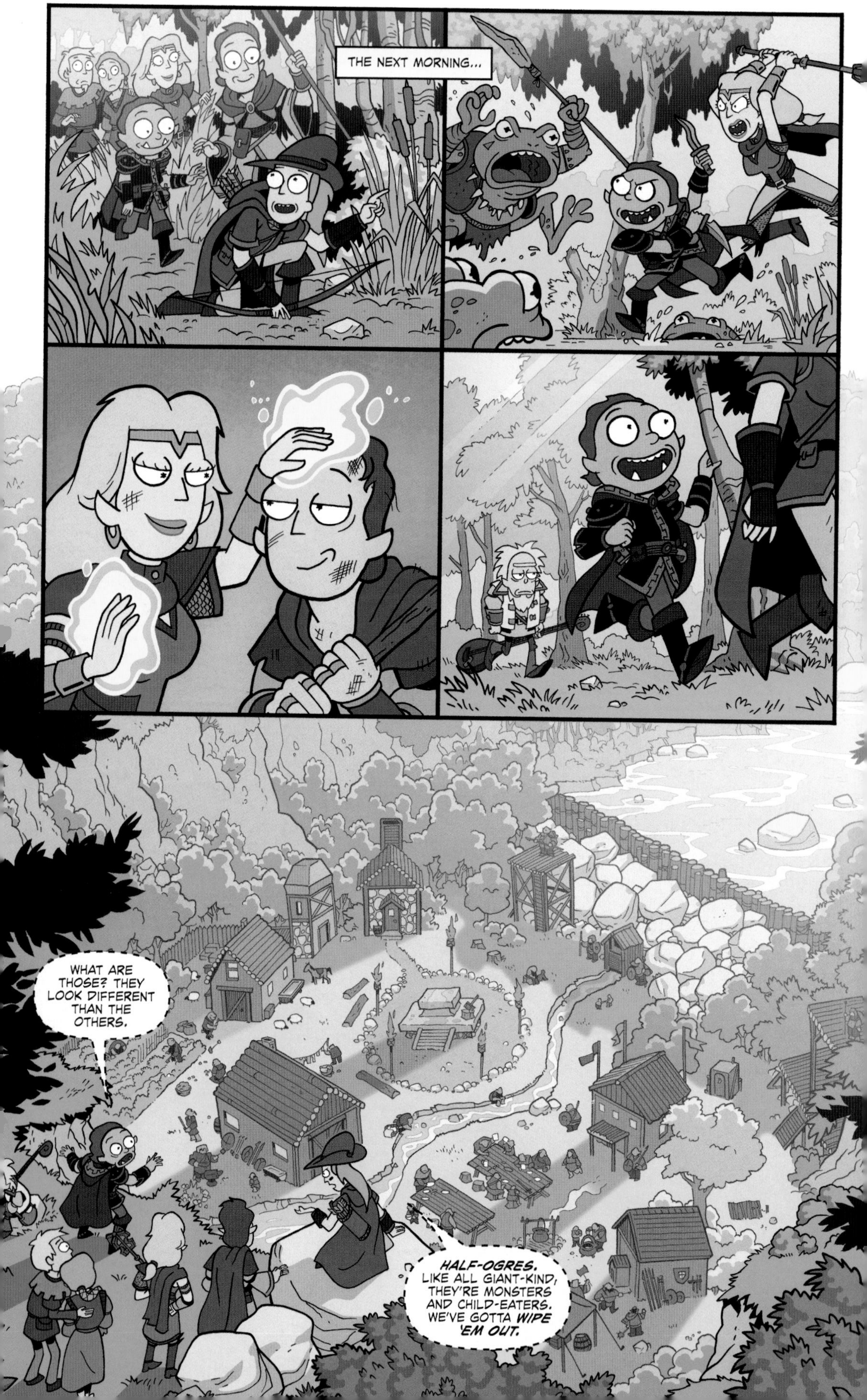
THE NEXT MORNING...
WHAT ARE THOSE? THEY LOOK DIFFERENT THAN THE OTHERS.
HALF-OGRES. LIKE ALL GIANT-KIND, THEY'RE MONSTERS AND CHILD-EATERS. WE'VE GOTTA WIPE 'EM OUT.

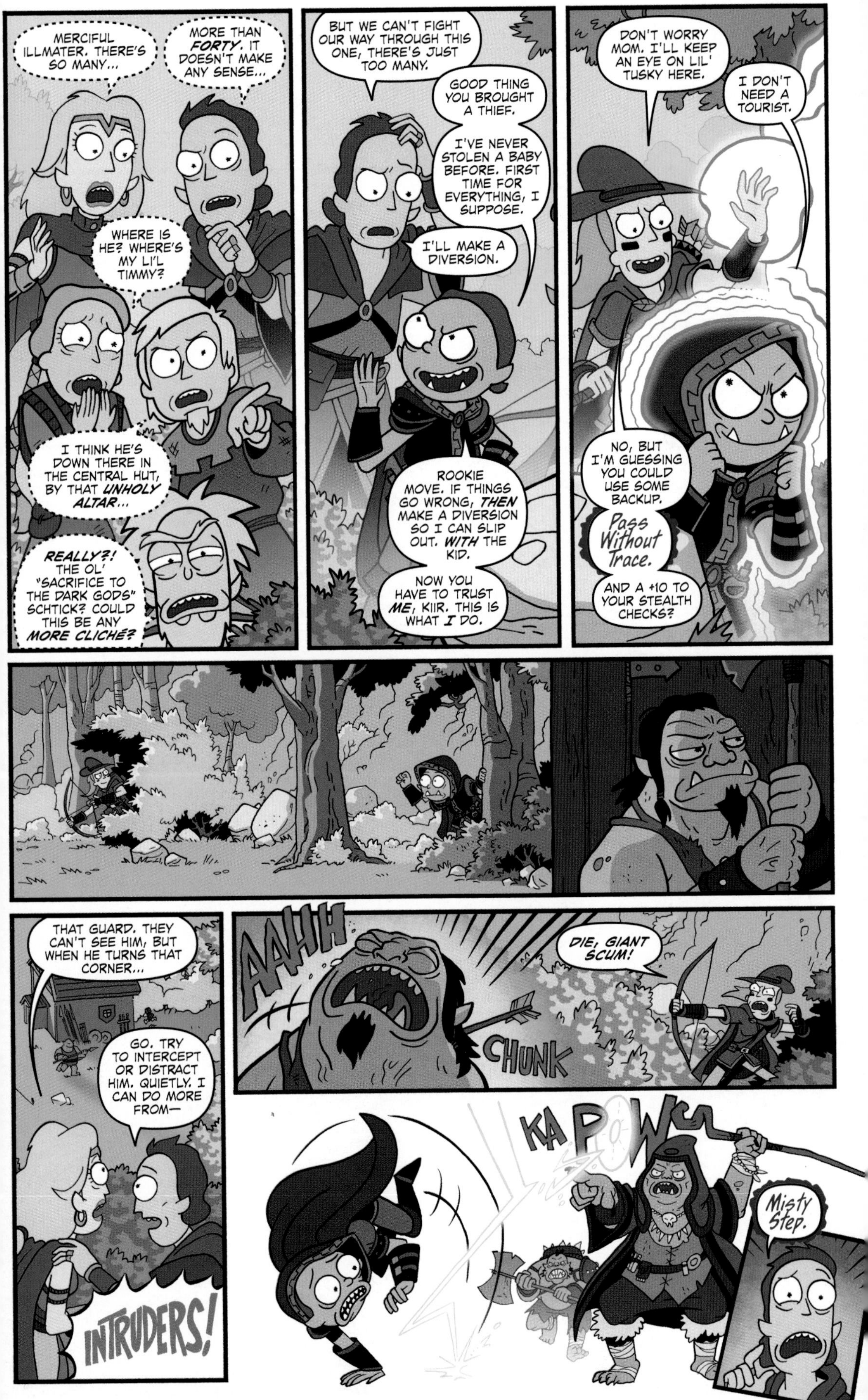
MERCIFUL ILLMATER. THERE'S SO MANY...
MORE THAN FORTY. IT DOESN'T MAKE ANY SENSE...
WHERE IS HE? WHERE'S MY LI'L TIMMY?
I THINK HE'S DOWN THERE IN THE CENTRAL HUT, BY THAT UNHOLY ALTAR...
REALLY?! THE OL' "SACRIFICE TO THE DARK GODS" SCHTICK? COULD THIS BE ANY MORE CLICHÉ?
BUT WE CAN'T FIGHT OUR WAY THROUGH THIS ONE, THERE'S JUST TOO MANY.
GOOD THING YOU BROUGHT A THIEF.
I'VE NEVER STOLEN A BABY BEFORE. FIRST TIME FOR EVERYTHING, I SUPPOSE.
I'LL MAKE A DIVERSION.
ROOKIE MOVE. IF THINGS GO WRONG, THEN MAKE A DIVERSION SO I CAN SLIP OUT. WITH THE KID.
NOW YOU HAVE TO TRUST ME, KIIR. THIS IS WHAT I DO.
DON'T WORRY MOM. I'LL KEEP AN EYE ON LIL' TUSKY HERE.
I DON'T NEED A TOURIST.
NO, BUT I'M GUESSING YOU COULD USE SOME BACKUP.
Pass Without Trace.
AND A +10 TO YOUR STEALTH CHECKS?
THAT GUARD. THEY CAN'T SEE HIM, BUT WHEN HE TURNS THAT CORNER...
GO. TRY TO INTERCEPT OR DISTRACT HIM. QUIETLY. I CAN DO MORE FROM—
INTRUDERS!
AAHH
DIE, GIANT SCUM!
CHUNK
KAPOWGA
Misty Step.

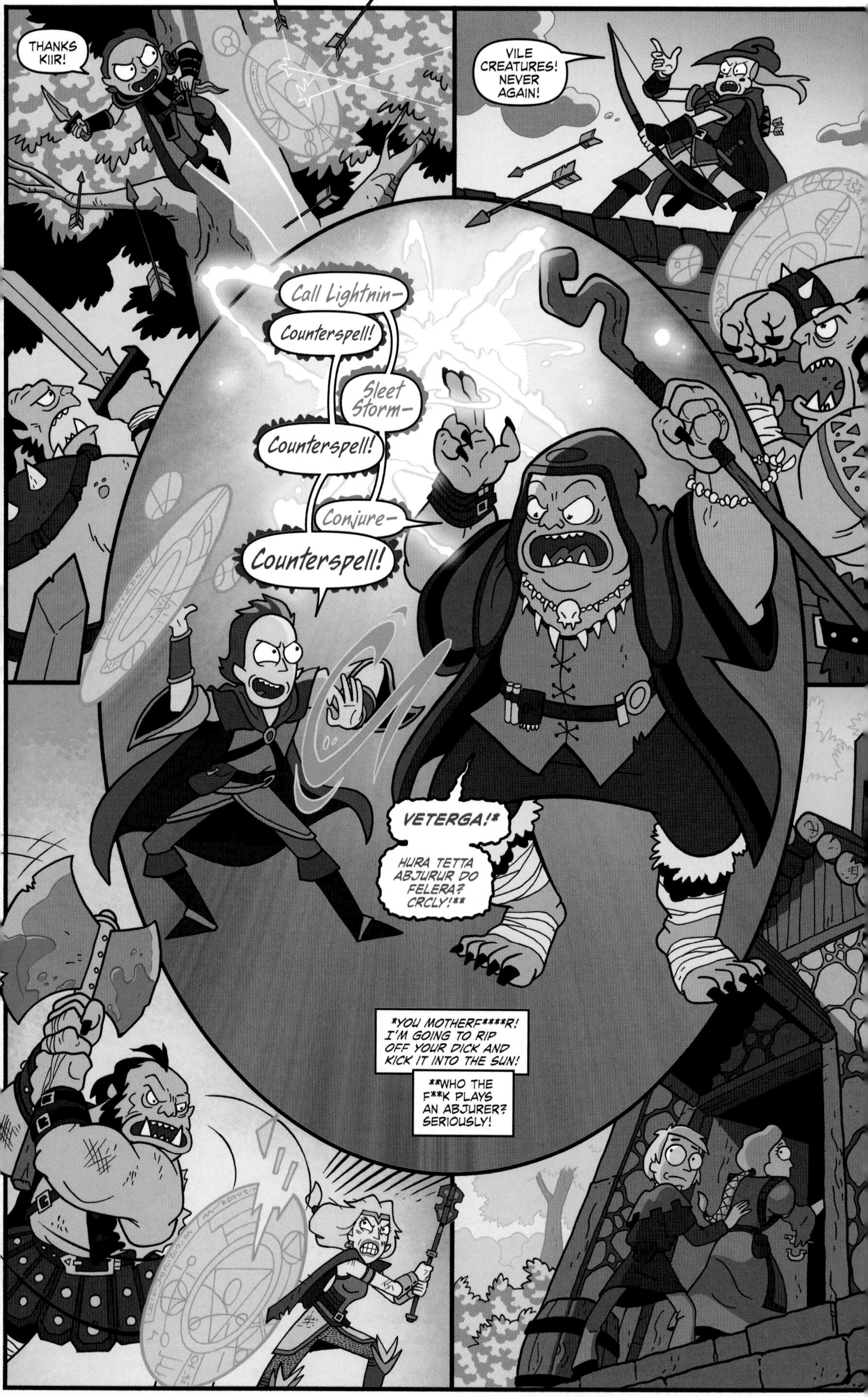

THANKS KIIR!
VILE CREATURES! NEVER AGAIN!
Call Lightnin-
Counterspell!
Sleet Storm-
Counterspell!
Conjure-
Counterspell!
VETERGA!*
HURA TETTA ABJURUR DO FELERA? CRCLY!**
*YOU MOTHERF****R! I'M GOING TO RIP OFF YOUR DICK AND KICK IT INTO THE SUN!
WHO THE FK PLAYS AN ABJURER? SERIOUSLY!

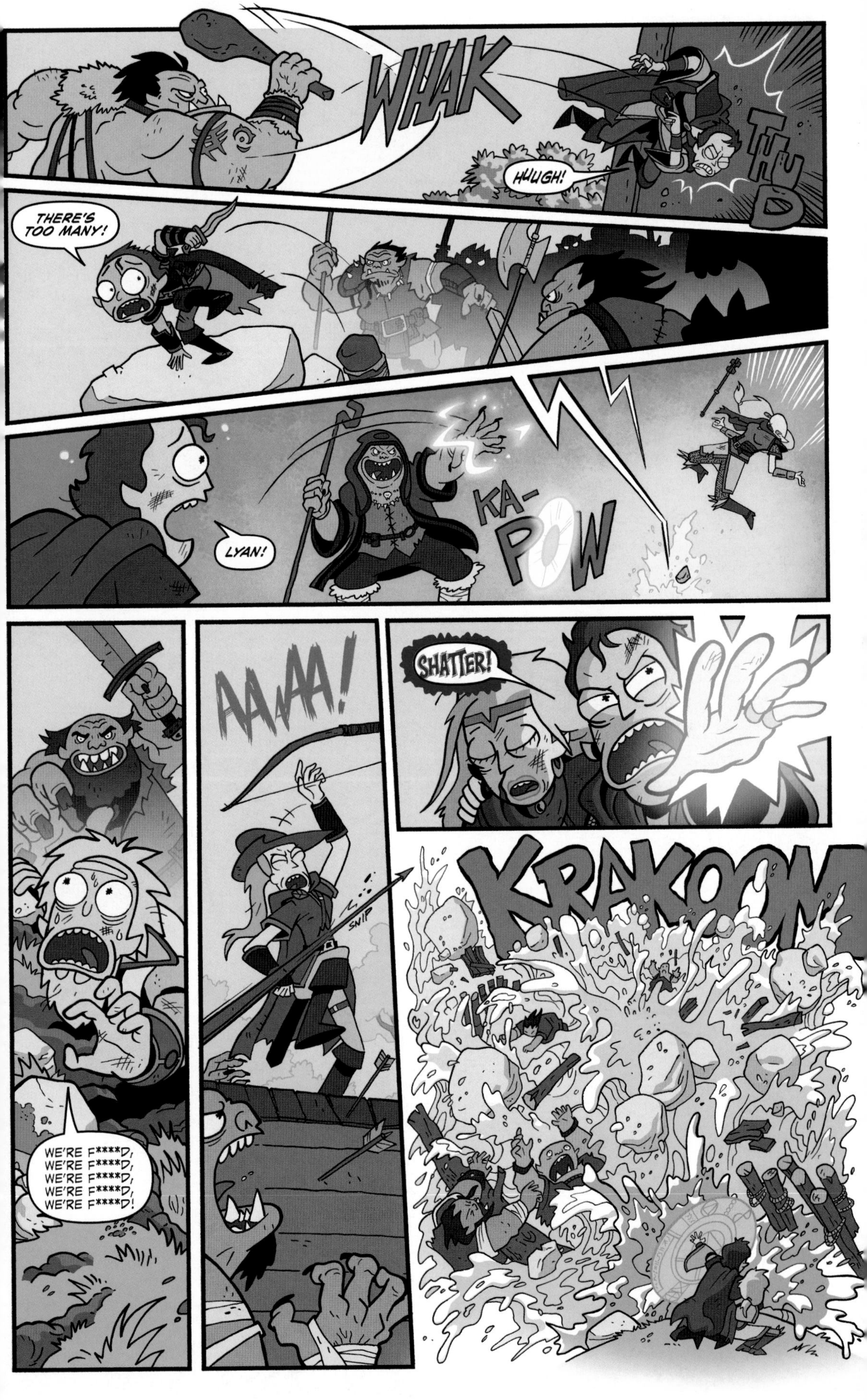
WHAK
HUUGH!
THUD
THERE'S TOO MANY!
LYAN!
KA-POW
AAAAA!
SNIP
SHATTER!
WE'RE F****D,
WE'RE F****D,
WE'RE F****D,
WE'RE F****D,
WE'RE F****D!
KRAKOOM

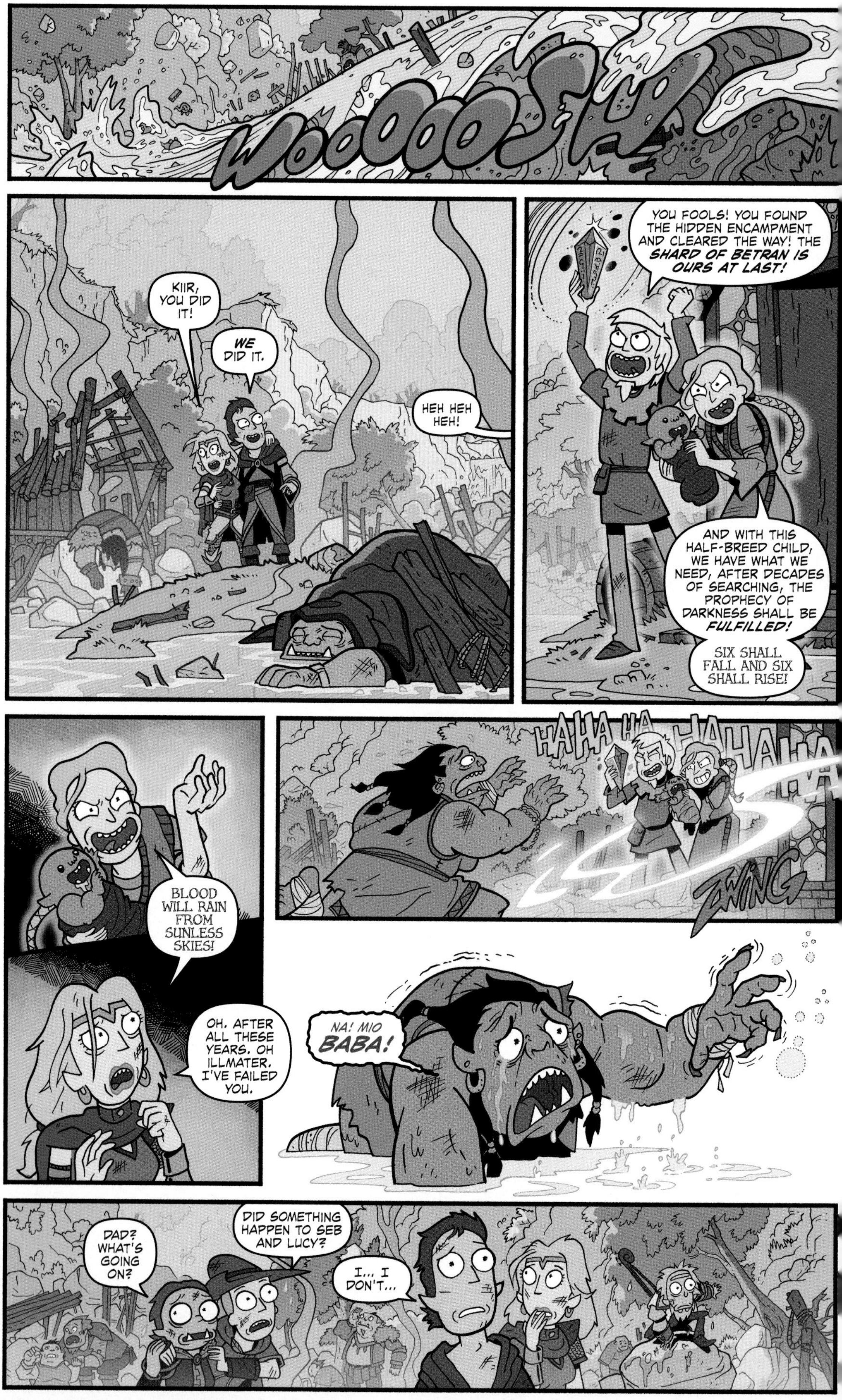
WOOOOOSH
KIIR, YOU DID IT!
WE DID IT.
HEH HEH HEH!
YOU FOOLS! YOU FOUND THE HIDDEN ENCAMPMENT AND CLEARED THE WAY! THE SHARD OF BETRAN IS OURS AT LAST!
AND WITH THIS HALF-BREED CHILD, WE HAVE WHAT WE NEED, AFTER DECADES OF SEARCHING, THE PROPHECY OF DARKNESS SHALL BE FULFILLED!
SIX SHALL FALL AND SIX SHALL RISE!
BLOOD WILL RAIN FROM SUNLESS SKIES!
HAHAHA HA HAHAHA
ZWING
OH. AFTER ALL THESE YEARS. OH ILLMATER. I'VE FAILED YOU.
NA! MIO BABA!
DAD? WHAT'S GOING ON?
DID SOMETHING HAPPEN TO SEB AND LUCY?
I... I DON'T...

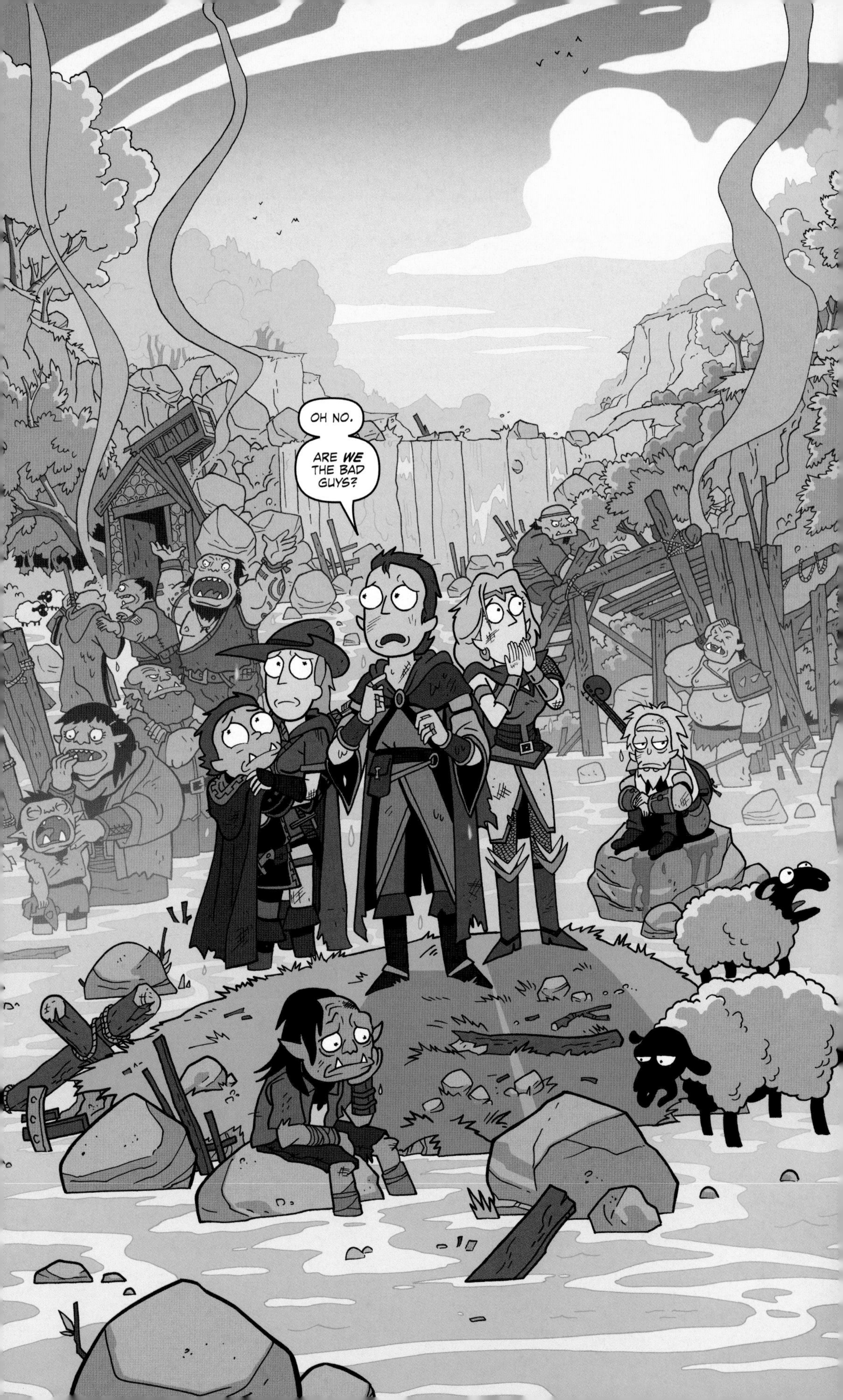
OH NO.
ARE *WE* THE BAD GUYS?

Art by Troy Little

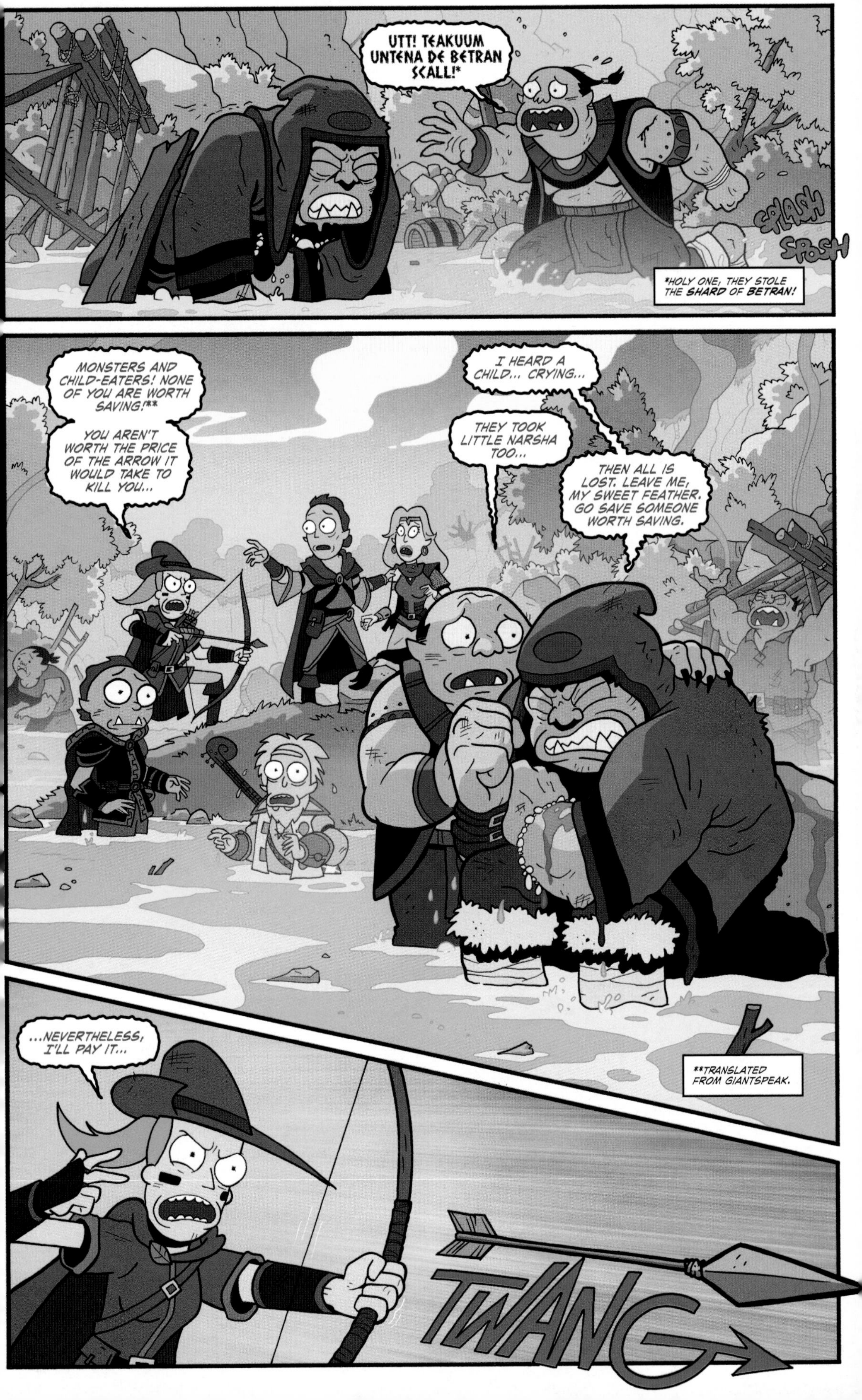
UTT! TEAKUUM UNTENA DE BETRAN SCALL!*
SPLASH
SPOSH
*HOLY ONE, THEY STOLE THE SHARD OF BETRAN!
MONSTERS AND CHILD-EATERS! NONE OF YOU ARE WORTH SAVING!**
YOU AREN'T WORTH THE PRICE OF THE ARROW IT WOULD TAKE TO KILL YOU...
I HEARD A CHILD... CRYING...
THEY TOOK LITTLE NARSHA TOO...
THEN ALL IS LOST. LEAVE ME, MY SWEET FEATHER. GO SAVE SOMEONE WORTH SAVING.
**TRANSLATED FROM GIANTSPEAK.
...NEVERTHELESS, I'LL PAY IT...
TWANG

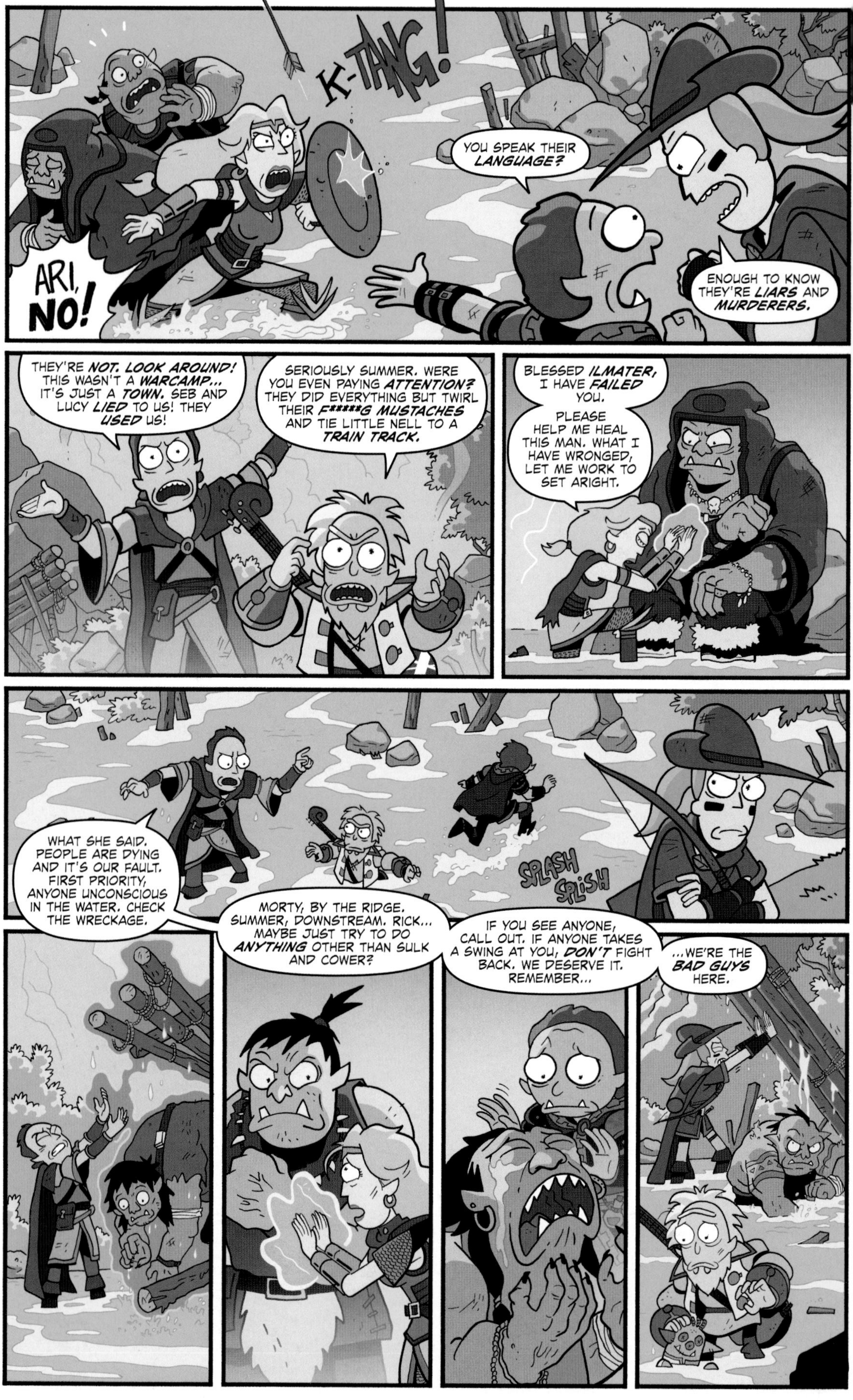
K-TANG!
ARI, NO!
YOU SPEAK THEIR LANGUAGE?
ENOUGH TO KNOW THEY'RE LIARS AND MURDERERS.
THEY'RE NOT. LOOK AROUND! THIS WASN'T A WARCAMP... IT'S JUST A TOWN. SEB AND LUCY LIED TO US! THEY USED US!
SERIOUSLY SUMMER. WERE YOU EVEN PAYING ATTENTION? THEY DID EVERYTHING BUT TWIRL THEIR F*****G MUSTACHES AND TIE LITTLE NELL TO A TRAIN TRACK.
BLESSED ILMATER, I HAVE FAILED YOU.
PLEASE HELP ME HEAL THIS MAN. WHAT I HAVE WRONGED, LET ME WORK TO SET ARIGHT.
WHAT SHE SAID. PEOPLE ARE DYING AND IT'S OUR FAULT. FIRST PRIORITY, ANYONE UNCONSCIOUS IN THE WATER. CHECK THE WRECKAGE.
SPLASH SPLISH
MORTY, BY THE RIDGE. SUMMER, DOWNSTREAM. RICK... MAYBE JUST TRY TO DO ANYTHING OTHER THAN SULK AND COWER?
IF YOU SEE ANYONE, CALL OUT. IF ANYONE TAKES A SWING AT YOU, DON'T FIGHT BACK. WE DESERVE IT. REMEMBER...
...WE'RE THE BAD GUYS HERE.

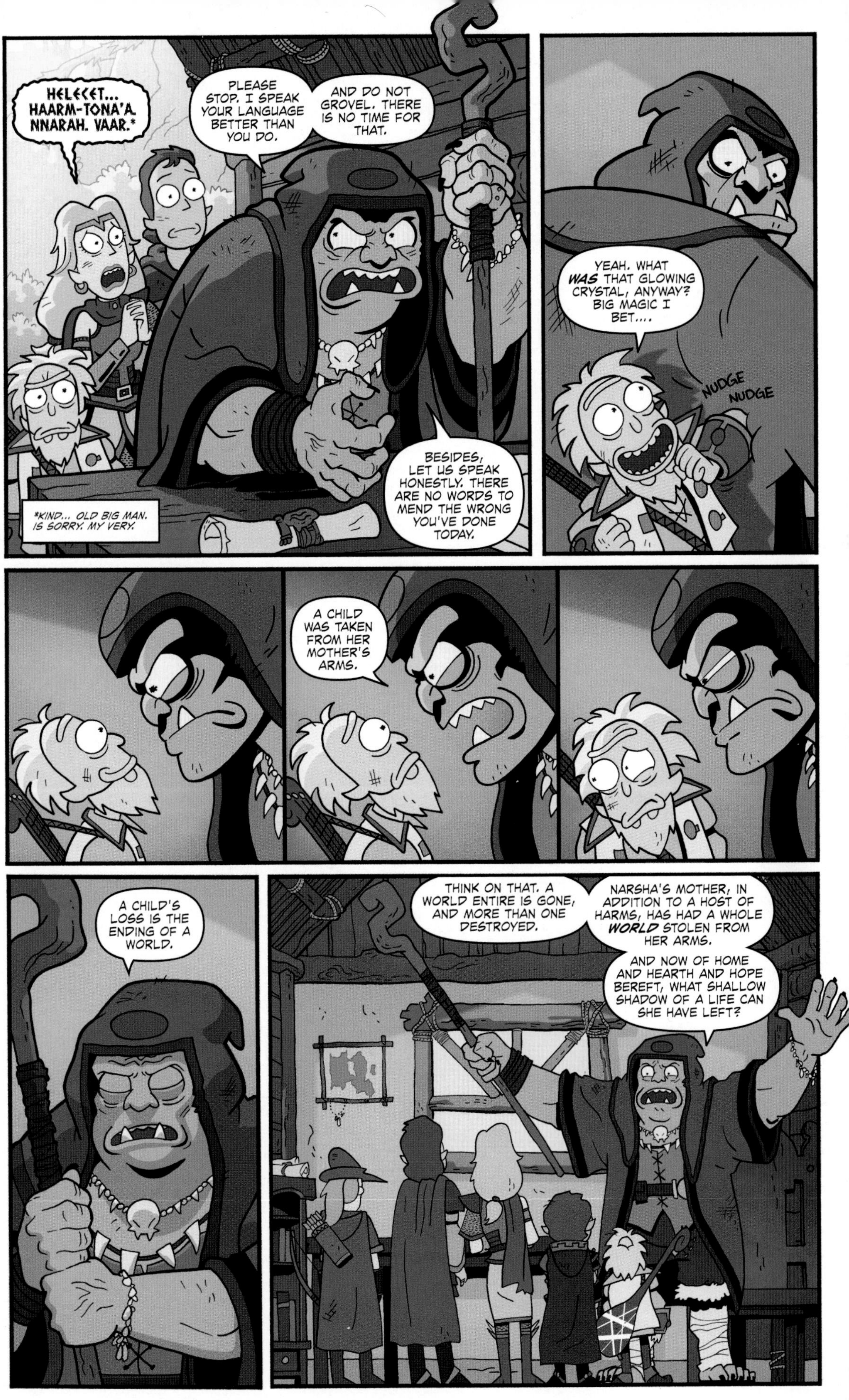
HELECCET... HAARM-TONA'A. NNARAH. VAAR.*
PLEASE STOP. I SPEAK YOUR LANGUAGE BETTER THAN YOU DO.
AND DO NOT GROVEL. THERE IS NO TIME FOR THAT.
BESIDES, LET US SPEAK HONESTLY. THERE ARE NO WORDS TO MEND THE WRONG YOU'VE DONE TODAY.
*KIND... OLD BIG MAN. IS SORRY. MY VERY.
YEAH. WHAT WAS THAT GLOWING CRYSTAL, ANYWAY? BIG MAGIC I BET....
NUDGE NUDGE
A CHILD WAS TAKEN FROM HER MOTHER'S ARMS.
A CHILD'S LOSS IS THE ENDING OF A WORLD.
THINK ON THAT. A WORLD ENTIRE IS GONE, AND MORE THAN ONE DESTROYED.
NARSHA'S MOTHER, IN ADDITION TO A HOST OF HARMS, HAS HAD A WHOLE WORLD STOLEN FROM HER ARMS.
AND NOW OF HOME AND HEARTH AND HOPE BEREFT, WHAT SHALLOW SHADOW OF A LIFE CAN SHE HAVE LEFT?

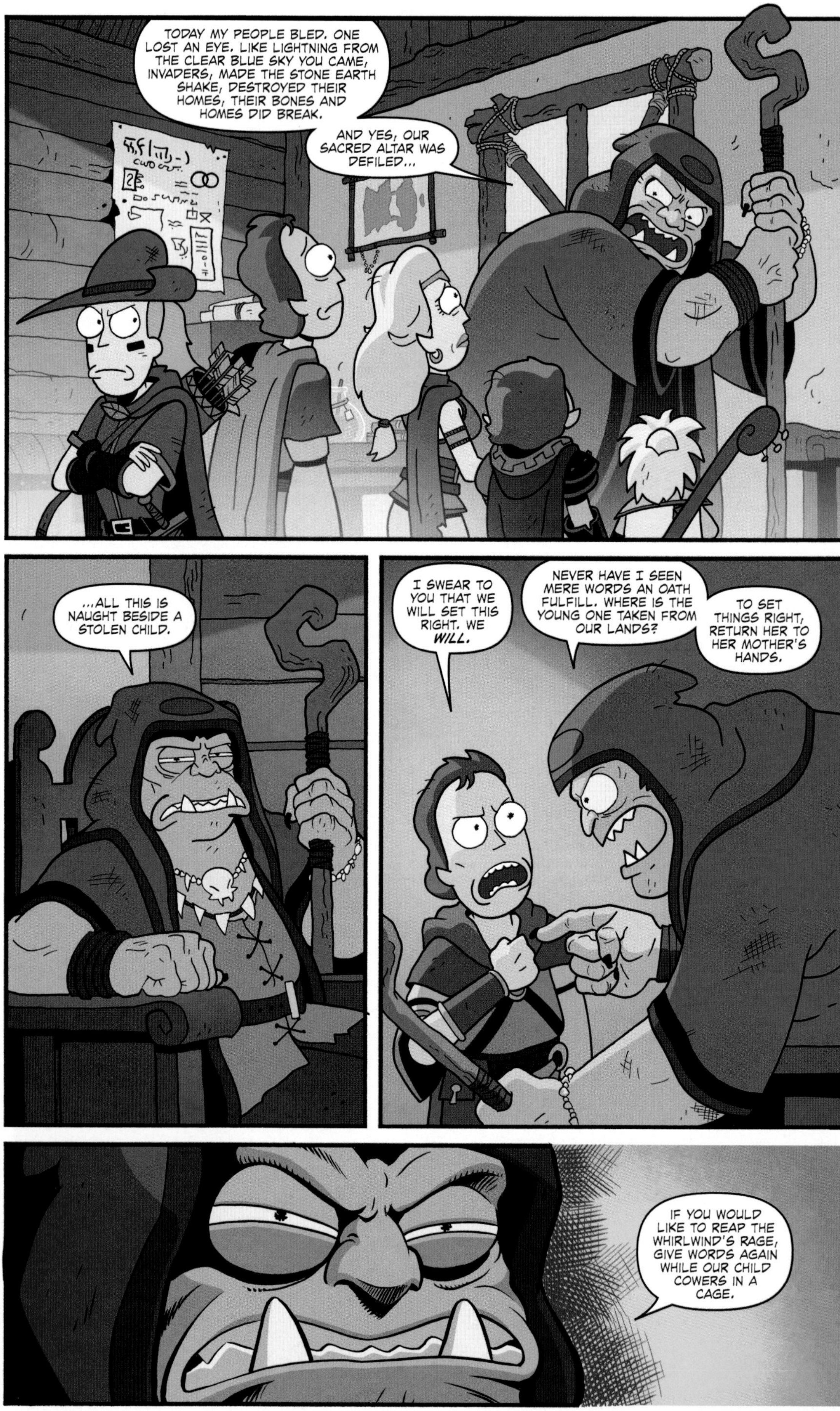
TODAY MY PEOPLE BLED. ONE LOST AN EYE. LIKE LIGHTNING FROM THE CLEAR BLUE SKY YOU CAME, INVADERS, MADE THE STONE EARTH SHAKE, DESTROYED THEIR HOMES, THEIR BONES AND HOMES DID BREAK.
AND YES, OUR SACRED ALTAR WAS DEFILED...
...ALL THIS IS NAUGHT BESIDE A STOLEN CHILD.
I SWEAR TO YOU THAT WE WILL SET THIS RIGHT. WE *WILL.*
NEVER HAVE I SEEN MERE WORDS AN OATH FULFILL. WHERE IS THE YOUNG ONE TAKEN FROM OUR LANDS?
TO SET THINGS RIGHT, RETURN HER TO HER MOTHER'S HANDS.
IF YOU WOULD LIKE TO REAP THE WHIRLWIND'S RAGE, GIVE WORDS AGAIN WHILE OUR CHILD COWERS IN A CAGE.

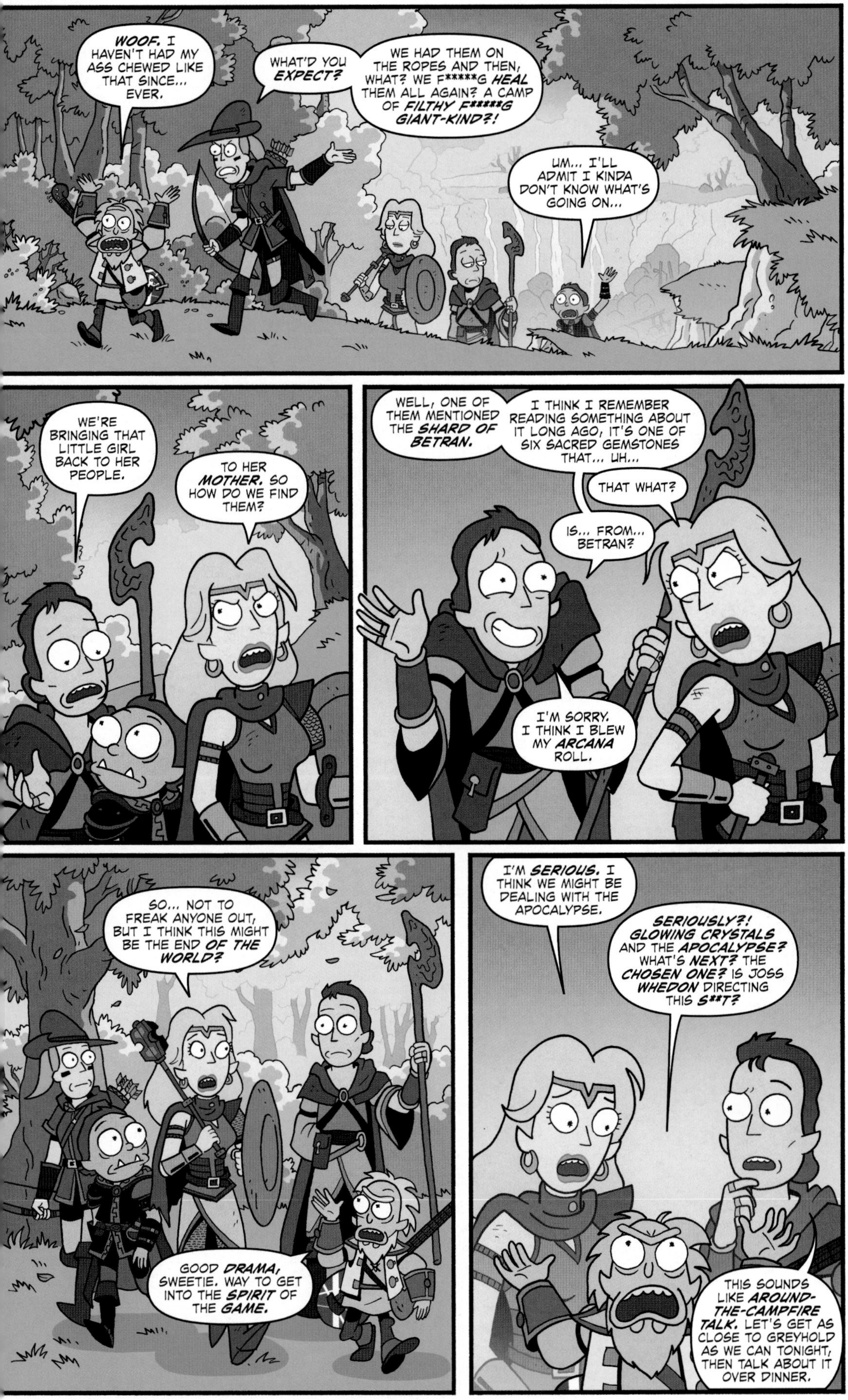
WOOF. I HAVEN'T HAD MY ASS CHEWED LIKE THAT SINCE... EVER.
WHAT'D YOU EXPECT?
WE HAD THEM ON THE ROPES AND THEN, WHAT? WE F*****G HEAL THEM ALL AGAIN? A CAMP OF FILTHY F*****G GIANT-KIND?!
UM... I'LL ADMIT I KINDA DON'T KNOW WHAT'S GOING ON...
WE'RE BRINGING THAT LITTLE GIRL BACK TO HER PEOPLE.
TO HER MOTHER. SO HOW DO WE FIND THEM?
WELL, ONE OF THEM MENTIONED THE SHARD OF BETRAN.
I THINK I REMEMBER READING SOMETHING ABOUT IT LONG AGO, IT'S ONE OF SIX SACRED GEMSTONES THAT... UH...
THAT WHAT?
IS... FROM... BETRAN?
I'M SORRY. I THINK I BLEW MY ARCANA ROLL.
SO... NOT TO FREAK ANYONE OUT, BUT I THINK THIS MIGHT BE THE END OF THE WORLD?
GOOD DRAMA, SWEETIE. WAY TO GET INTO THE SPIRIT OF THE GAME.
I'M SERIOUS. I THINK WE MIGHT BE DEALING WITH THE APOCALYPSE.
SERIOUSLY?! GLOWING CRYSTALS AND THE APOCALYPSE? WHAT'S NEXT? THE CHOSEN ONE? IS JOSS WHEDON DIRECTING THIS S**T?
THIS SOUNDS LIKE AROUND-THE-CAMPFIRE TALK. LET'S GET AS CLOSE TO GREYHOLD AS WE CAN TONIGHT, THEN TALK ABOUT IT OVER DINNER.

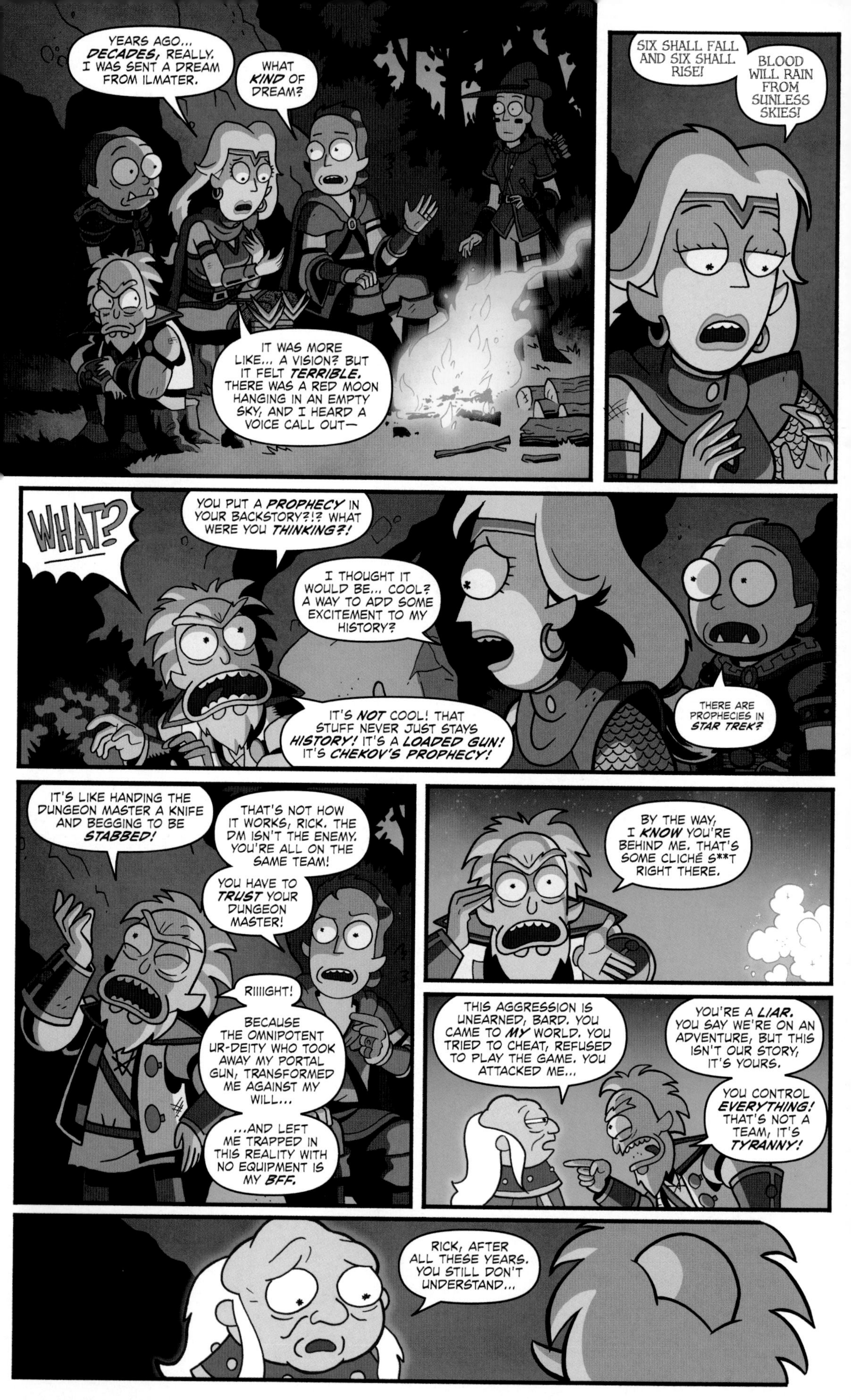
YEARS AGO... DECADES, REALLY. I WAS SENT A DREAM FROM ILMATER.
WHAT KIND OF DREAM?
IT WAS MORE LIKE... A VISION? BUT IT FELT TERRIBLE. THERE WAS A RED MOON HANGING IN AN EMPTY SKY, AND I HEARD A VOICE CALL OUT—
SIX SHALL FALL AND SIX SHALL RISE!
BLOOD WILL RAIN FROM SUNLESS SKIES!
WHAT?
YOU PUT A PROPHECY IN YOUR BACKSTORY?!? WHAT WERE YOU THINKING?!
I THOUGHT IT WOULD BE... COOL? A WAY TO ADD SOME EXCITEMENT TO MY HISTORY?
IT'S NOT COOL! THAT STUFF NEVER JUST STAYS HISTORY! IT'S A LOADED GUN! IT'S CHEKOV'S PROPHECY!
THERE ARE PROPHECIES IN STAR TREK?
IT'S LIKE HANDING THE DUNGEON MASTER A KNIFE AND BEGGING TO BE STABBED!
THAT'S NOT HOW IT WORKS, RICK. THE DM ISN'T THE ENEMY. YOU'RE ALL ON THE SAME TEAM!
YOU HAVE TO TRUST YOUR DUNGEON MASTER!
RIIIIGHT!
BECAUSE THE OMNIPOTENT UR-DEITY WHO TOOK AWAY MY PORTAL GUN, TRANSFORMED ME AGAINST MY WILL...
...AND LEFT ME TRAPPED IN THIS REALITY WITH NO EQUIPMENT IS MY BFF.
BY THE WAY, I KNOW YOU'RE BEHIND ME. THAT'S SOME CLICHÉ S**T RIGHT THERE.
THIS AGGRESSION IS UNEARNED, BARD. YOU CAME TO MY WORLD. YOU TRIED TO CHEAT, REFUSED TO PLAY THE GAME. YOU ATTACKED ME...
YOU'RE A LIAR. YOU SAY WE'RE ON AN ADVENTURE, BUT THIS ISN'T OUR STORY, IT'S YOURS.
YOU CONTROL EVERYTHING! THAT'S NOT A TEAM, IT'S TYRANNY!
RICK, AFTER ALL THESE YEARS. YOU STILL DON'T UNDERSTAND...

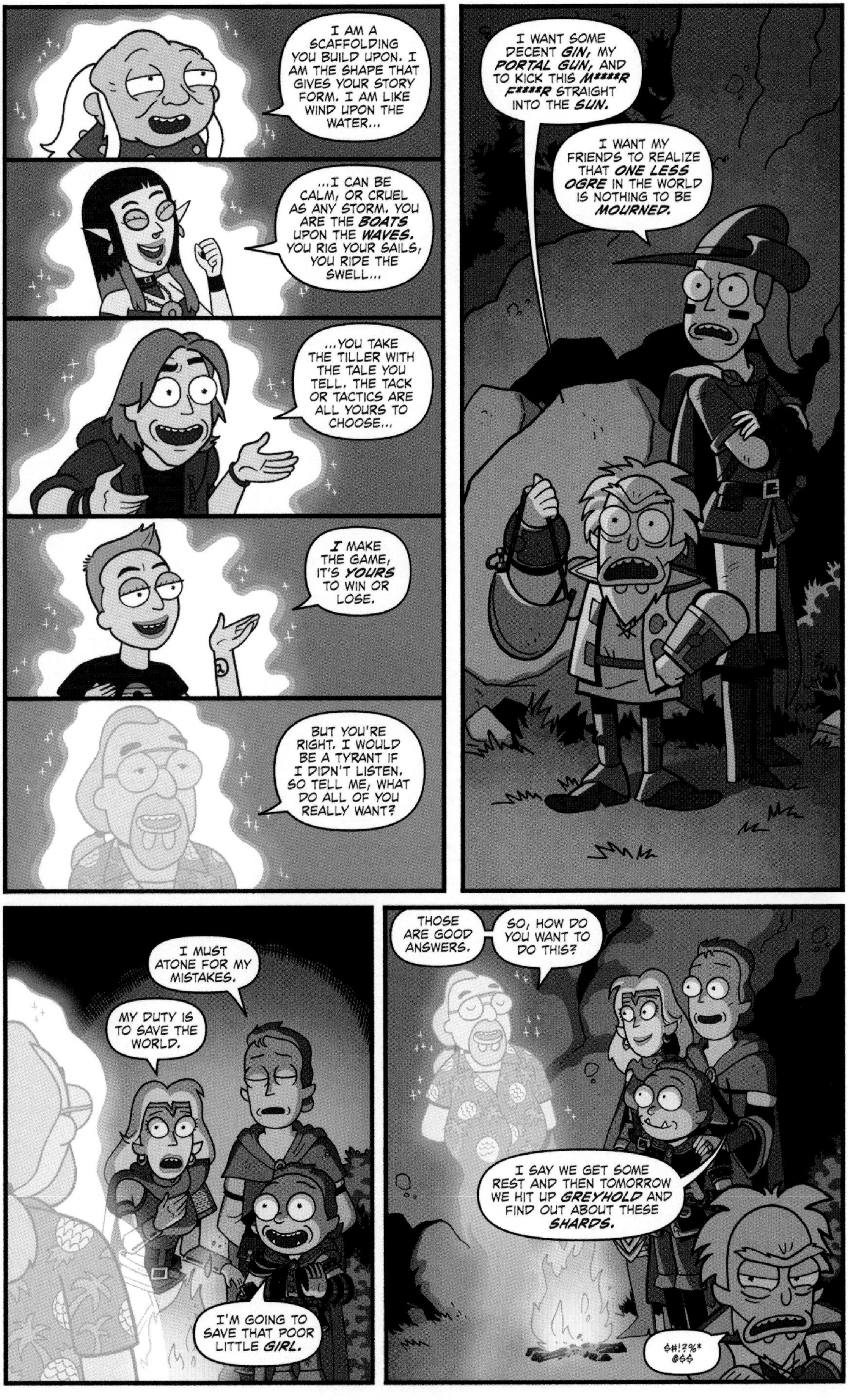
I AM A SCAFFOLDING YOU BUILD UPON. I AM THE SHAPE THAT GIVES YOUR STORY FORM. I AM LIKE WIND UPON THE WATER...
...I CAN BE CALM, OR CRUEL AS ANY STORM. YOU ARE THE BOATS UPON THE WAVES. YOU RIG YOUR SAILS, YOU RIDE THE SWELL...
...YOU TAKE THE TILLER WITH THE TALE YOU TELL. THE TACK OR TACTICS ARE ALL YOURS TO CHOOSE...
I MAKE THE GAME, IT'S YOURS TO WIN OR LOSE.
BUT YOU'RE RIGHT. I WOULD BE A TYRANT IF I DIDN'T LISTEN. SO TELL ME, WHAT DO ALL OF YOU REALLY WANT?
I WANT SOME DECENT GIN, MY PORTAL GUN, AND TO KICK THIS M****R F*****R STRAIGHT INTO THE SUN.
I WANT MY FRIENDS TO REALIZE THAT ONE LESS OGRE IN THE WORLD IS NOTHING TO BE MOURNED.
I MUST ATONE FOR MY MISTAKES.
MY DUTY IS TO SAVE THE WORLD.
I'M GOING TO SAVE THAT POOR LITTLE GIRL.
THOSE ARE GOOD ANSWERS.
SO, HOW DO YOU WANT TO DO THIS?
I SAY WE GET SOME REST AND THEN TOMORROW WE HIT UP GREYHOLD AND FIND OUT ABOUT THESE SHARDS.
$#!?%* @$$

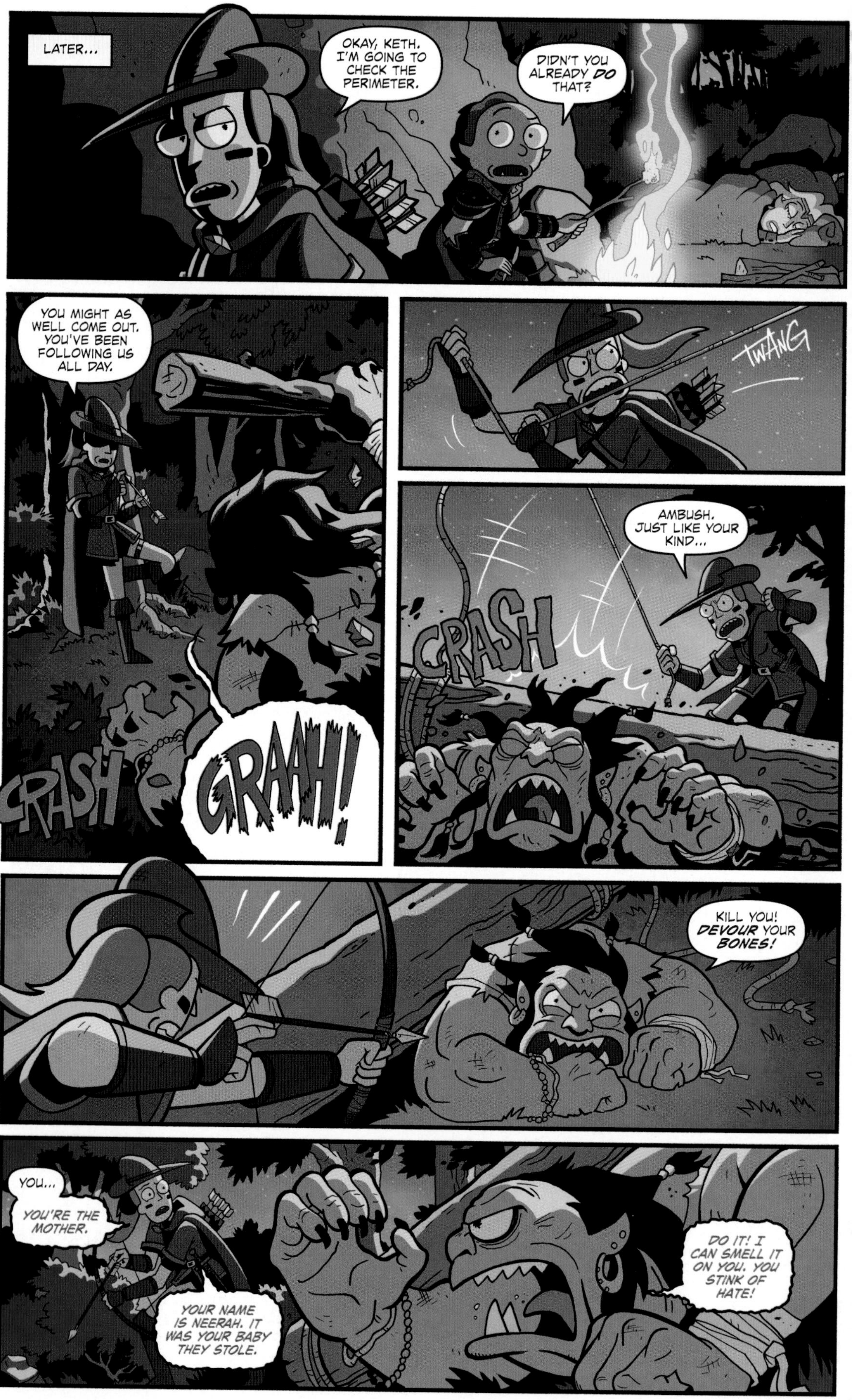
LATER...
OKAY, KETH. I'M GOING TO CHECK THE PERIMETER.
DIDN'T YOU ALREADY *DO* THAT?
YOU MIGHT AS WELL COME OUT. YOU'VE BEEN FOLLOWING US ALL DAY.
CRASH
GRAAH!
TWANG
AMBUSH. JUST LIKE YOUR KIND...
CRASH
KILL YOU! ***DEVOUR*** YOUR ***BONES!***
YOU...
YOU'RE THE MOTHER.
YOUR NAME IS NEERAH. IT WAS YOUR BABY THEY STOLE.
DO IT! I CAN SMELL IT ON YOU. YOU STINK OF HATE!

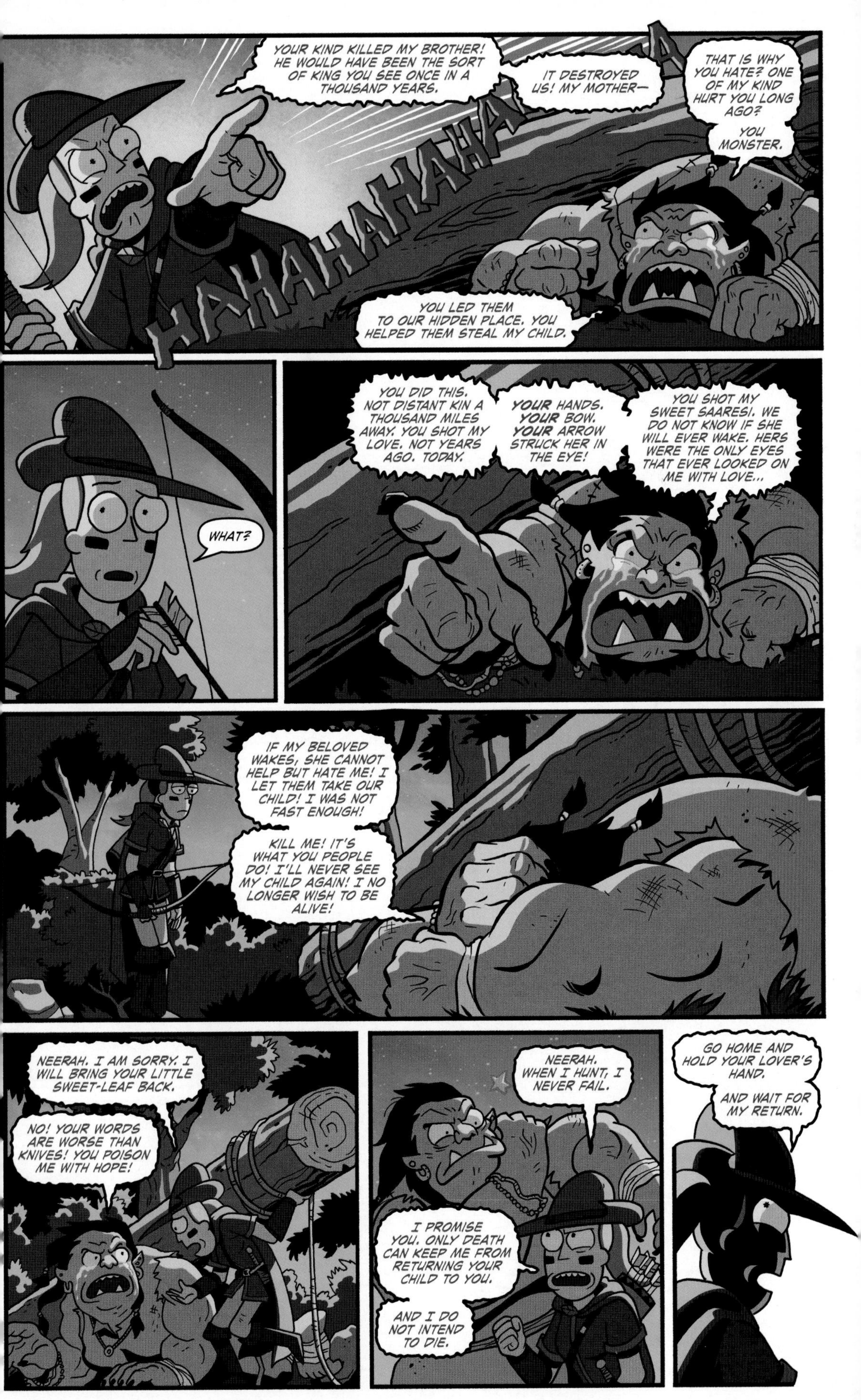
YOUR KIND KILLED MY BROTHER! HE WOULD HAVE BEEN THE SORT OF KING YOU SEE ONCE IN A THOUSAND YEARS.
IT DESTROYED US! MY MOTHER—
HAHAHAHAHAHAHA
THAT IS WHY YOU HATE? ONE OF MY KIND HURT YOU LONG AGO?
YOU MONSTER.
YOU LED THEM TO OUR HIDDEN PLACE. YOU HELPED THEM STEAL MY CHILD.
WHAT?
YOU DID THIS. NOT DISTANT KIN A THOUSAND MILES AWAY. YOU SHOT MY LOVE. NOT YEARS AGO. TODAY.
YOUR HANDS. YOUR BOW. YOUR ARROW STRUCK HER IN THE EYE!
YOU SHOT MY SWEET SAARESI. WE DO NOT KNOW IF SHE WILL EVER WAKE. HERS WERE THE ONLY EYES THAT EVER LOOKED ON ME WITH LOVE...
IF MY BELOVED WAKES, SHE CANNOT HELP BUT HATE ME! I LET THEM TAKE OUR CHILD! I WAS NOT FAST ENOUGH!
KILL ME! IT'S WHAT YOU PEOPLE DO! I'LL NEVER SEE MY CHILD AGAIN! I NO LONGER WISH TO BE ALIVE!
NEERAH. I AM SORRY. I WILL BRING YOUR LITTLE SWEET-LEAF BACK.
NO! YOUR WORDS ARE WORSE THAN KNIVES! YOU POISON ME WITH HOPE!
NEERAH. WHEN I HUNT, I NEVER FAIL.
I PROMISE YOU. ONLY DEATH CAN KEEP ME FROM RETURNING YOUR CHILD TO YOU.
AND I DO NOT INTEND TO DIE.
GO HOME AND HOLD YOUR LOVER'S HAND.
AND WAIT FOR MY RETURN.

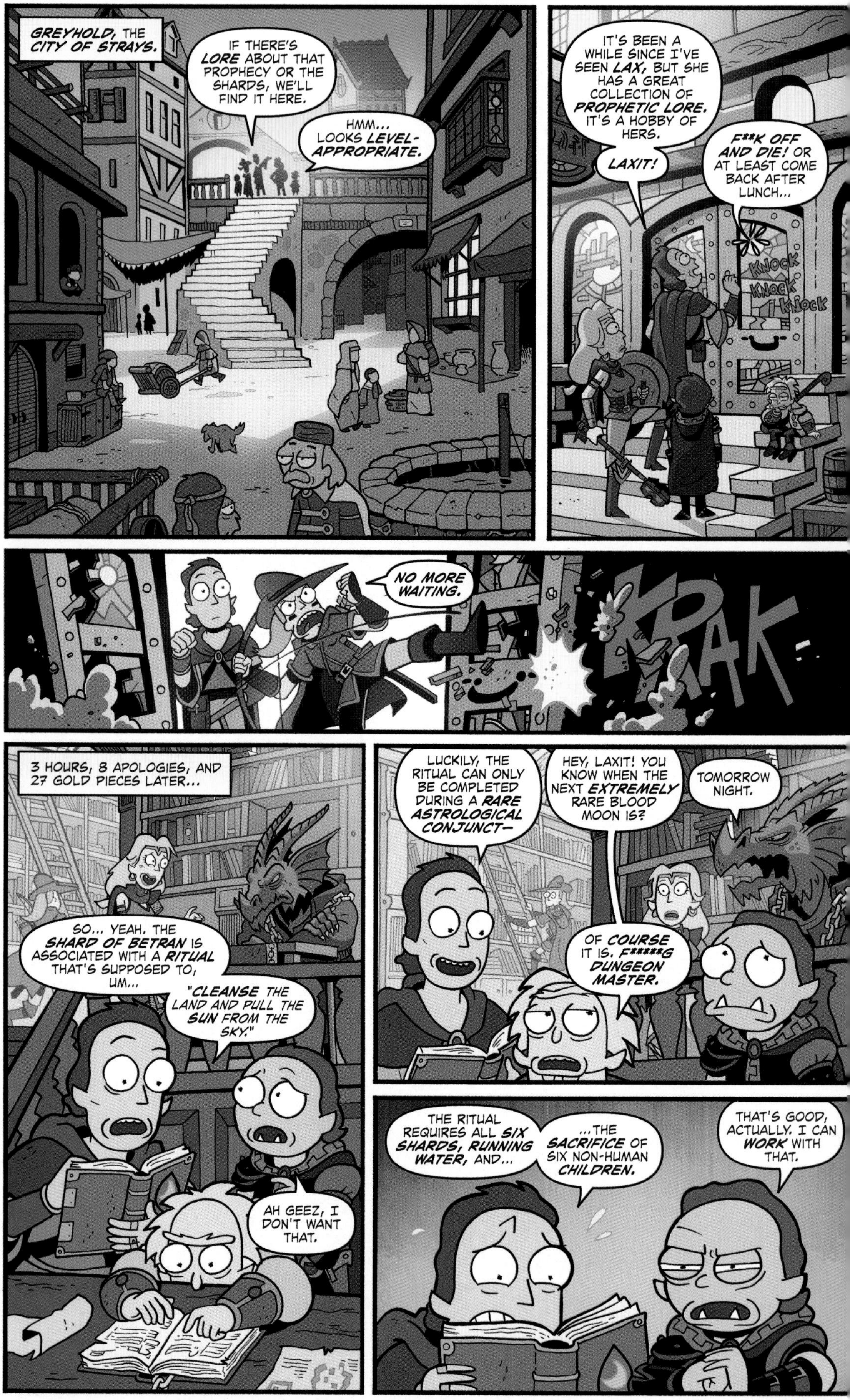

GREYHOLD, THE CITY OF STRAYS.
IF THERE'S LORE ABOUT THAT PROPHECY OR THE SHARDS, WE'LL FIND IT HERE.
HMM... LOOKS LEVEL-APPROPRIATE.
IT'S BEEN A WHILE SINCE I'VE SEEN LAX, BUT SHE HAS A GREAT COLLECTION OF PROPHETIC LORE. IT'S A HOBBY OF HERS.
LAXIT!
F**K OFF AND DIE! OR AT LEAST COME BACK AFTER LUNCH...
KNOCK KNOCK KNOCK
NO MORE WAITING.
KRAK
3 HOURS, 8 APOLOGIES, AND 27 GOLD PIECES LATER...
SO... YEAH. THE SHARD OF BETRAN IS ASSOCIATED WITH A RITUAL THAT'S SUPPOSED TO, UM...
"CLEANSE THE LAND AND PULL THE SUN FROM THE SKY."
AH GEEZ, I DON'T WANT THAT.
LUCKILY, THE RITUAL CAN ONLY BE COMPLETED DURING A RARE ASTROLOGICAL CONJUNCT—
HEY, LAXIT! YOU KNOW WHEN THE NEXT EXTREMELY RARE BLOOD MOON IS?
TOMORROW NIGHT.
OF COURSE IT IS. F*****G DUNGEON MASTER.
THE RITUAL REQUIRES ALL SIX SHARDS, RUNNING WATER, AND...
...THE SACRIFICE OF SIX NON-HUMAN CHILDREN.
THAT'S GOOD, ACTUALLY. I CAN WORK WITH THAT.

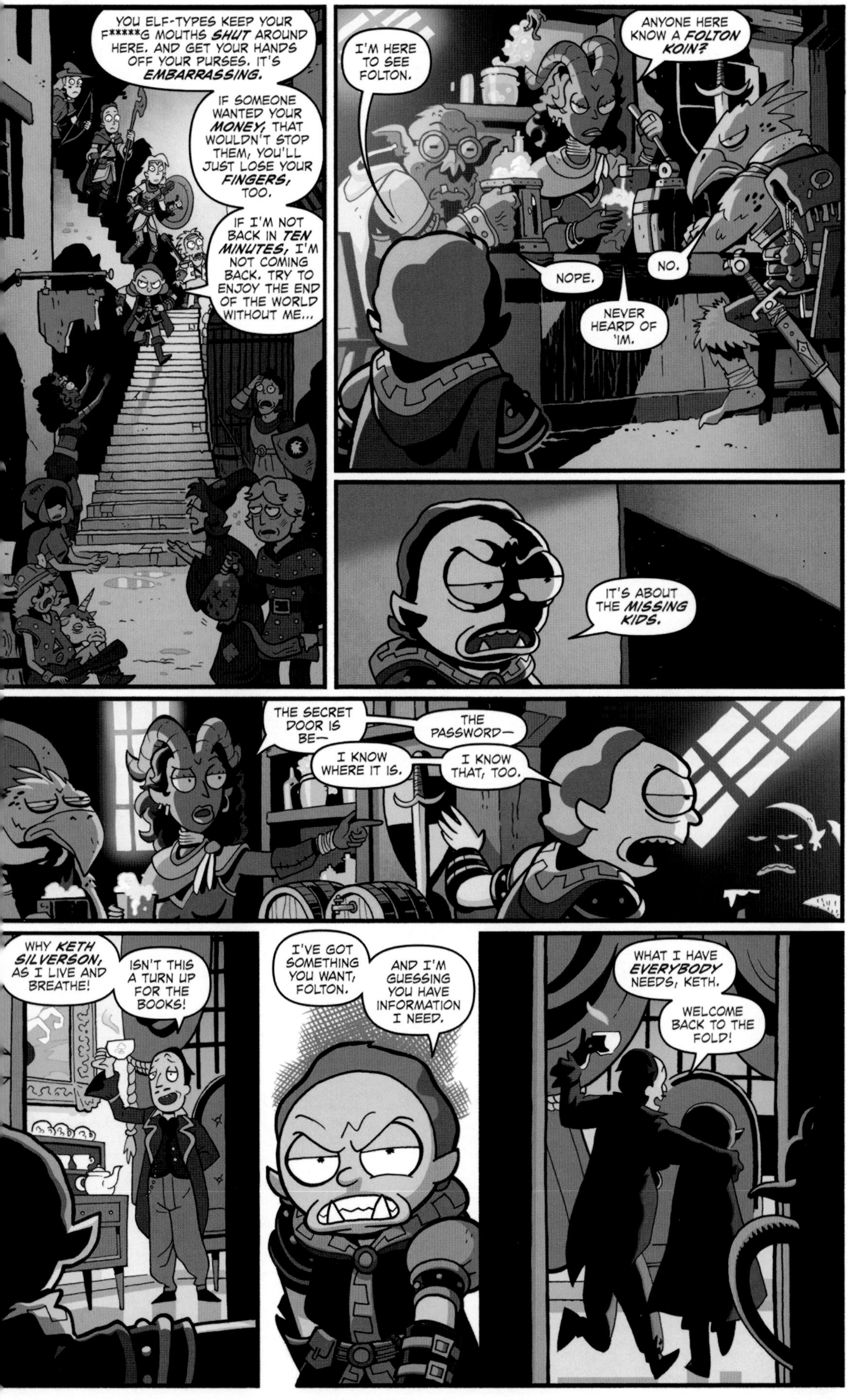

YOU ELF-TYPES KEEP YOUR F*****G MOUTHS SHUT AROUND HERE. AND GET YOUR HANDS OFF YOUR PURSES. IT'S EMBARRASSING.
IF SOMEONE WANTED YOUR MONEY, THAT WOULDN'T STOP THEM, YOU'LL JUST LOSE YOUR FINGERS, TOO.
IF I'M NOT BACK IN TEN MINUTES, I'M NOT COMING BACK. TRY TO ENJOY THE END OF THE WORLD WITHOUT ME...
ANYONE HERE KNOW A FOLTON KOIN?
I'M HERE TO SEE FOLTON.
NOPE.
NO.
NEVER HEARD OF 'IM.
IT'S ABOUT THE MISSING KIDS.
THE SECRET DOOR IS BE—
THE PASSWORD—
I KNOW WHERE IT IS.
I KNOW THAT, TOO.
WHY KETH SILVERSON, AS I LIVE AND BREATHE!
ISN'T THIS A TURN UP FOR THE BOOKS!
I'VE GOT SOMETHING YOU WANT, FOLTON.
AND I'M GUESSING YOU HAVE INFORMATION I NEED.
WHAT I HAVE EVERYBODY NEEDS, KETH.
WELCOME BACK TO THE FOLD!

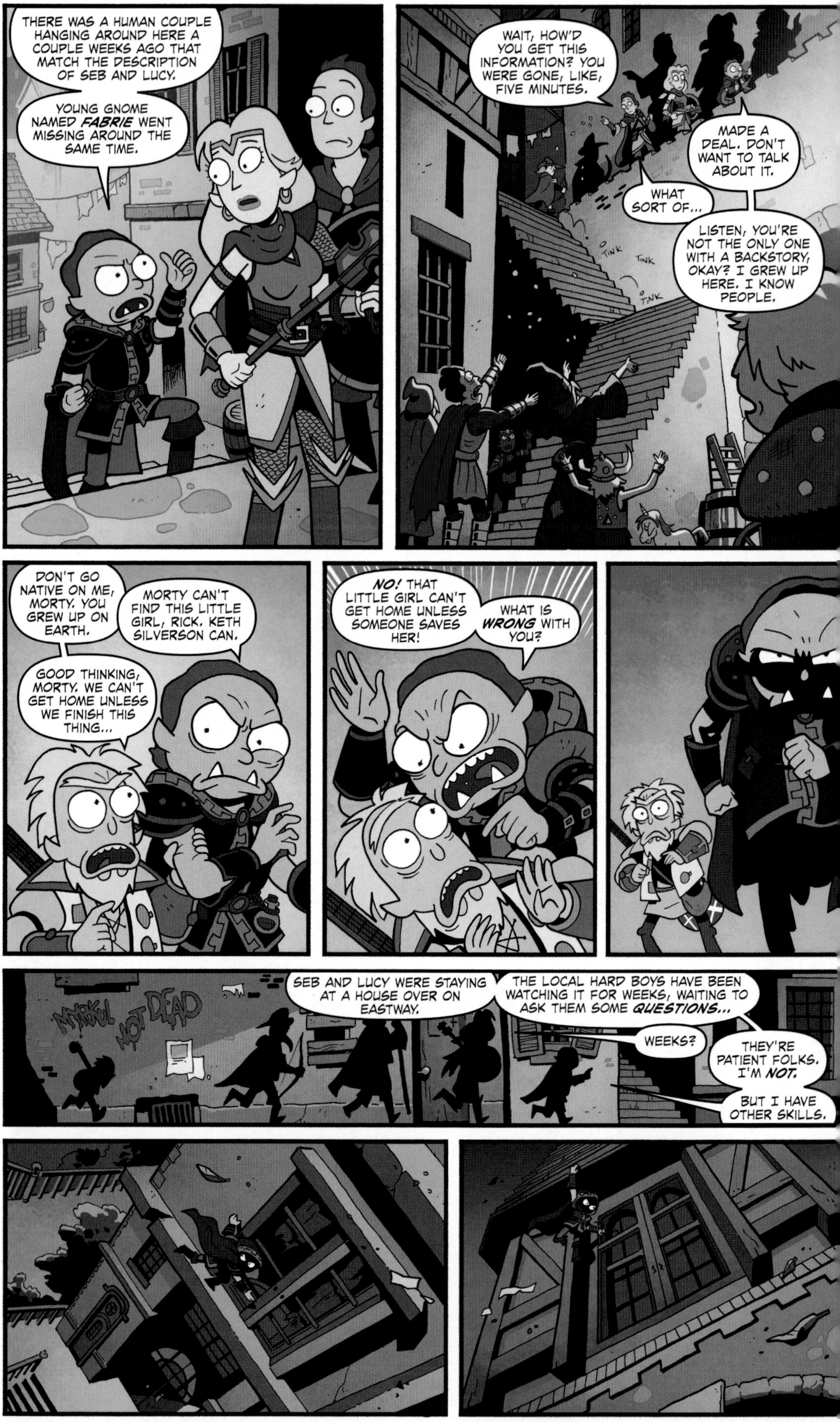
THERE WAS A HUMAN COUPLE HANGING AROUND HERE A COUPLE WEEKS AGO THAT MATCH THE DESCRIPTION OF SEB AND LUCY.
YOUNG GNOME NAMED *FABRIE* WENT MISSING AROUND THE SAME TIME.
WAIT, HOW'D YOU GET THIS INFORMATION? YOU WERE GONE, LIKE, FIVE MINUTES.
MADE A DEAL. DON'T WANT TO TALK ABOUT IT.
WHAT SORT OF...
LISTEN, YOU'RE NOT THE ONLY ONE WITH A BACKSTORY, OKAY? I GREW UP HERE. I KNOW PEOPLE.
TINK
TINK
TINK
DON'T GO NATIVE ON ME, MORTY. YOU GREW UP ON EARTH.
MORTY CAN'T FIND THIS LITTLE GIRL, RICK. KETH SILVERSON CAN.
GOOD THINKING, MORTY. WE CAN'T GET HOME UNLESS WE FINISH THIS THING...
NO! THAT LITTLE GIRL CAN'T GET HOME UNLESS SOMEONE SAVES HER!
WHAT IS *WRONG* WITH YOU?
SEB AND LUCY WERE STAYING AT A HOUSE OVER ON EASTWAY.
THE LOCAL HARD BOYS HAVE BEEN WATCHING IT FOR WEEKS, WAITING TO ASK THEM SOME *QUESTIONS...*
WEEKS?
THEY'RE PATIENT FOLKS. I'M *NOT.*
BUT I HAVE OTHER SKILLS.
MYRKUL NOT DEAD

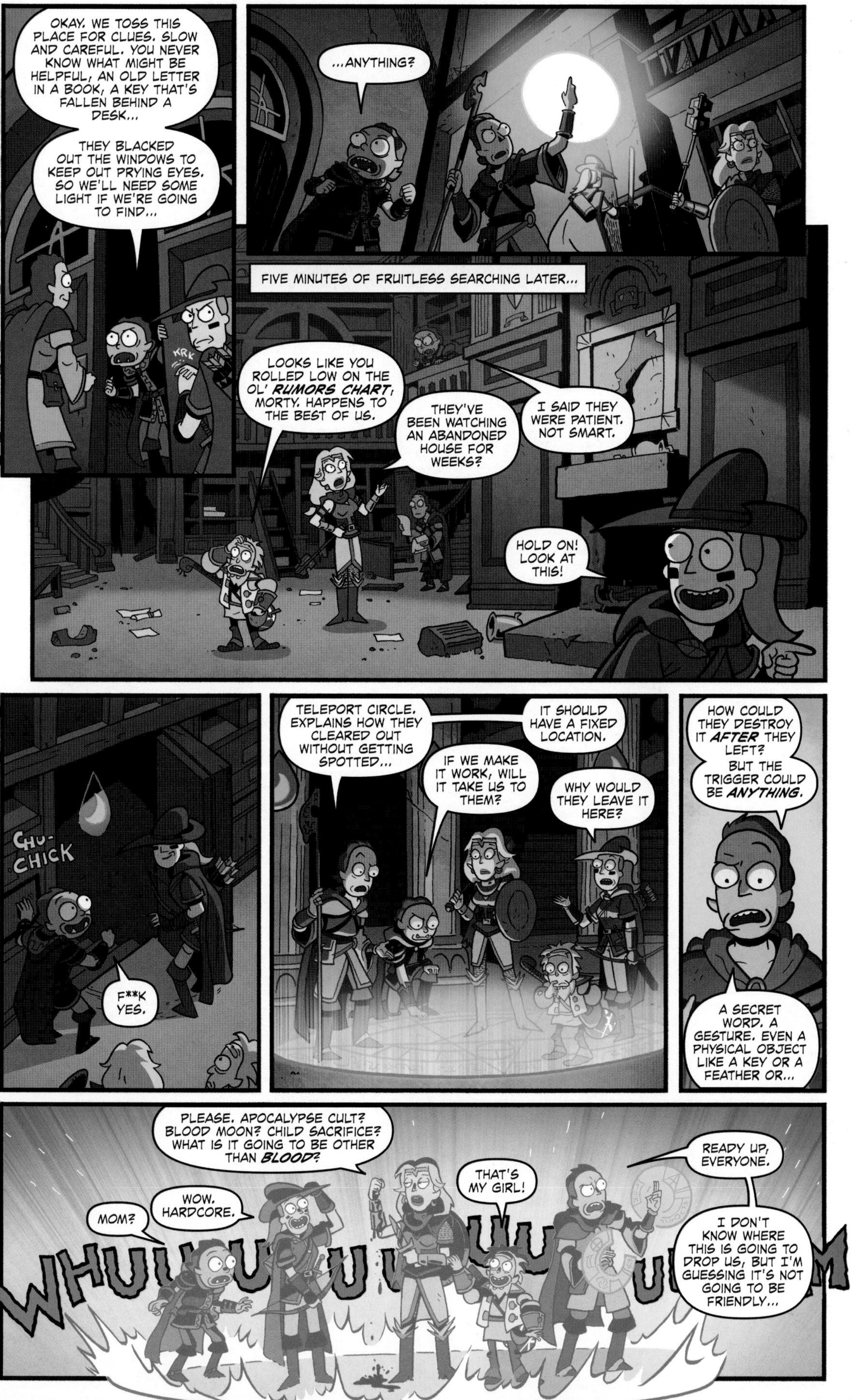
OKAY. WE TOSS THIS PLACE FOR CLUES. SLOW AND CAREFUL. YOU NEVER KNOW WHAT MIGHT BE HELPFUL, AN OLD LETTER IN A BOOK, A KEY THAT'S FALLEN BEHIND A DESK...
THEY BLACKED OUT THE WINDOWS TO KEEP OUT PRYING EYES. SO WE'LL NEED SOME LIGHT IF WE'RE GOING TO FIND...
KRK
...ANYTHING?
FIVE MINUTES OF FRUITLESS SEARCHING LATER...
LOOKS LIKE YOU ROLLED LOW ON THE OL' RUMORS CHART, MORTY. HAPPENS TO THE BEST OF US.
THEY'VE BEEN WATCHING AN ABANDONED HOUSE FOR WEEKS?
I SAID THEY WERE PATIENT. NOT SMART.
HOLD ON! LOOK AT THIS!
CHU-CHICK
F**K YES.
TELEPORT CIRCLE. EXPLAINS HOW THEY CLEARED OUT WITHOUT GETTING SPOTTED...
IT SHOULD HAVE A FIXED LOCATION.
IF WE MAKE IT WORK, WILL IT TAKE US TO THEM?
WHY WOULD THEY LEAVE IT HERE?
HOW COULD THEY DESTROY IT AFTER THEY LEFT?
BUT THE TRIGGER COULD BE ANYTHING.
A SECRET WORD. A GESTURE. EVEN A PHYSICAL OBJECT LIKE A KEY OR A FEATHER OR...
PLEASE. APOCALYPSE CULT? BLOOD MOON? CHILD SACRIFICE? WHAT IS IT GOING TO BE OTHER THAN BLOOD?
MOM?
WOW. HARDCORE.
THAT'S MY GIRL!
READY UP, EVERYONE.
I DON'T KNOW WHERE THIS IS GOING TO DROP US, BUT I'M GUESSING IT'S NOT GOING TO BE FRIENDLY...
WHUUUUUUUUUM

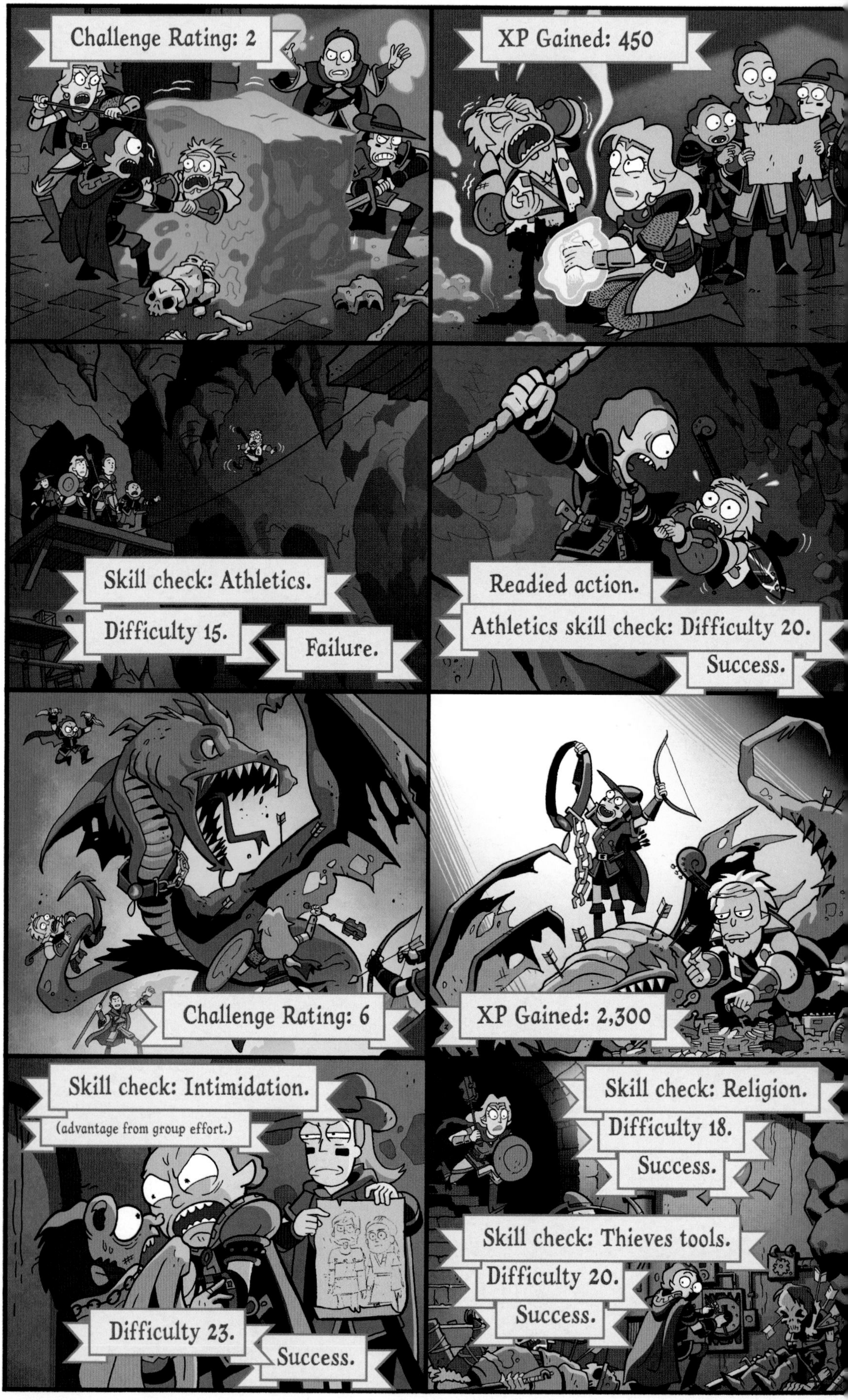
Challenge Rating: 2
XP Gained: 450
Skill check: Athletics.
Difficulty 15.
Failure.
Readied action.
Athletics skill check: Difficulty 20.
Success.
Challenge Rating: 6
XP Gained: 2,300
Skill check: Intimidation.
(advantage from group effort.)
Difficulty 23.
Success.
Skill check: Religion.
Difficulty 18.
Success.
Skill check: Thieves tools.
Difficulty 20.
Success.

WE'RE CLEAR.

OKAY EVERYONE, LET'S GRAB A SHORT REST.

WHY NOT A LONG REST?

THAT WAY YOU CAN GET *ALL* YOUR SPELLS BACK. AND I NEED A F*****G NAP.

GREAT IDEA, RICK.

HEY EVERYONE! SOME EVIL SONS OF B*****S ARE GOING TO KILL A BUNCH OF CHILDREN TONIGHT.

WE'VE BEEN UNDERGROUND FOR A WHILE AND DON'T KNOW EXACTLY WHAT TIME IT IS. OR WHEN THE BLOOD MOON WILL RISE, OR HOW FAR WE STILL HAVE TO GO BEFORE WE FIND THEM...

...THAT SAID, WHO WANTS TO SLEEP FOR 8 HOURS. ANYONE? SHOW OF HANDS?

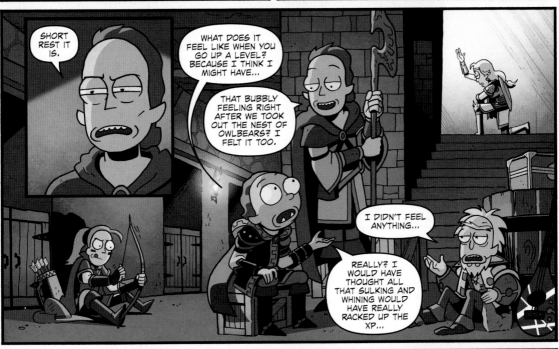

SHORT REST IT IS.

WHAT DOES IT FEEL LIKE WHEN YOU GO UP A LEVEL? BECAUSE I THINK I MIGHT HAVE...

THAT BUBBLY FEELING RIGHT AFTER WE TOOK OUT THE NEST OF OWLBEARS? I FELT IT TOO.

I DIDN'T FEEL ANYTHING...

REALLY? I WOULD HAVE THOUGHT ALL THAT SULKING AND WHINING WOULD HAVE REALLY RACKED UP THE XP...

HEY NOW! I'M—

RICK, WHY DON'T YOU GO KEEP LOOKOUT? SOME OF US HAVE SPELLS TO PREPARE.

EVERYONE ELSE, REMEMBER TO TAKE YOUR FULL RECOVERY. I HAVE A FEELING THE WORST IS YET TO COME.

UM... DAD? I KNOW WE HAVE NUMBERS FOR STRENGTH AND INTELLIGENCE AND STUFF. IS THERE A STAT FOR, LIKE, COOLNESS?
TOK TOK
TOK
WELL GRAMPA RICK SEEMS REALLY... DIFFERENT.
CHARISMA MAKES YOU MORE ARTICULATE AND CHARMING, BUT NOT REALLY COOL PER SE. WHY DO YOU ASK?
NICE SHOT, ARI!
THANKS DAD!
HA! MORTY, RICK'S NEVER BEEN COOL.
WHAT? BUT HE'S—
B... WHAT DO YOU MEAN?
DON'T GET ME WRONG: HE LOOKS COOL. ALL THE TIME. BUT HE'S NOT.
HE'S JUST ABLE TO DO COOL THINGS. BIG DIFFERENCE.
STABBY
YOU'VE GOT EYES. LOOK AT HIM...
THERE HE IS. SAME AS ALWAYS. SNARKY. BITTER. SELF-CENTERED AS A GYROSCOPE.
IF YOU TAKE AWAY WHAT HE CAN DO, YOU SEE WHAT HE IS.
AND IT ISN'T PRETTY.
KICK
THE THING IS, BARDS ARE GREAT THESE DAYS. HE COULD FIGHT. HE EVEN HAS SPELLS...
HE'S JUST NOT INTERESTED IN HELPING. NEVER HAS BEEN. HE'S ONLY INTERESTED IN AMUSING HIMSELF.
WHAK
HE COULD FEED PEOPLE. CURE CANCER. BUT HE DOESN'T. HE MAKES DEATH RAYS AND GETS HIGH.
RIGHT NOW, I'M NOT COOL. I CAN JUST DO MAGIC.
THOUGH DON'T GET ME WRONG. I LOVE HAVING HIGH INTELLIGENCE AND CHARISMA. IT'S SO EASY TO UNDERSTAND ALL THIS...
...TO KNOW MY OWN MIND AND SAY EXACTLY WHAT I MEAN.
THE DIFFERENCE BETWEEN ME AND RICK ISN'T THAT HE'S COOL AND I'M NOT.
IT'S THAT I'M NOT GOOD AT CARING FOR PEOPLE. BUT RICK, HE ISN'T GOOD AT CARING ABOUT THEM.
QUIET! SOMETHING'S HAPPENING IN THE BIG ROOM UP AHEAD!

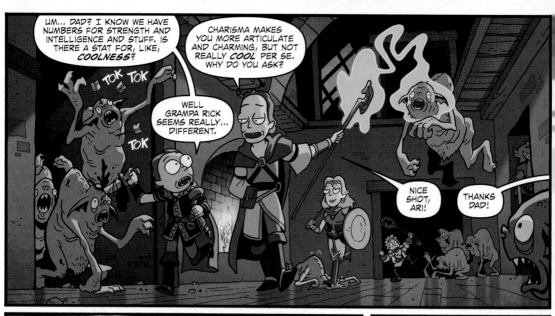

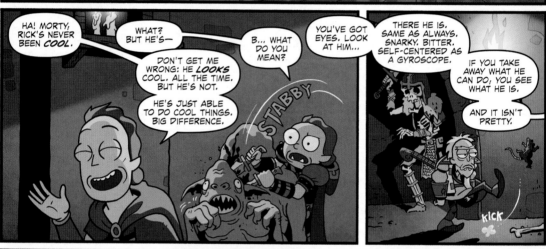

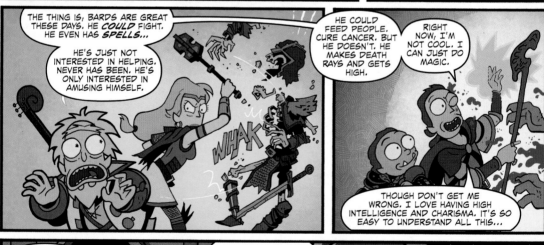

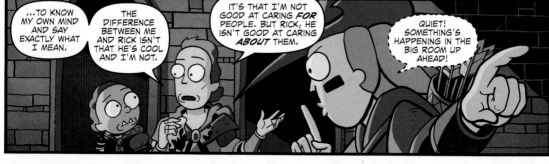

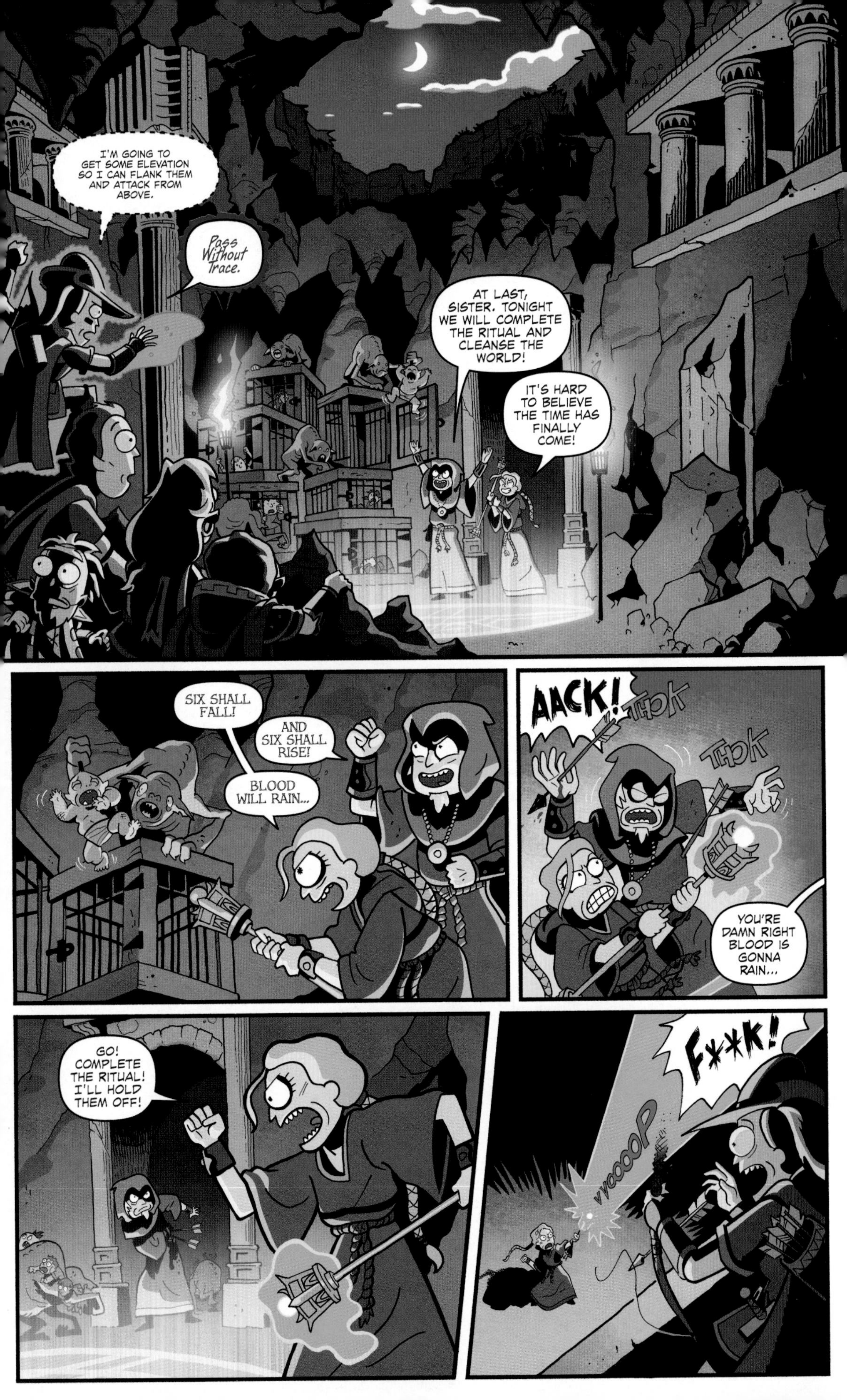
I'M GOING TO GET SOME ELEVATION SO I CAN FLANK THEM AND ATTACK FROM ABOVE.
Pass Without Trace.
AT LAST, SISTER. TONIGHT WE WILL COMPLETE THE RITUAL AND CLEANSE THE WORLD!
IT'S HARD TO BELIEVE THE TIME HAS FINALLY COME!
SIX SHALL FALL!
AND SIX SHALL RISE!
BLOOD WILL RAIN...
AACK!
THOK
THOK
YOU'RE DAMN RIGHT BLOOD IS GONNA RAIN...
GO! COMPLETE THE RITUAL! I'LL HOLD THEM OFF!
F**K!
VVOOOOP

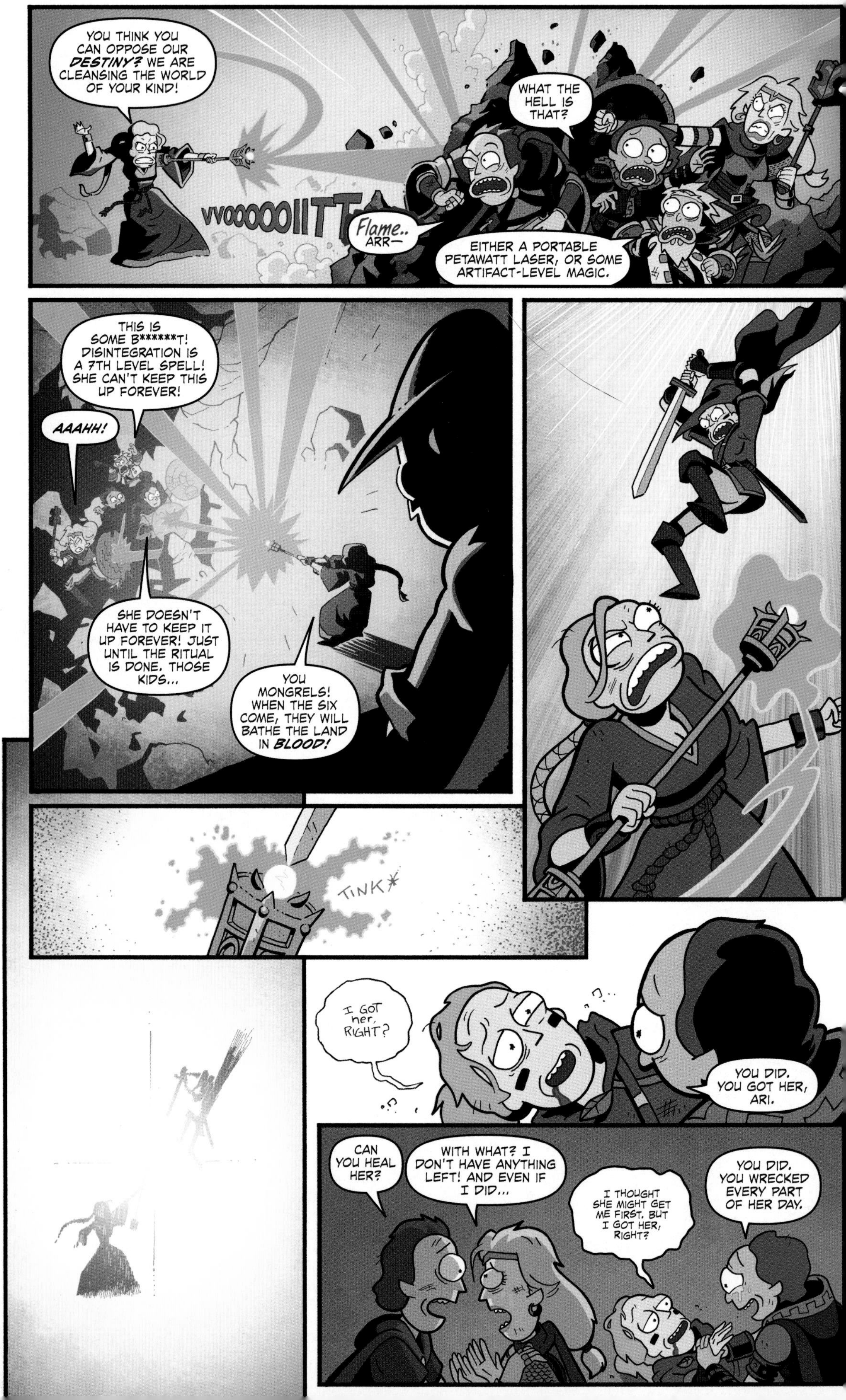
YOU THINK YOU CAN OPPOSE OUR DESTINY? WE ARE CLEANSING THE WORLD OF YOUR KIND!
WHAT THE HELL IS THAT?
VVOOOOOIIITT
Flame.. ARR—
EITHER A PORTABLE PETAWATT LASER, OR SOME ARTIFACT-LEVEL MAGIC.
THIS IS SOME B******T! DISINTEGRATION IS A 7TH LEVEL SPELL! SHE CAN'T KEEP THIS UP FOREVER!
AAAHH!
SHE DOESN'T HAVE TO KEEP IT UP FOREVER! JUST UNTIL THE RITUAL IS DONE. THOSE KIDS...
YOU MONGRELS! WHEN THE SIX COME, THEY WILL BATHE THE LAND IN BLOOD!
TINK
I GOT her, RIGHT?
YOU DID. YOU GOT HER, ARI.
CAN YOU HEAL HER?
WITH WHAT? I DON'T HAVE ANYTHING LEFT! AND EVEN IF I DID...
I THOUGHT SHE MIGHT GET ME FIRST. BUT I GOT HER, RIGHT?
YOU DID. YOU WRECKED EVERY PART OF HER DAY.

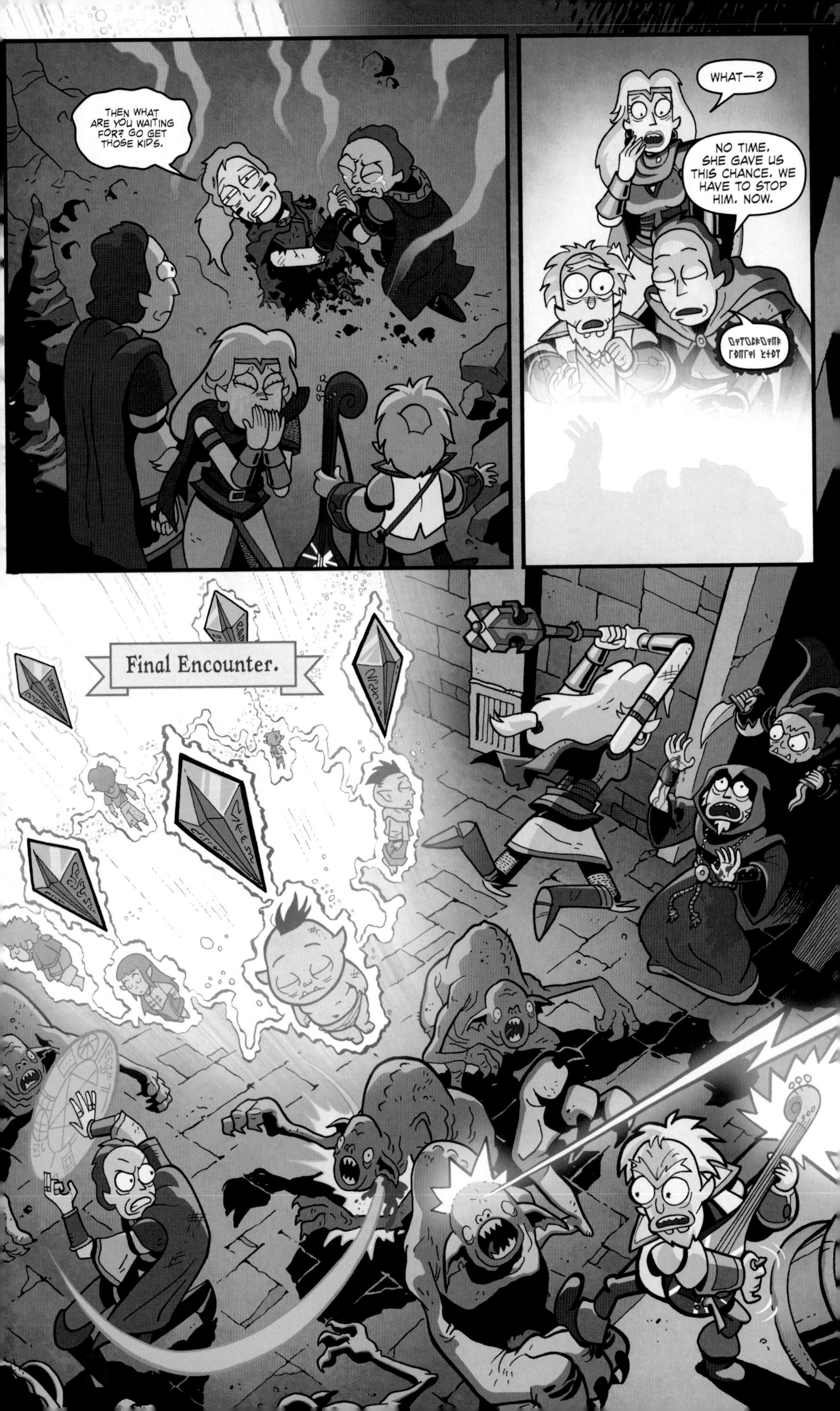
THEN WHAT ARE YOU WAITING FOR? GO GET THOSE KIDS.
WHAT—?
NO TIME. SHE GAVE US THIS CHANCE. WE HAVE TO STOP HIM. NOW.
Final Encounter.

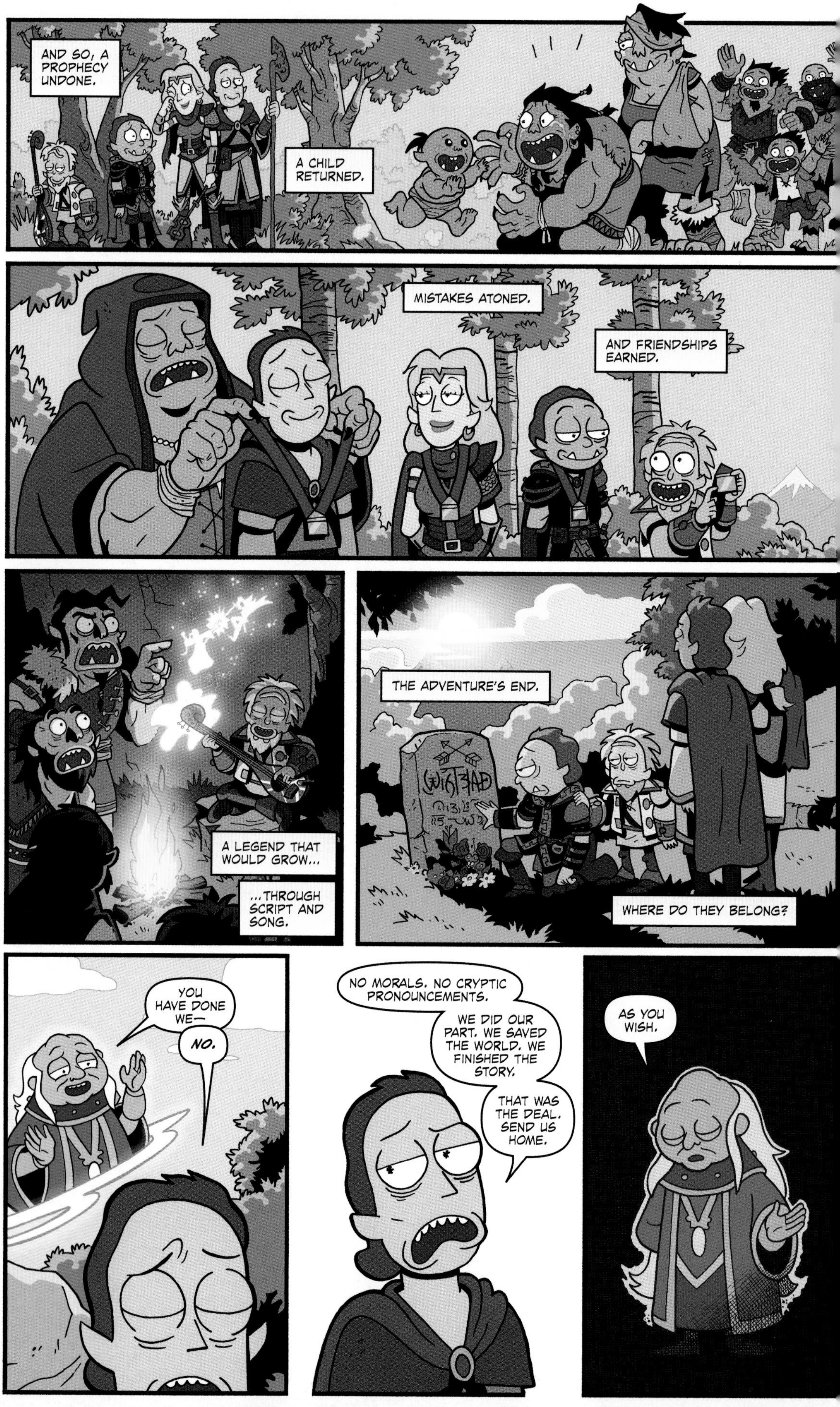
AND SO, A PROPHECY UNDONE.
A CHILD RETURNED.
MISTAKES ATONED.
AND FRIENDSHIPS EARNED.
A LEGEND THAT WOULD GROW...
...THROUGH SCRIPT AND SONG.
THE ADVENTURE'S END.
WHERE DO THEY BELONG?
YOU HAVE DONE WE—
NO.
NO MORALS. NO CRYPTIC PRONOUNCEMENTS.
WE DID OUR PART. WE SAVED THE WORLD. WE FINISHED THE STORY.
THAT WAS THE DEAL. SEND US HOME.
AS YOU WISH.

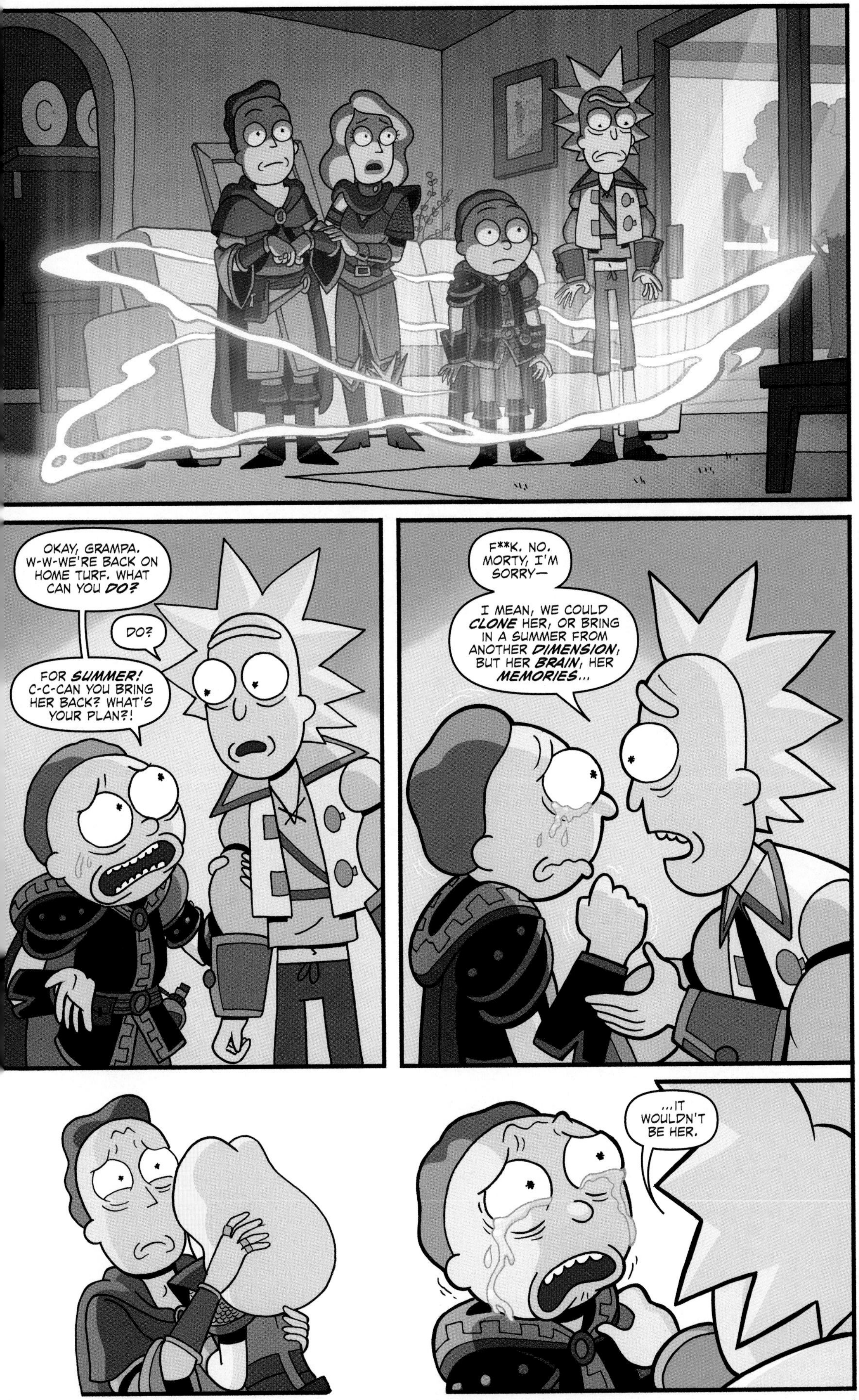
OKAY, GRAMPA. W-W-WE'RE BACK ON HOME TURF. WHAT CAN YOU *DO?*
DO?
FOR *SUMMER!* C-C-CAN YOU BRING HER BACK? WHAT'S YOUR PLAN?!
F**K. NO. MORTY, I'M SORRY—
I MEAN, WE COULD *CLONE* HER, OR BRING IN A SUMMER FROM ANOTHER *DIMENSION*, BUT HER *BRAIN*, HER *MEMORIES*...
...IT WOULDN'T BE HER.

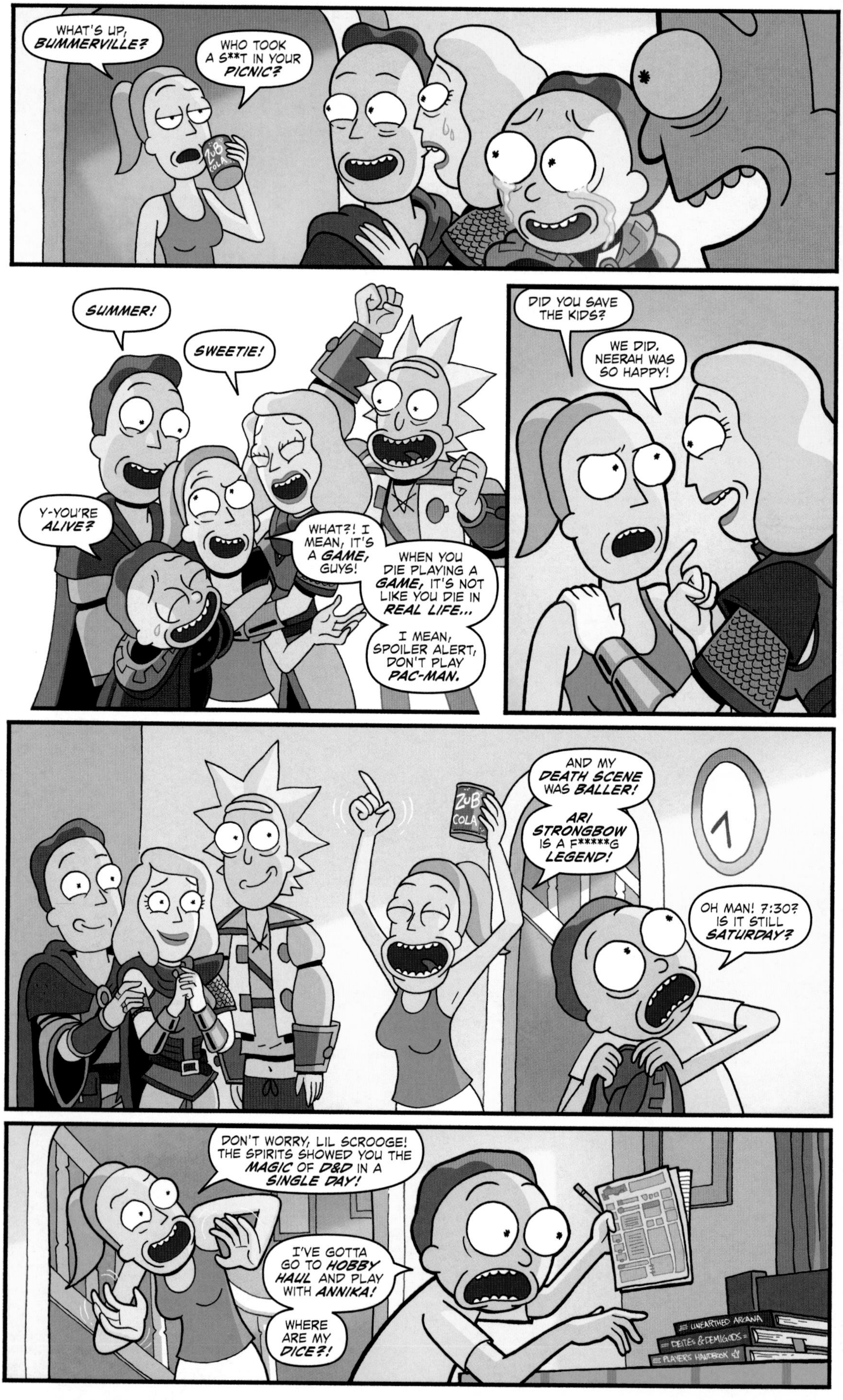
WHAT'S UP, BUMMERVILLE?
WHO TOOK A S**T IN YOUR PICNIC?
SUMMER!
SWEETIE!
Y-YOU'RE ALIVE?
WHAT?! I MEAN, IT'S A GAME, GUYS!
WHEN YOU DIE PLAYING A GAME, IT'S NOT LIKE YOU DIE IN REAL LIFE...
I MEAN, SPOILER ALERT, DON'T PLAY PAC-MAN.
DID YOU SAVE THE KIDS?
WE DID. NEERAH WAS SO HAPPY!
AND MY DEATH SCENE WAS BALLER!
ARI STRONGBOW IS A F*****G LEGEND!
OH MAN! 7:30? IS IT STILL SATURDAY?
DON'T WORRY, LIL SCROOGE! THE SPIRITS SHOWED YOU THE MAGIC OF D&D IN A SINGLE DAY!
I'VE GOTTA GO TO HOBBY HAUL AND PLAY WITH ANNIKA!
WHERE ARE MY DICE?!
UNEARTHED ARCANA
DEITIES & DEMIGODS
PLAYER'S HANDBOOK

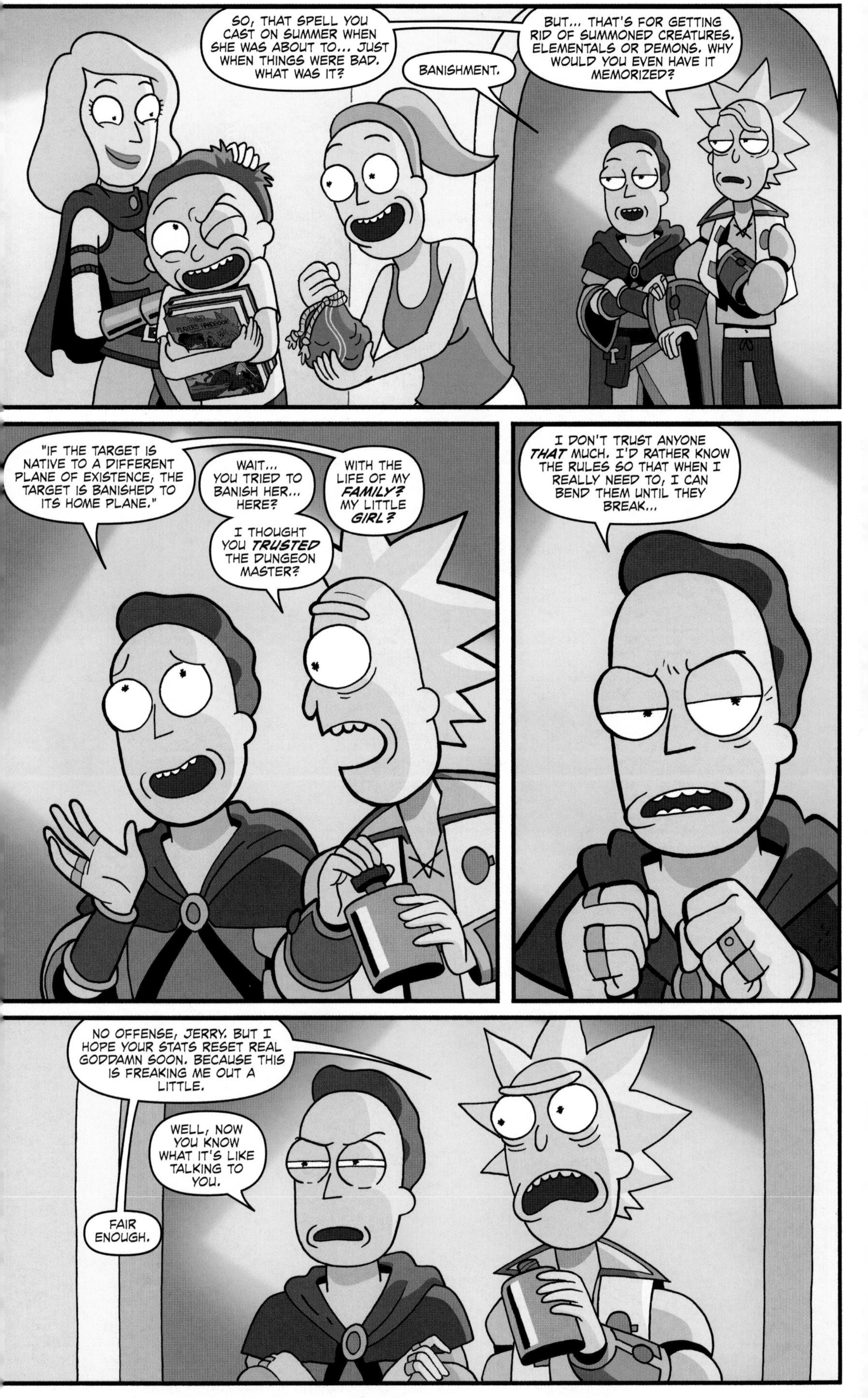
SO, THAT SPELL YOU CAST ON SUMMER WHEN SHE WAS ABOUT TO... JUST WHEN THINGS WERE BAD. WHAT WAS IT?
BANISHMENT.
BUT... THAT'S FOR GETTING RID OF SUMMONED CREATURES. ELEMENTALS OR DEMONS. WHY WOULD YOU EVEN HAVE IT MEMORIZED?
PLAYER'S HANDBOOK
"IF THE TARGET IS NATIVE TO A DIFFERENT PLANE OF EXISTENCE, THE TARGET IS BANISHED TO ITS HOME PLANE."
WAIT... YOU TRIED TO BANISH HER... HERE?
WITH THE LIFE OF MY *FAMILY?* MY LITTLE *GIRL?*
I THOUGHT YOU *TRUSTED* THE DUNGEON MASTER?
I DON'T TRUST ANYONE *THAT* MUCH. I'D RATHER KNOW THE RULES SO THAT WHEN I REALLY NEED TO, I CAN BEND THEM UNTIL THEY BREAK...
NO OFFENSE, JERRY. BUT I HOPE YOUR STATS RESET REAL GODDAMN SOON. BECAUSE THIS IS FREAKING ME OUT A LITTLE.
WELL, NOW YOU KNOW WHAT IT'S LIKE TALKING TO YOU.
FAIR ENOUGH.

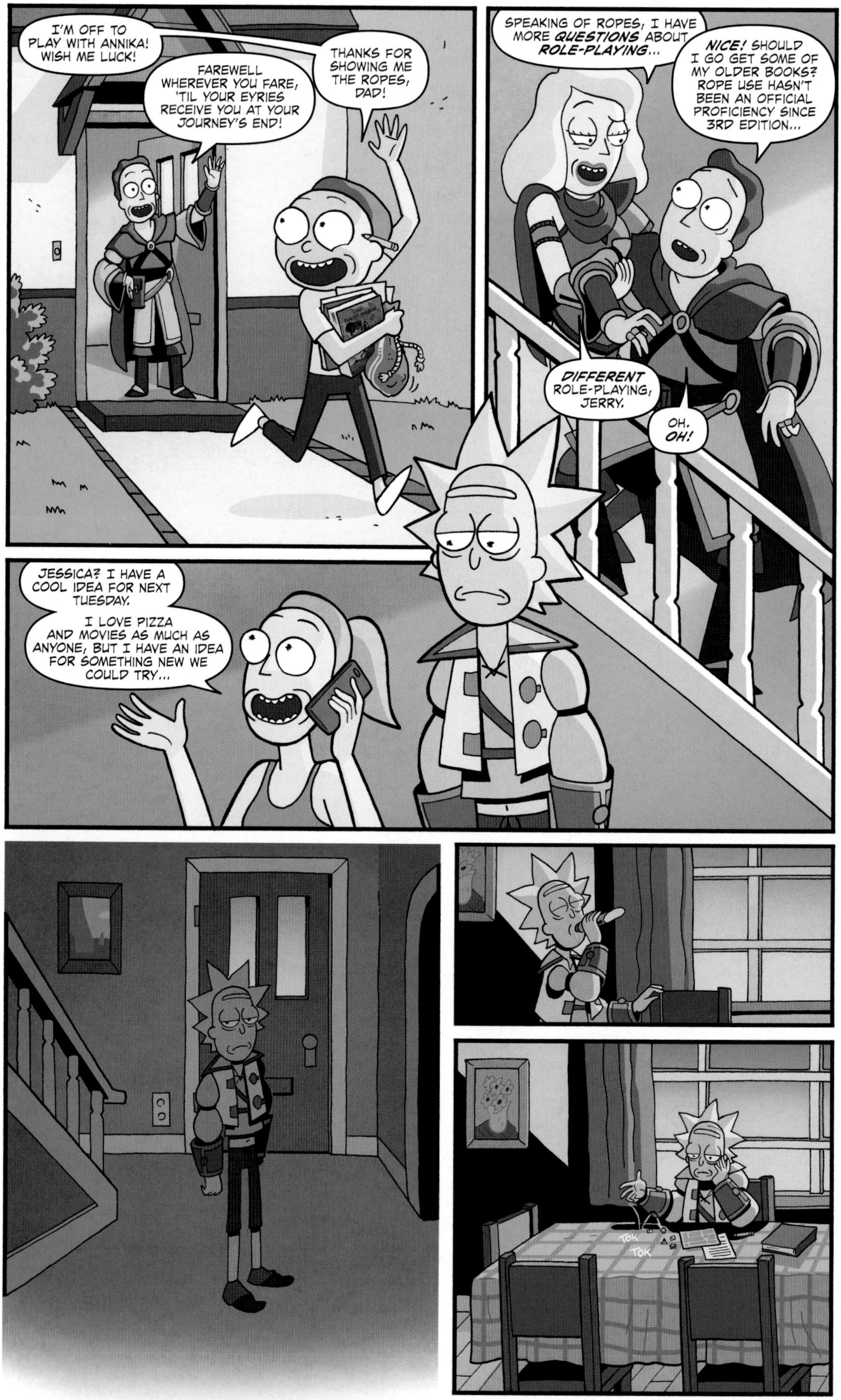
I'M OFF TO PLAY WITH ANNIKA! WISH ME LUCK!
FAREWELL WHEREVER YOU FARE, 'TIL YOUR EYRIES RECEIVE YOU AT YOUR JOURNEY'S END!
THANKS FOR SHOWING ME THE ROPES, DAD!
SPEAKING OF ROPES, I HAVE MORE QUESTIONS ABOUT ROLE-PLAYING...
NICE! SHOULD I GO GET SOME OF MY OLDER BOOKS? ROPE USE HASN'T BEEN AN OFFICIAL PROFICIENCY SINCE 3RD EDITION...
DIFFERENT ROLE-PLAYING, JERRY.
OH. OH!
JESSICA? I HAVE A COOL IDEA FOR NEXT TUESDAY.
I LOVE PIZZA AND MOVIES AS MUCH AS ANYONE, BUT I HAVE AN IDEA FOR SOMETHING NEW WE COULD TRY...
TOK
TOK

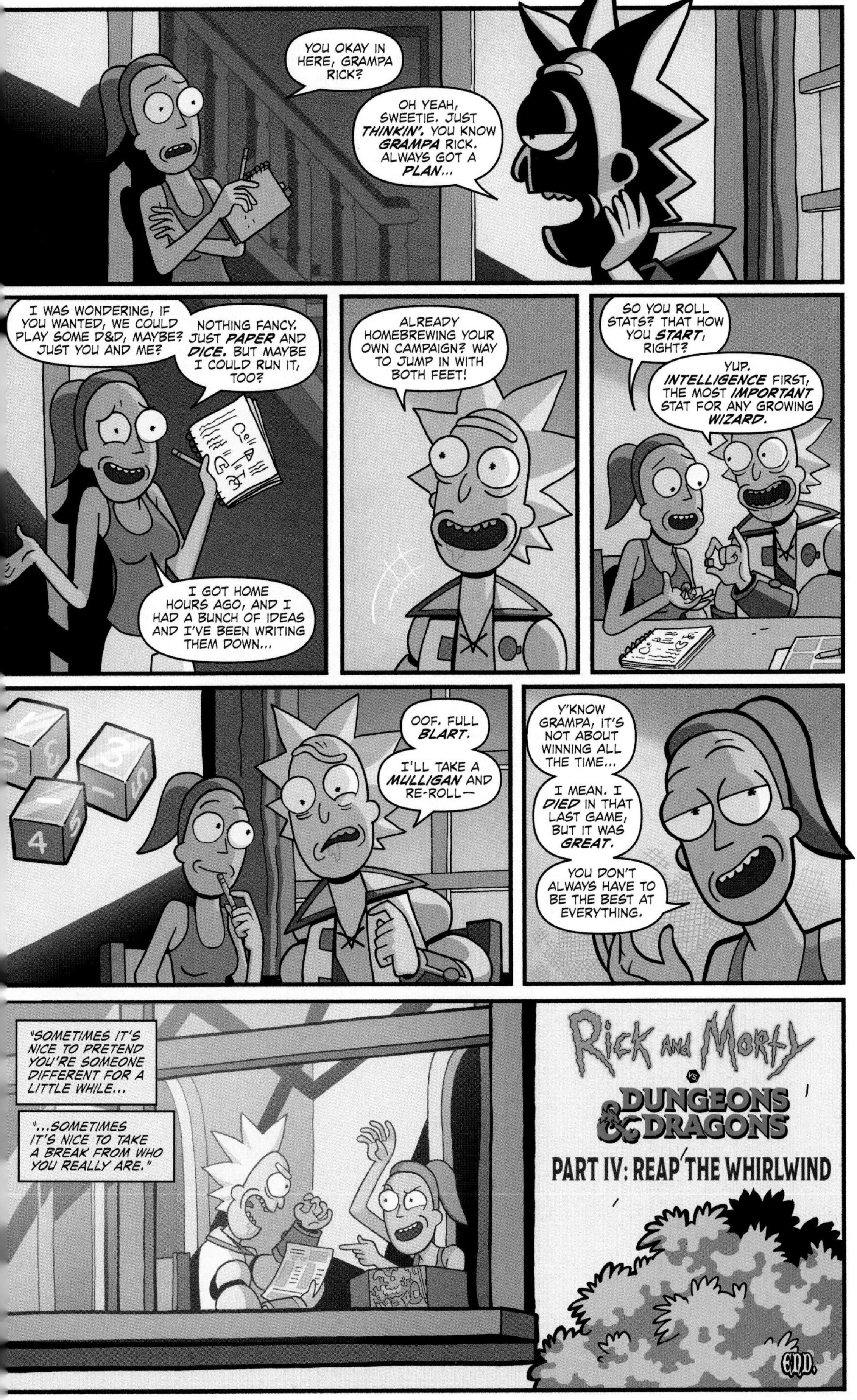

YOU OKAY IN HERE, GRAMPA RICK?
OH YEAH, SWEETIE. JUST THINKIN'. YOU KNOW GRAMPA RICK. ALWAYS GOT A PLAN...
I WAS WONDERING, IF YOU WANTED, WE COULD PLAY SOME D&D, MAYBE? JUST YOU AND ME?
NOTHING FANCY. JUST PAPER AND DICE. BUT MAYBE I COULD RUN IT, TOO?
I GOT HOME HOURS AGO, AND I HAD A BUNCH OF IDEAS AND I'VE BEEN WRITING THEM DOWN...
ALREADY HOMEBREWING YOUR OWN CAMPAIGN? WAY TO JUMP IN WITH BOTH FEET!
SO YOU ROLL STATS? THAT HOW YOU START, RIGHT?
YUP. INTELLIGENCE FIRST, THE MOST IMPORTANT STAT FOR ANY GROWING WIZARD.
OOF. FULL BLART.
I'LL TAKE A MULLIGAN AND RE-ROLL—
Y'KNOW GRAMPA, IT'S NOT ABOUT WINNING ALL THE TIME...
I MEAN. I DIED IN THAT LAST GAME, BUT IT WAS GREAT.
YOU DON'T ALWAYS HAVE TO BE THE BEST AT EVERYTHING.
"SOMETIMES IT'S NICE TO PRETEND YOU'RE SOMEONE DIFFERENT FOR A LITTLE WHILE...
"...SOMETIMES IT'S NICE TO TAKE A BREAK FROM WHO YOU REALLY ARE."
RICK AND MORTY VS. DUNGEONS & DRAGONS
PART IV: REAP THE WHIRLWIND
END.

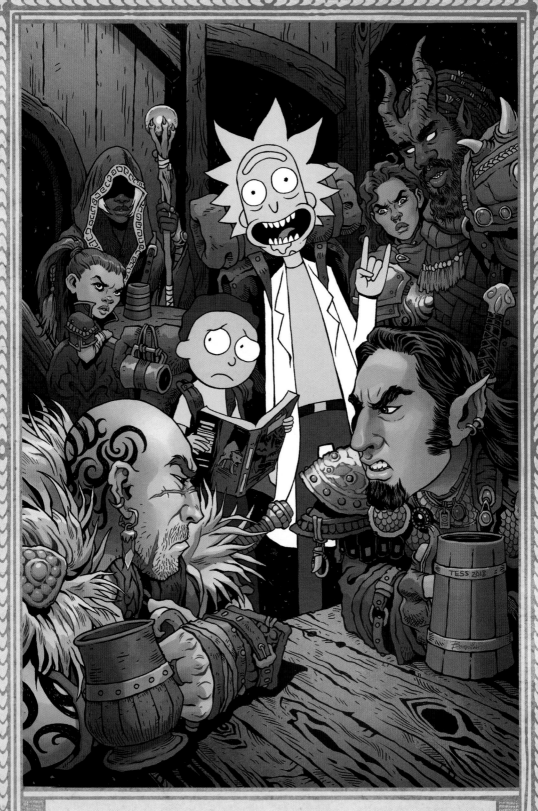

Art by Tess Fowler Colors by Tamra Bonvillain

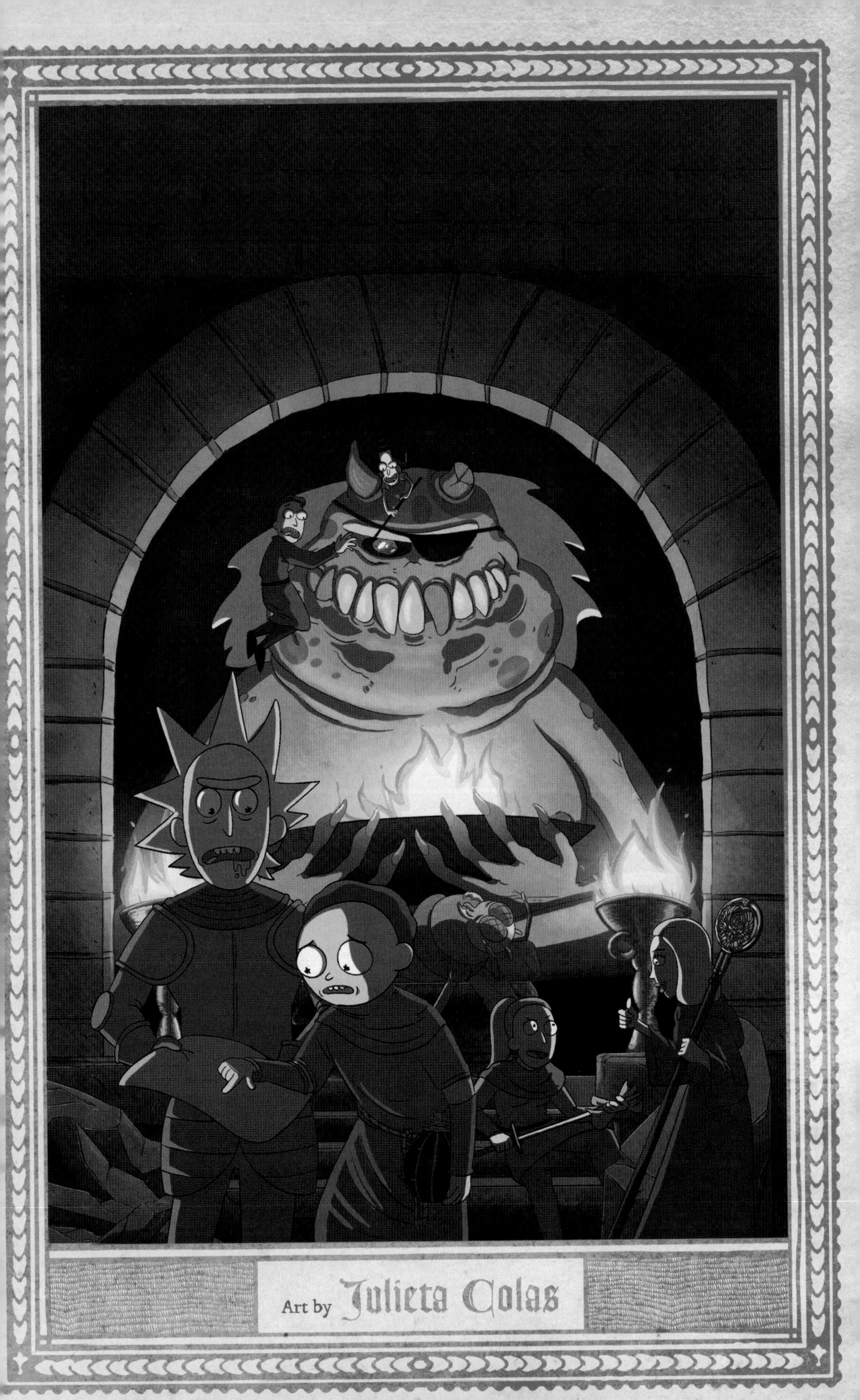

Art by Julieta Colas

Rick and Morty vs. Dungeons & Dragons

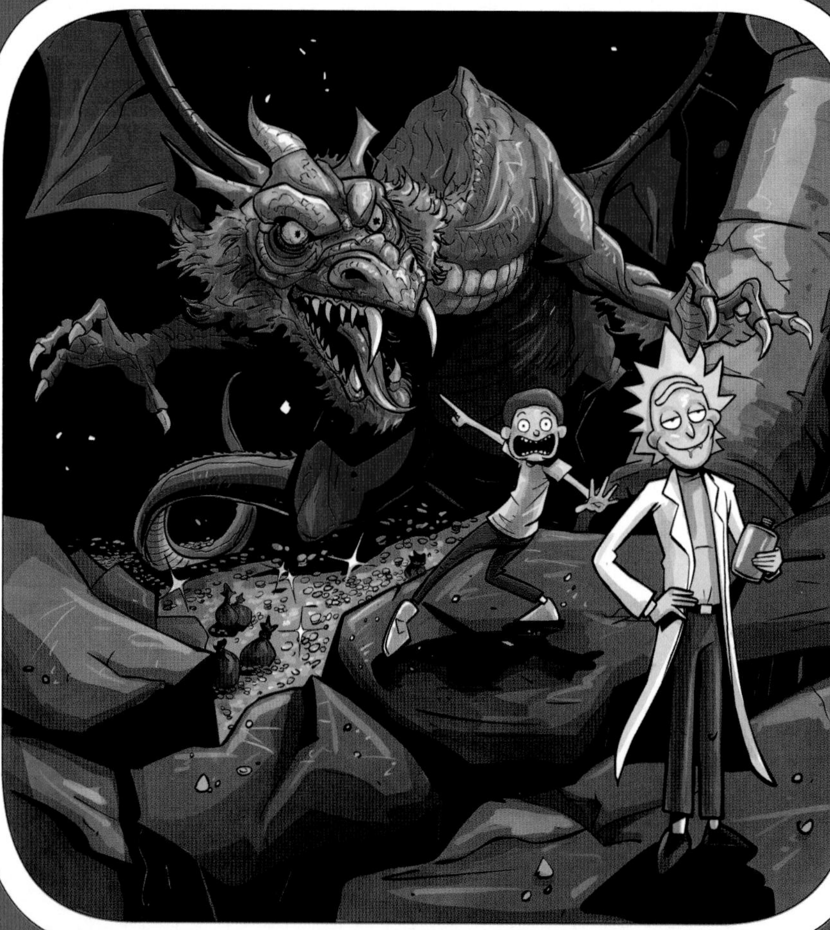

Alex Cormack '2018

Art by Alex Cormack

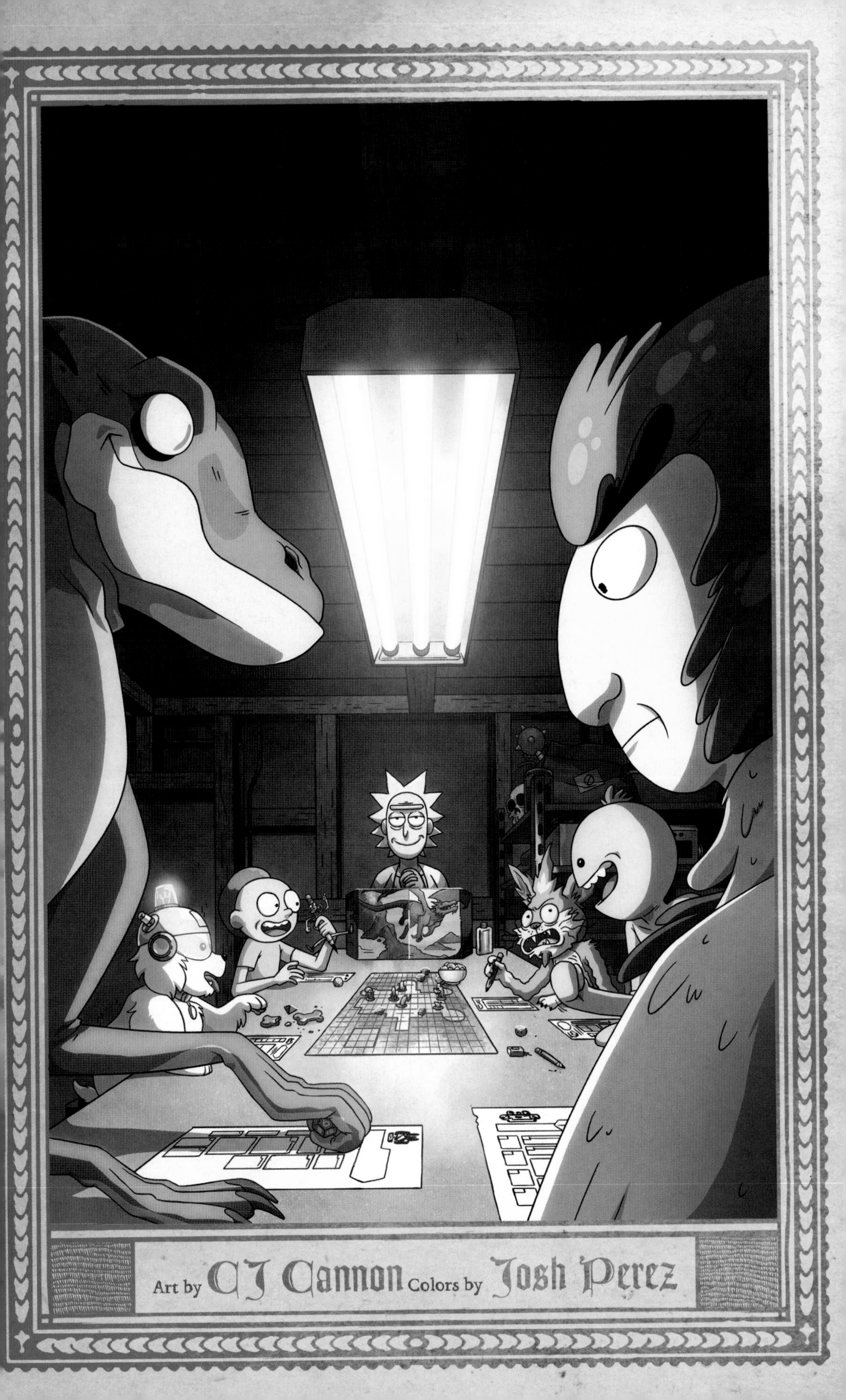

Art by CJ Cannon Colors by Josh Perez

Art by **Agnes Garbowska** Color Assist by **Lauren Perry**

Art by **Alex Kotkin** Colors by **Ivan Nunes**

Art by **Marc Ellerby** Colors by **Sarah Stern**

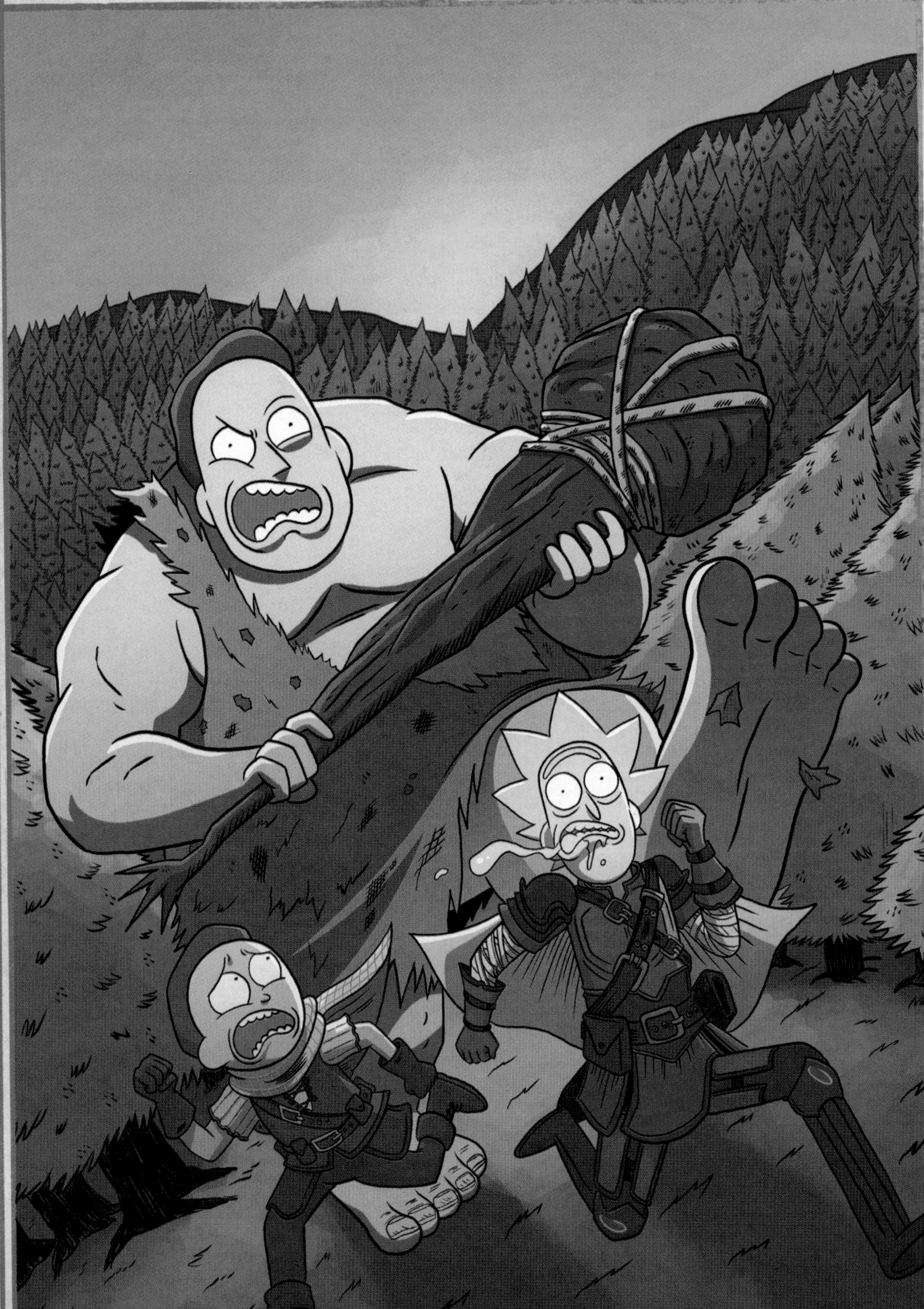

Art by Marc Ellerby Colors by Sarah Stern

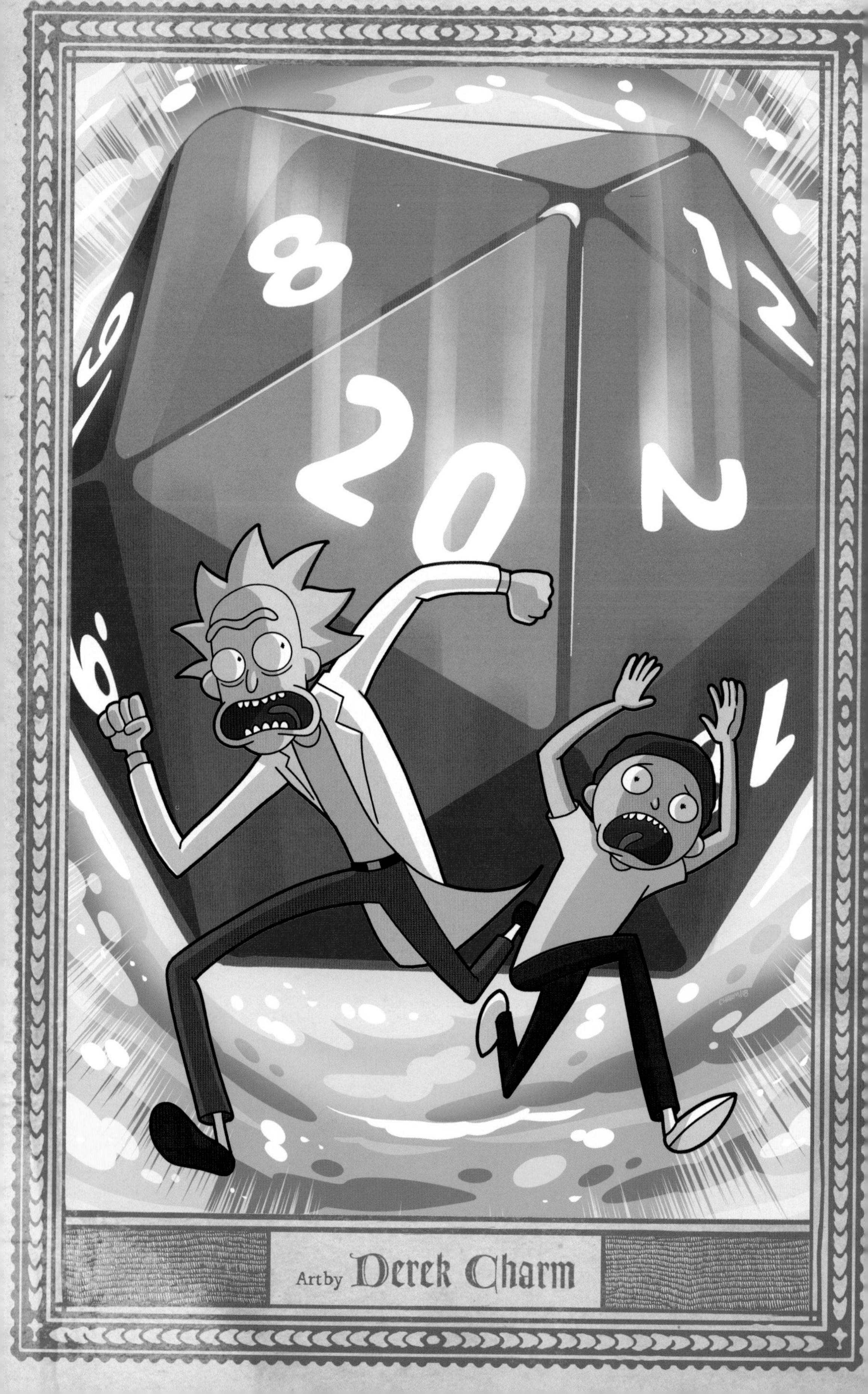

Art by Derek Charm

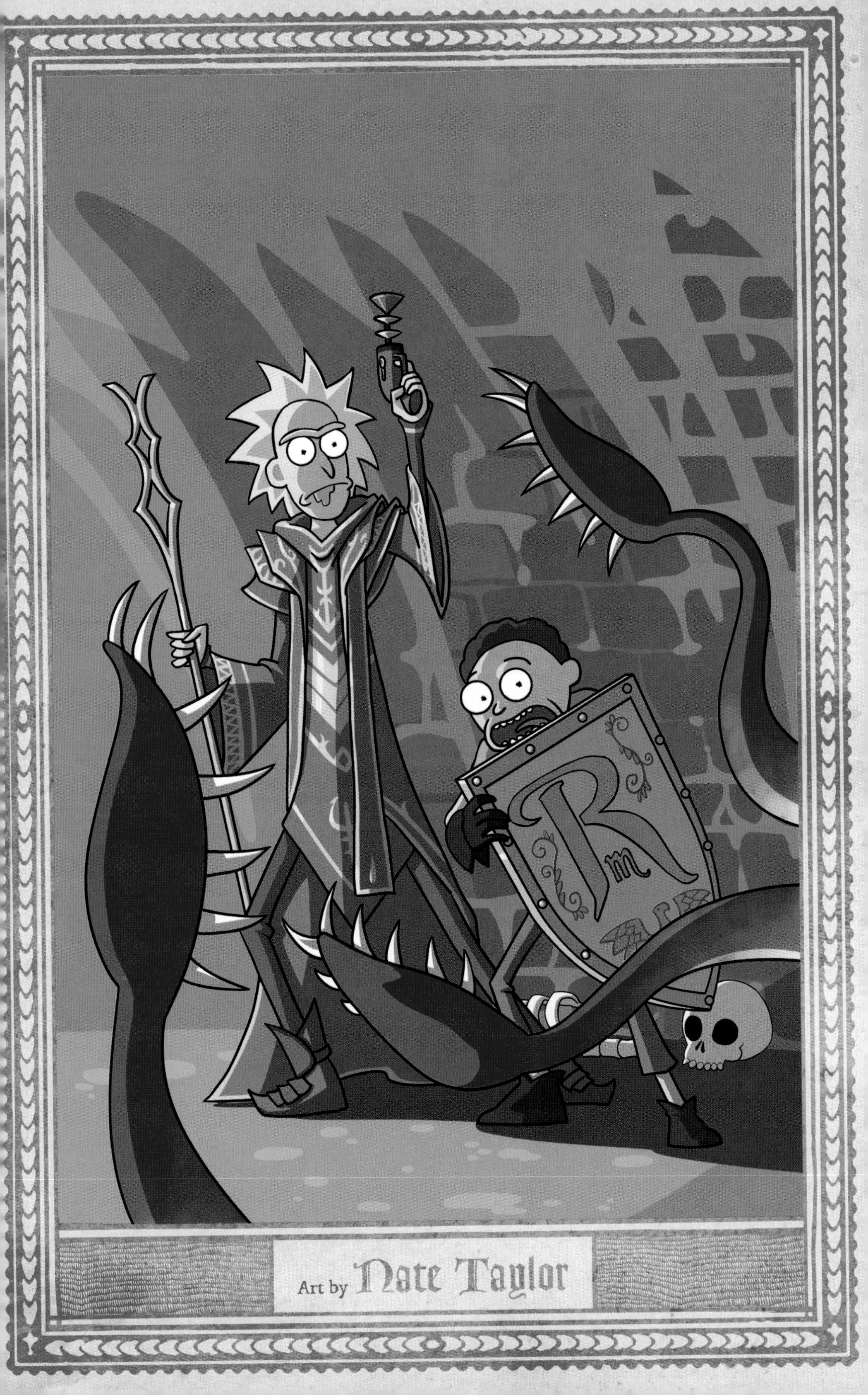

Art by Nate Taylor

Art by Marie Enger

Art by **Tess Fowler** Colors by **Tamra Bonvillain**

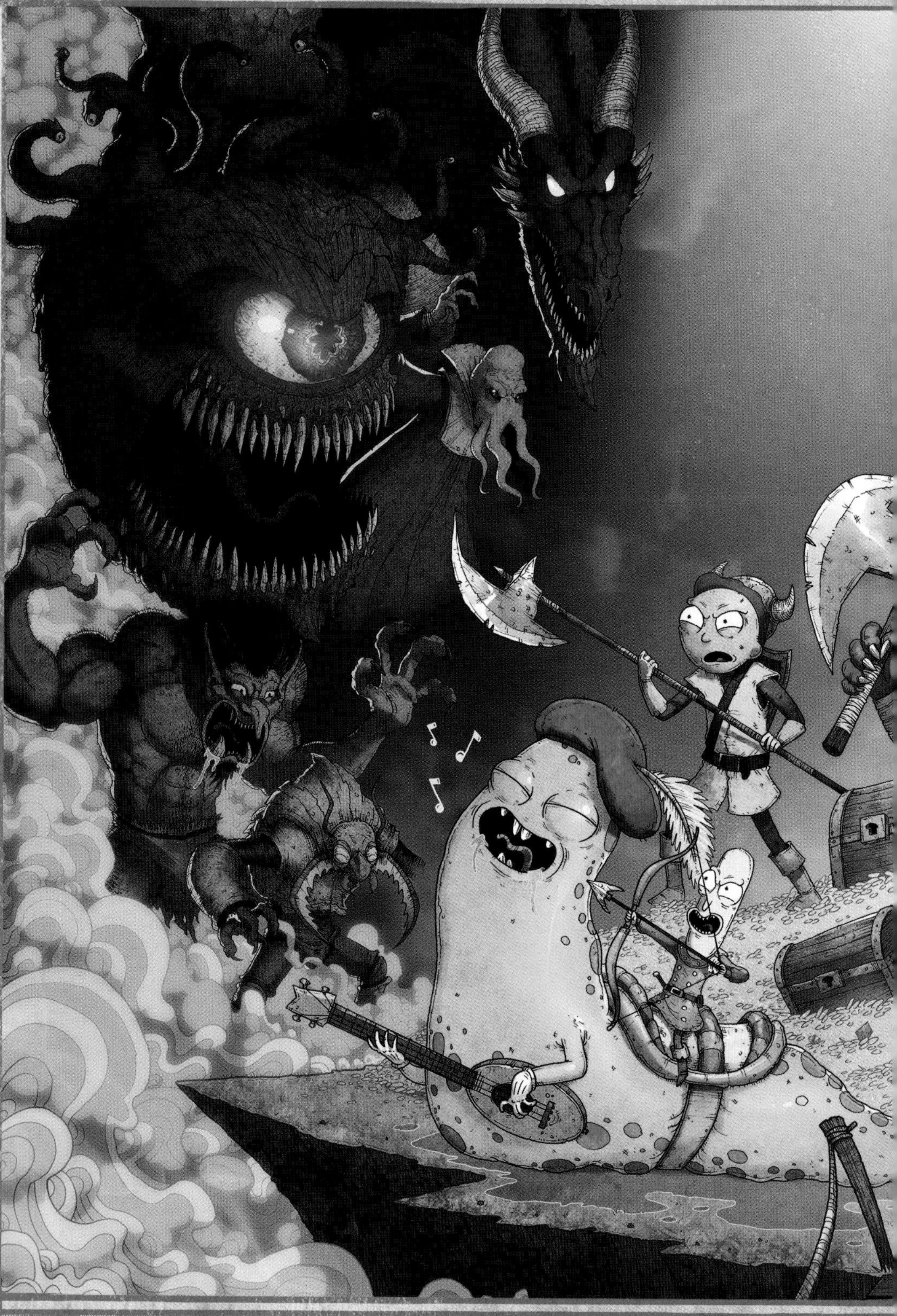
Art by Mike Vasquez

Colors by Josh Perez

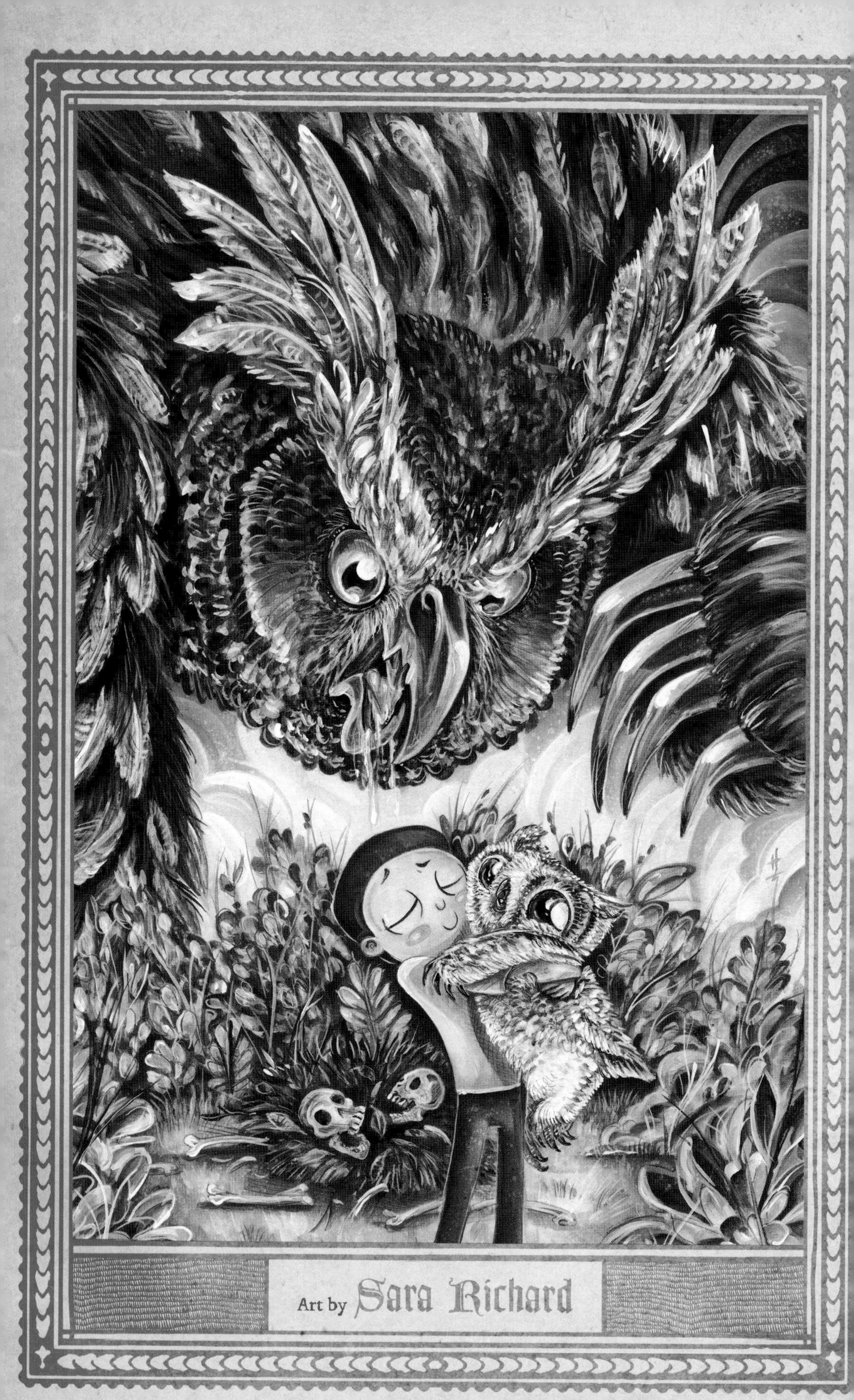

Art by Sara Richard

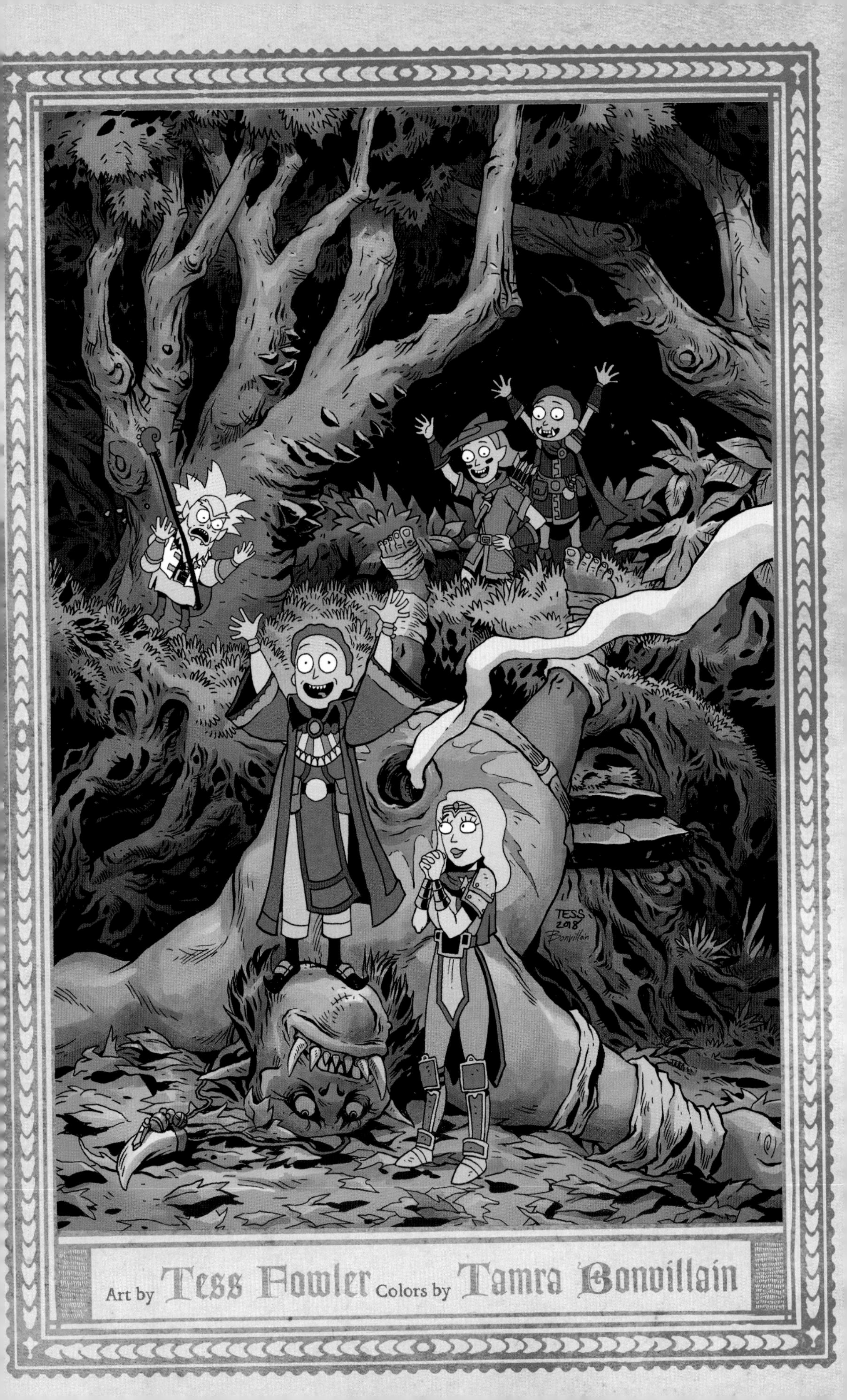
TESS 2018 Bonvillain

Art by Tess Fowler Colors by Tamra Bonvillain

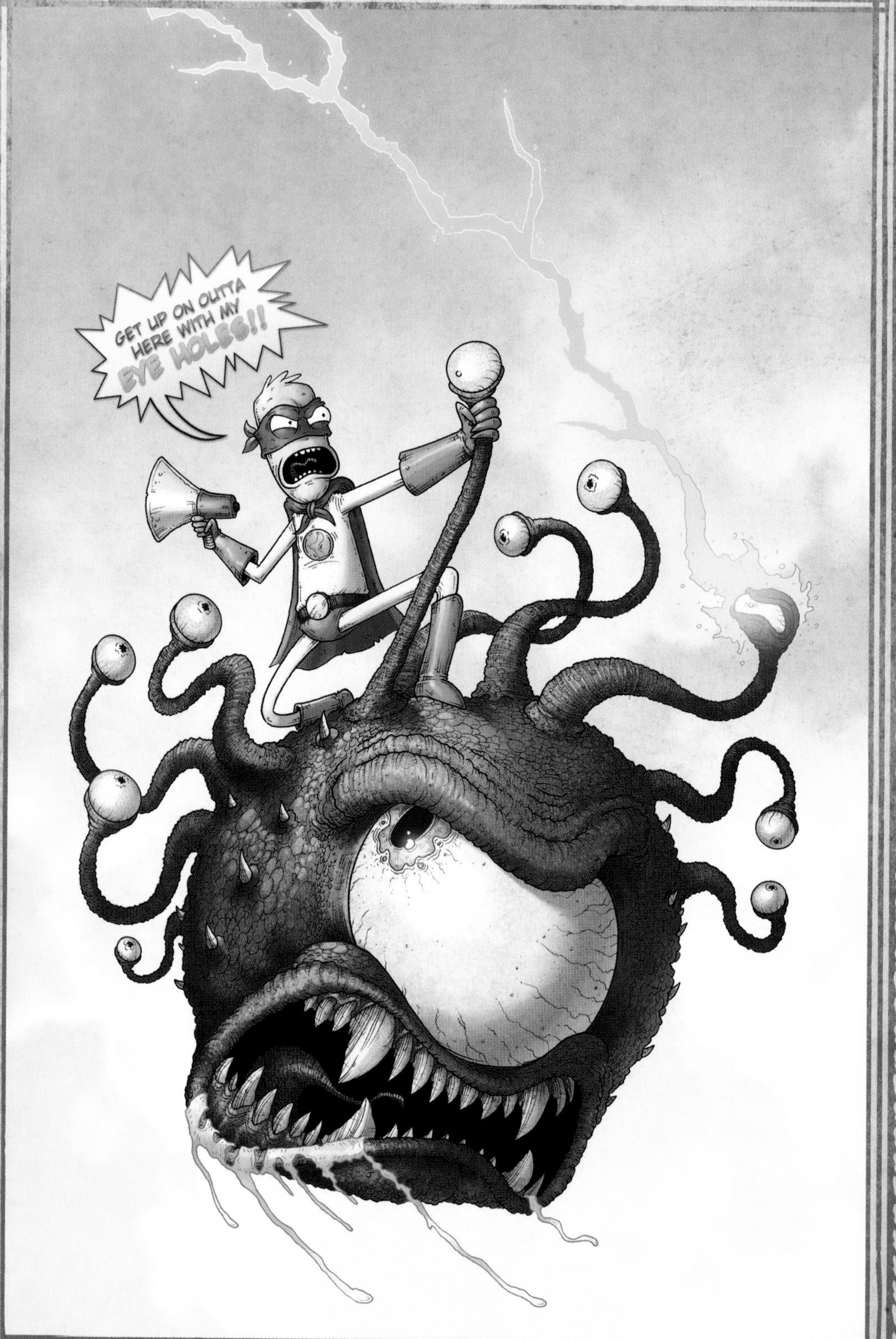
GET UP ON OUTTA HERE WITH MY EYE HOLES!!

Art by Mike Vasquez Colors by Josh Perez

Art by **Mike Vasquez** Colors by **Josh Perez**

Art by **Tess Fowler** Colors by **Tamra Bonvillain**

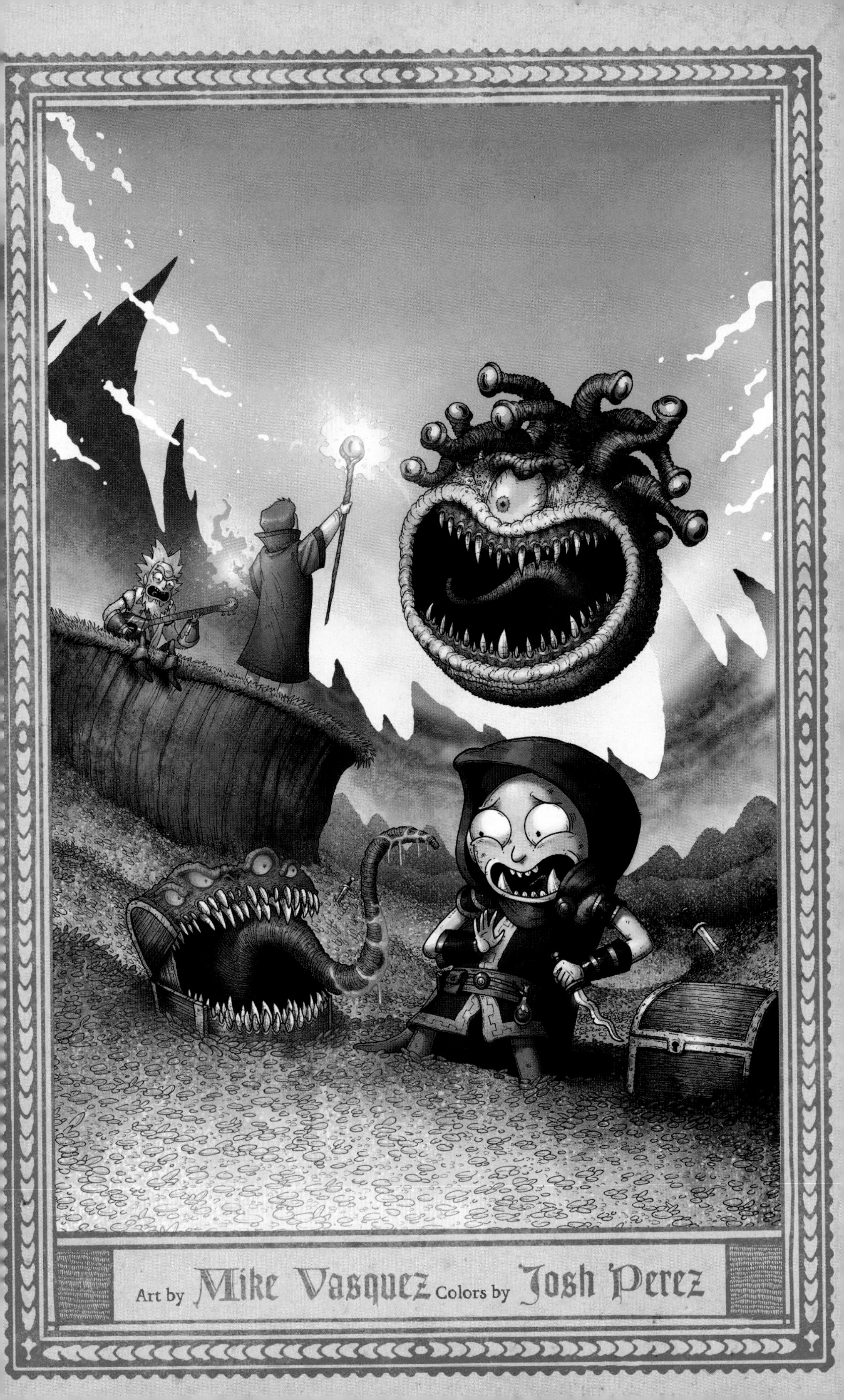

Art by Mike Vasquez Colors by Josh Perez

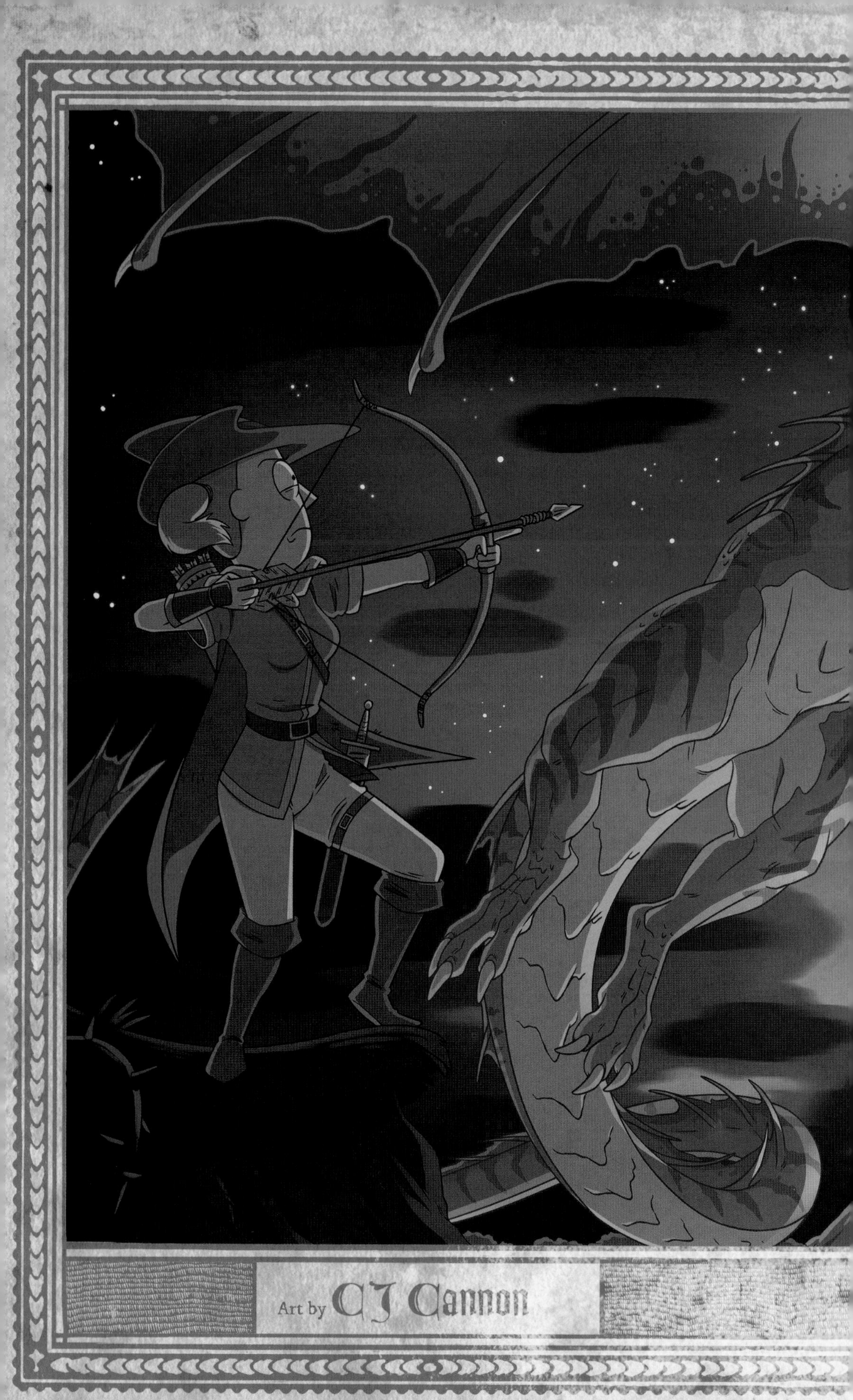

Art by CJ Cannon

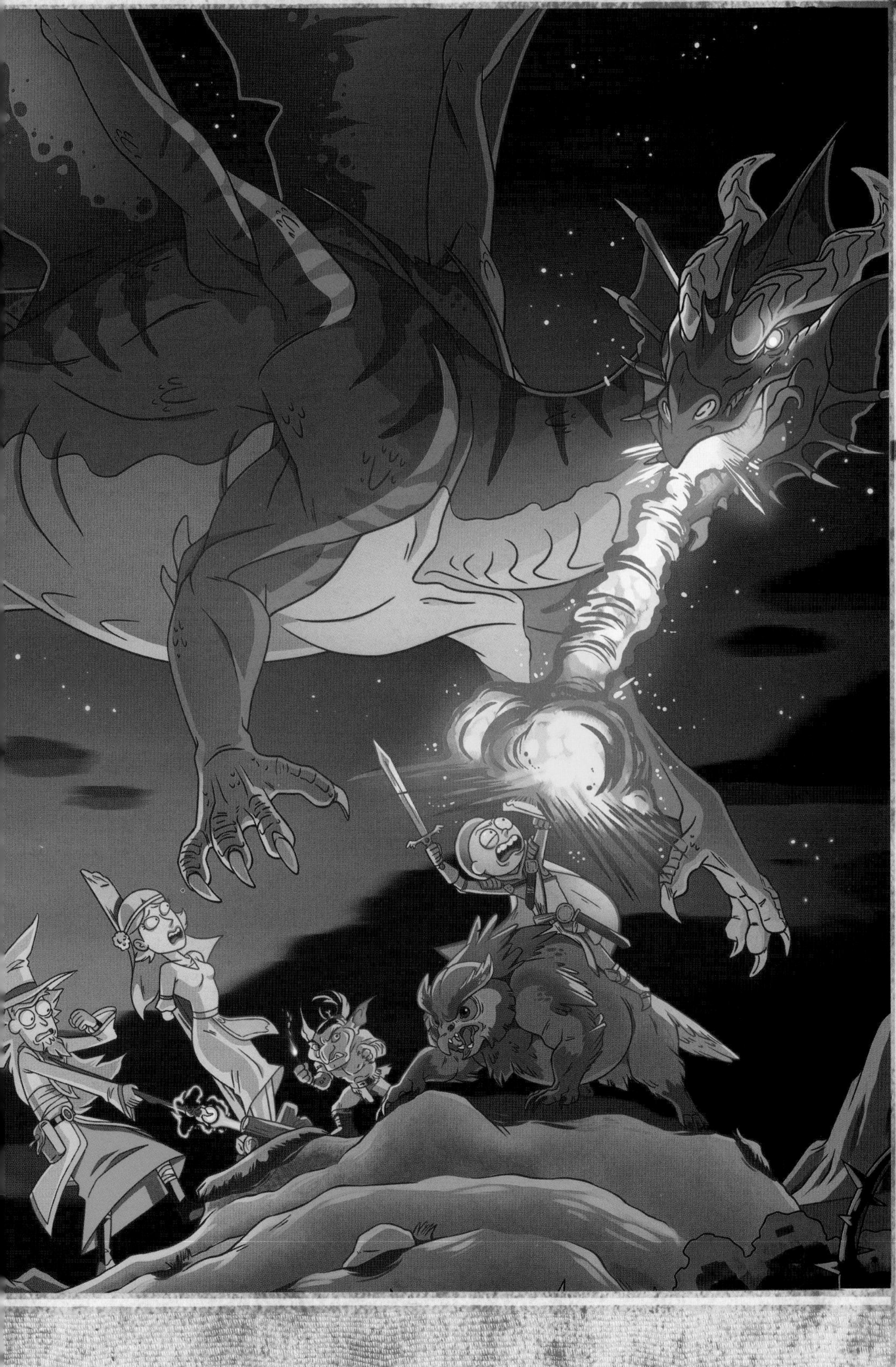

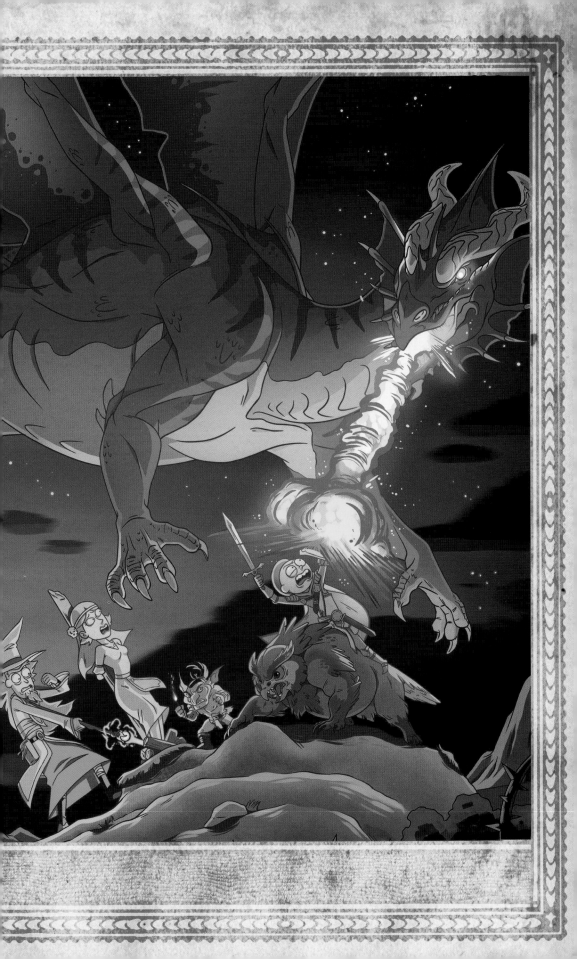

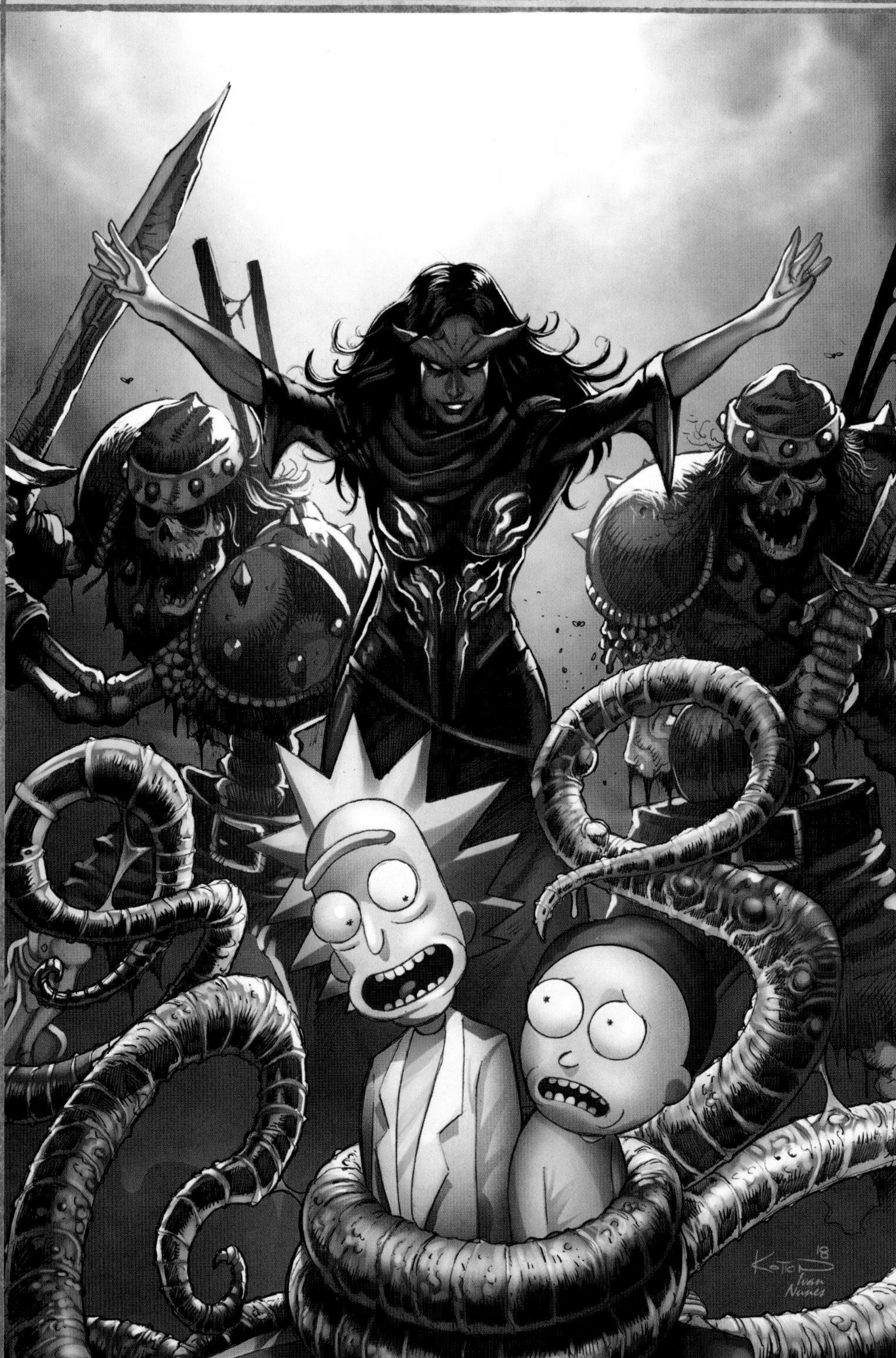

Art by Alex Kotkin Colors by Ivan Nunes

DUNGEONS & DRAGONS®

CHARACTER NAME

| CLASS & LEVEL | BACKGROUND | PLAYER NAME |
| RACE | ALIGNMENT | EXPERIENCE POINTS |

STRENGTH

DEXTERITY

CONSTITUTION

INTELLIGENCE

WISDOM

CHARISMA

INSPIRATION

PROFICIENCY BONUS

- O ___ Strength
- O ___ Dexterity
- O ___ Constitution
- O ___ Intelligence
- O ___ Wisdom
- O ___ Charisma

SAVING THROWS

- O ___ Acrobatics (Dex)
- O ___ Animal Handling (Wis)
- O ___ Arcana (Int)
- O ___ Athletics (Str)
- O ___ Deception (Cha)
- O ___ History (Int)
- O ___ Insight (Wis)
- O ___ Intimidation (Cha)
- O ___ Investigation (Int)
- O ___ Medicine (Wis)
- O ___ Nature (Int)
- O ___ Perception (Wis)
- O ___ Performance (Cha)
- O ___ Persuasion (Cha)
- O ___ Religion (Int)
- O ___ Sleight of Hand (Dex)
- O ___ Stealth (Dex)
- O ___ Survival (Wis)

SKILLS

PASSIVE WISDOM (PERCEPTION)

PERSONALITY TRAITS

IDEALS

BONDS

FLAWS

ARMOR CLASS

INITIATIVE

SPEED

Hit Point Maximum

CURRENT HIT POINTS

TEMPORARY HIT POINTS

Total

HIT DICE

SUCCESSES O O O
FAILURES O O O

DEATH SAVES

FEATURES & TRAITS

| NAME | ATK BONUS | DAMAGE/TYPE |

ATTACKS & SPELLCASTING

CP
SP
EP
GP
PP

OTHER PROFICIENCIES & LANGUAGES

EQUIPMENT

DUNGEONS & DRAGONS®

CHARACTER NAME: Keth Silverson

Rogue 6	Urchin	Morty Smith
CLASS & LEVEL	BACKGROUND	PLAYER NAME
Half-Orc	Chaotic Good	14,000
RACE	ALIGNMENT	EXPERIENCE POINTS

PERSONALITY TRAITS: Has trouble saying no to pretty girls. And mad scientists.

BONDS: You know what? What's mine is actually just mine. Give it back.

IDEALS: What's mine is yours, and what's yours is mine.

FLAWS: I have trouble trusting my allies. Especially Rick.

STRENGTH
+0
(10)

DEXTERITY
+3
(16)

CONSTITUTION
+3
(16)

INTELLIGENCE
+1
(12)

WISDOM
-1
(8)

CHARISMA
+2
(14)

INSPIRATION

PROFICIENCY BONUS: +3

SAVING THROWS
- O +0 Strength
- ◉ +6 Dexterity
- O +3 Constitution
- ◉ +4 Intelligence
- O -1 Wisdom
- O +2 Charisma

SKILLS
- ◉ +6 Acrobatics (Dex)
- O -1 Animal Handling (Wis)
- O +1 Arcana (Int)
- ◉ +3 Athletics (Str)
- ◉ +5 Deception (Cha)
- O +1 History (Int)
- O -1 Insight (Wis)
- ◉ +8 Intimidation (Cha)
- O +1 Investigation (Int)
- O -1 Medicine (Wis)
- O +1 Nature (Int)
- ◉ +2 Perception (Wis)
- O +2 Performance (Cha)
- O +2 Persuasion (Cha)
- O +1 Religion (Int)
- ◉ +9 Sleight of Hand (Dex)
- ◉ +9 Stealth (Dex)
- O -1 Survival (Wis)

PASSIVE WISDOM (PERCEPTION): 14

Languages: Common, Orc

Proficiencies:
Hand Crossbow,
Disguise Kit,
Light Armor,
Longsword, Rapier,
Shortsword,
Simple Weapons,
Thieves' Tools
(double proficiency)

OTHER PROFICIENCIES & LANGUAGES

ARMOR CLASS
15

INITIATIVE
+3

SPEED
30ft

Hit Point Maximum: 43

CURRENT HIT POINTS

TEMPORARY HIT POINTS

Total: 6d8
HIT DICE

DEATH SAVES
SUCCESSES O-O-O
FAILURES O-O-O

ATTACKS & SPELLCASTING

NAME	ATK BONUS	DAMAGE/TYPE
Dagger	+6	1d4+3 piercing
Dagger	+6	1d4+3 piercing

EQUIPMENT
- 0 - Leather Armor
- 0 - Dagger
- 0 - Dagger
- 0 - Acid (vial)
- 15 - Alchemist's Fire (flask)
- 0 - Antitoxin
- Caltrops (bag of 20)
- Backpack (2)
- Crowbar (2)
- Hammer (2)
- Piton (20)
- Torch (20)
- Tinderbox (2)
- Rations (1 day) (21)
- Waterskin (2)
- Rope, Hempen (50 feet) (3)
- Pouch
- Thieves' Tools

FEATURES & TRAITS

Rogue Features (Thief):
- Sneak Attack (3d6)
- Thieves' Cant
- Cunning Action
- Fast Hands
- Second-Story Work
- Dual Wielder
- Uncanny Dodge

Racial Traits:
- Darkvision
- Menacing
- Relentless Endurance
- Savage Attacks

Urchin:
- City Secrets

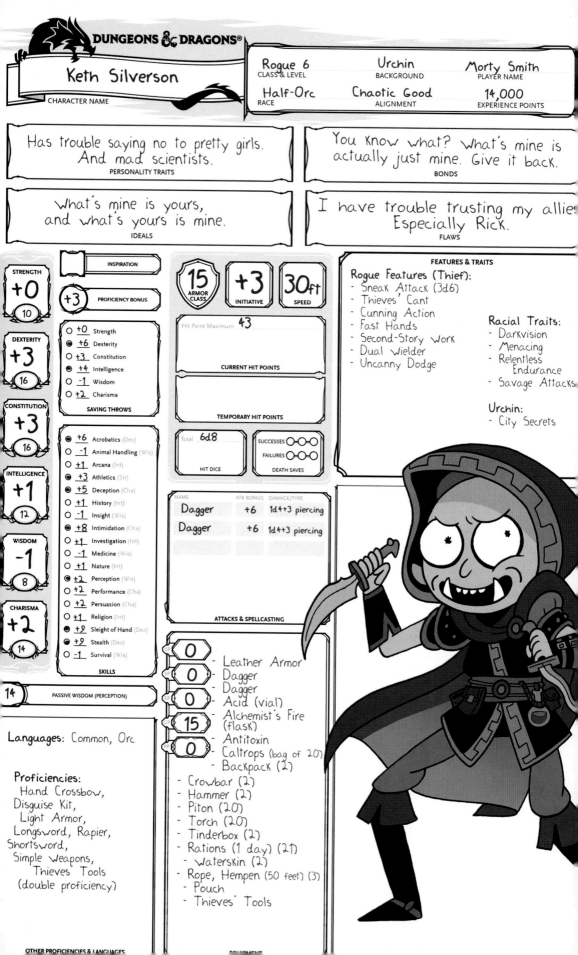

DUNGEONS & DRAGONS®

CHARACTER NAME: Ari Strongbow

Ranger 6	Outlander	Summer Smith
CLASS & LEVEL	BACKGROUND	PLAYER NAME
Half-Elf	Neutral Good	14,000
RACE	ALIGNMENT	EXPERIENCE POINTS

PERSONALITY TRAITS: Don't forgive, don't forget.

BONDS: You aren't worth the cost of the arrows it would take to kill you.

IDEALS: I will have vengeance for my brother's murder, and the betrayal that caused it.

FLAWS: Kind of a drama bomb.

INSPIRATION

PROFICIENCY BONUS: +3

STRENGTH
1
+3

Saving Throws:
- ● +4 Strength
- ● +6 Dexterity
- ○ +0 Constitution
- ○ +1 Intelligence
- ○ +2 Wisdom
- ○ +0 Charisma

DEXTERITY
3
+7

CONSTITUTION
0
+0

INTELLIGENCE
1
+3

WISDOM
2
+5

CHARISMA
0
+0

Skills:
- ● +6 Acrobatics (Dex)
- ● +5 Animal Handling (Wis)
- ○ +1 Arcana (Int)
- ● +4 Athletics (Str)
- ○ +0 Deception (Cha)
- ○ +1 History (Int)
- ○ +2 Insight (Wis)
- ○ +0 Intimidation (Cha)
- ○ +1 Investigation (Int)
- ○ +2 Medicine (Wis)
- ● +4 Nature (Int)
- ● +5 Perception (Wis)
- ○ +0 Performance (Cha)
- ○ +0 Persuasion (Cha)
- ○ +1 Religion (Int)
- ○ +3 Sleight of Hand (Dex)
- ● +6 Stealth (Dex)
- ● +5 Survival (Wis)

PASSIVE WISDOM (PERCEPTION)

Languages: Common, Draconic, Elvish, Giant, Orc, Sylvan

Armor: Light Armor, Medium Armor, Shields

Weapons: Martial Weapons, Simple Weapons, Sarcasm

Tools: Flute

ARMOR CLASS: 13

INITIATIVE: +3

SPEED: 30ft

Hit Point Maximum: 40

CURRENT HIT POINTS

TEMPORARY HIT POINTS

Hit Dice Total: 6d10

Death Saves:
- SUCCESSES ○○○
- FAILURES ○○○

NAME	ATK BONUS	DAMAGE/TYPE
Longbow	+8	1d8+4 piercing
Shortsword	+7	1d6+4 piercing

Spells:
- Hunter's Mark & Cure Wounds
- Pass without Trace (Lvl 2)

ATTACKS & SPELLCASTING

- CP 0
- SP 0
- EP 0
- GP 15
- PP 0

- Shortsword
- Longbow
- Arrows (20)
- Hunting Trap
- Trophy
- Belt Pouch
- Set of Traveler's Clothes
- Dungeoneer's Pack
- Leather Armor

FEATURES & TRAITS

Ranger Features (Hunter):
- Favored enemy-Giants.
- Natural explorer-Forest, Mountains.
- Archery
- Spellcasting
- Extra attack
- Colossus Slayer

Racial Traits:
- Darkvision
- Fey Ancestry

Outlander:
- Wanderer

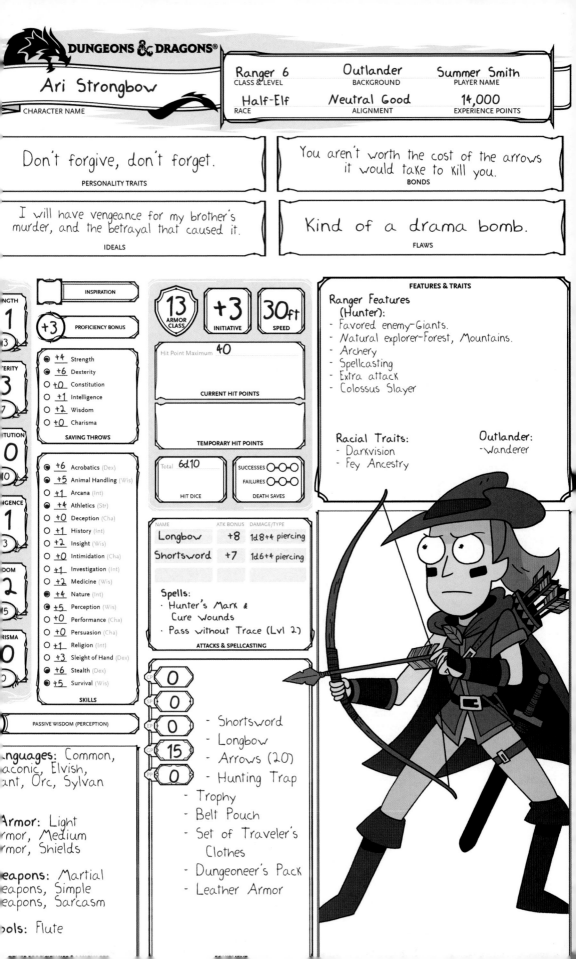

DUNGEONS & DRAGONS®

CHARACTER NAME: Kiir Bravian

Wizard 6	Sage	Jerry Smith
CLASS & LEVEL	BACKGROUND	PLAYER NAME
Half-Elf	Neutral Good	14,000
RACE	ALIGNMENT	EXPERIENCE POINTS

PERSONALITY TRAITS: Finally smart enough to realize you'll never be good enough.

BONDS: Finally courageous enough to fight for friends and family.

IDEALS: Power is cool, but only if used to protect the innocent.

FLAWS: No matter how hard you try, you will lose everything you love..

Ability Scores

STRENGTH -1 (8)

DEXTERITY +0 (10)

CONSTITUTION +2 (14)

INTELLIGENCE +3 (16)

WISDOM +1 (12)

CHARISMA +3 (16)

INSPIRATION

PROFICIENCY BONUS +3

Saving Throws
- -1 Strength
- 0 Dexterity
- +2 Constitution
- ● +6 Intelligence
- ● +4 Wisdom
- +3 Charisma

Skills
- +0 Acrobatics (Dex)
- +1 Animal Handling (Wis)
- ● +6 Arcana (Int)
- -1 Athletics (Str)
- +3 Deception (Cha)
- ● +6 History (Int)
- +1 Insight (Wis)
- ● +6 Intimidation (Cha)
- +3 Investigation (Int)
- +1 Medicine (Wis)
- +3 Nature (Int)
- +1 Perception (Wis)
- ● +6 Performance (Cha)
- +3 Persuasion (Cha)
- +3 Religion (Int)
- 0 Sleight of Hand (Dex)
- 0 Stealth (Dex)
- +1 Survival (Wis)

PASSIVE WISDOM (PERCEPTION) 13

ARMOR CLASS 10

INITIATIVE +0

SPEED 30ft

Hit Point Maximum 38

CURRENT HIT POINTS

TEMPORARY HIT POINTS

HIT DICE Total 6d6

DEATH SAVES SUCCESSES ○○○ FAILURES ○○○

Attacks & Spellcasting

NAME	ATK BONUS	DAMAGE/TYPE
Unarmed	+2	0 Bludgeo

Spells:
Spell Attack +4
Spell Save DC -12
4 1st level spell slots
3 2nd level spell slots
3 3rd level spell slots

Features & Traits

Wizard:
- Spellcasting
- Arcane Tradition: School of Abjuration
- Abjuration Savant
- Arcane Ward
- Projected Ward
- Arcane Recovery
- Ritual Casting

Racial Traits:
- Darkvision
- Fey Ancestry
- Skill Versatility

Sage:
- Researcher

Currency
- CP 0
- SP 0
- EP 0
- GP 10
- PP 0

Equipment
- Component Pouch
- Scholar's Pack
- Spellbook
- Bottle of Black Ink
- Quill
- Small Knife
- Letter
- Set of Common Clothes
- Belt Pouch

Languages: Common, Elvish, Draconic, Gnomish, Sylvan

Armor: Light Armor, Medium Armor, Shields

Weapons: Martial Weapons, Simple Weapons, Sarcasm

Tools: Flute

OTHER PROFICIENCIES & LANGUAGES

EQUIPMENT

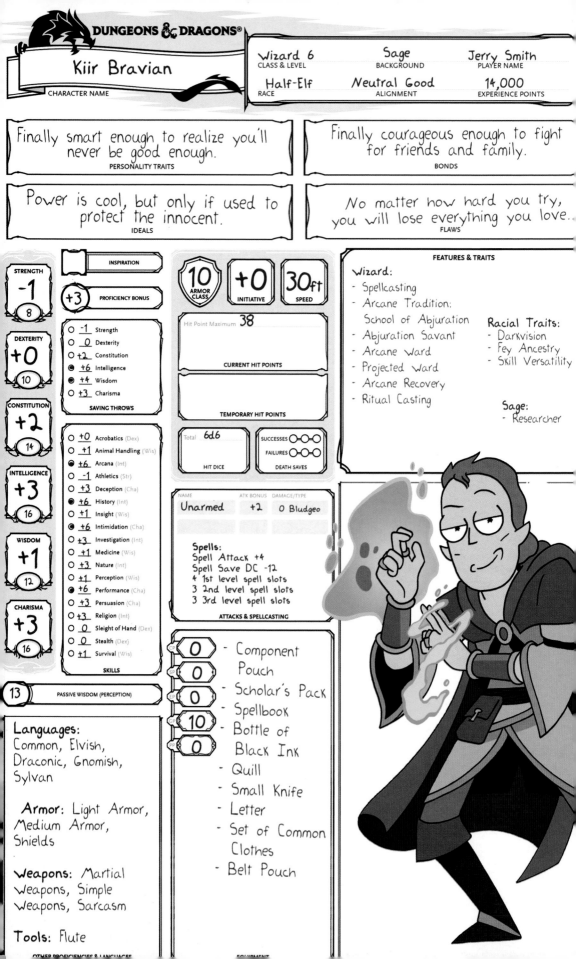

DUNGEONS & DRAGONS®

CHARACTER NAME: Lyan Amaranthia

Cleric 6 — CLASS & LEVEL	City Watch / Investigator — BACKGROUND	Beth Smith — PLAYER NAME
Wood Elf — RACE	Chaotic Good — ALIGNMENT	14,000 — EXPERIENCE POINTS

PERSONALITY TRAITS
Once abandoned yourself, you would never abandon someone who needs your help.

BONDS
All life is precious and should be preserved. (Especially horses.)

IDEALS
I believe in my heart that I am meant for great things.

FLAWS
Blind faith in nigh-omnipotent father-figures.

FEATURES & TRAITS

Cleric:
- Spellcasting
- Divine Domain: Life
- Disciple of Life
- Channel Divinity
  - Turn Undead
  - Preserve Life
  - Destroy Undead
- Blessed Healer

Racial Traits:
- Darkvision
- Fey Ancestry
- Keen Senses
- Trance
- Elf Weapon Training
- Fleet of Foot
- Mask of the Wild

City Watch:
- Investigator

INSPIRATION

PROFICIENCY BONUS: +3

NGTH 2
ERITY 1
TUTION 2
IGENCE 1
OM 3
ISMA 0

SAVING THROWS
- O +2 Strength
- O +1 Dexterity
- O +2 Constitution
- O −1 Intelligence
- ◉ +6 Wisdom
- ◉ +3 Charisma

SKILLS
- O +1 Acrobatics (Dex)
- O +3 Animal Handling (Wis)
- O −1 Arcana (Int)
- O +2 Athletics (Str)
- O +0 Deception (Cha)
- O −1 History (Int)
- ◉ +6 Insight (Wis)
- O +0 Intimidation (Cha)
- ◉ +2 Investigation (Int)
- O +3 Medicine (Wis)
- ◉ +6 Perception (Wis)
- O +0 Performance (Cha)
- ◉ +3 Persuasion (Cha)
- ◉ +2 Religion (Int)
- O +1 Sleight of Hand (Dex)
- O +1 Stealth (Dex)
- O +3 Survival (Wis)

PASSIVE WISDOM (PERCEPTION)

ARMOR CLASS: 17
INITIATIVE: +1
SPEED: 35ft

Hit Point Maximum: 45

CURRENT HIT POINTS

TEMPORARY HIT POINTS

HIT DICE Total 6d8

DEATH SAVES
SUCCESSES O O O
FAILURES O O O

ATTACKS & SPELLCASTING

NAME	ATK BONUS	DAMAGE/TYPE
Unarmed	+5	3 Bludgeon
Warhammer	+5	1d8+2 Bludgeon

Spells-Spell Attack +6
Spell Save DC -14

Prepared spells:
- Bless (lvl. 1)
- Cure Wounds (lvl. 1)
- Lesser Restoration (lvl. 2)
- Spiritual Weapon (lvl. 2)
- Beacon of Hope (lvl. 3)
- Revivify (lvl. 3)

EQUIPMENT

- 0 — Warhammer
- 0 — Shield
- 0 — Scale Mail Armor
- 10 — Priest's Pouch
- 0 — Holy Symbol
- Uniform
- Horn
- Set of Manacles

OTHER PROFICIENCIES & LANGUAGES

Languages: Common, ...ish, Giant, Orc

Armor: Heavy ...mor, Light Armor, ...edium Armor, ...ields

Weapons: Simple ...eapons, Longsword, ...ortsword, Shortbow, ...ngbow

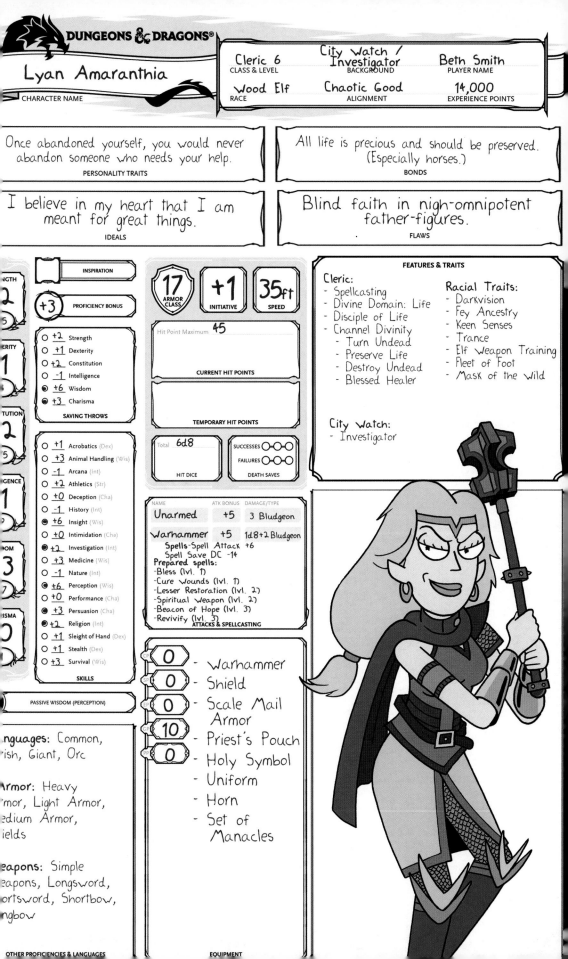

DUNGEONS & DRAGONS®

CHARACTER NAME: Gee-Whilickers Petalbutt

CLASS & LEVEL: Bard 4
BACKGROUND: Far Traveler
PLAYER NAME: Rick Sanchez
RACE: Rock Gnome
ALIGNMENT: Chaotic Neutral
EXPERIENCE POINTS: 2,700

PERSONALITY TRAITS: #@%$ you and #@%$ this.

IDEALS: When we get out of here, I will make all of you pay.

BONDS: I hate everything. This character sucks.

FLAWS: You're a Bard. This is basically your personal Hell.

Abilities

- **STRENGTH** +0 (10)
- **DEXTERITY** +1 (12)
- **CONSTITUTION** +2 (14)
- **INTELLIGENCE** +3 (17)
- **WISDOM** -1 (8)
- **CHARISMA** +2 (15)

INSPIRATION

PROFICIENCY BONUS +2

SAVING THROWS
- O +0 Strength
- ● +3 Dexterity
- O +2 Constitution
- O +3 Intelligence
- O -1 Wisdom
- ● +4 Charisma

SKILLS
- ● +2 Acrobatics (Dex)
- ● +0 Animal Handling (Wis)
- ● +4 Arcana (Int)
- ● +1 Athletics (Str)
- ● +3 Deception (Cha)
- ● +4 History (Int)
- ● +1 Insight (Wis)
- ● +3 Intimidation (Cha)
- ● +7 Investigation (Int)
- ● +1 Medicine (Wis)
- ● +4 Nature (Int)
- ● +1 Perception (Wis)
- ● +3 Performance (Cha)
- ● +6 Persuasion (Cha)
- ● +4 Religion (Int)
- ● +2 Sleight of Hand (Dex)
- ● +2 Stealth (Dex)
- ● +0 Survival (Wis)

PASSIVE WISDOM (PERCEPTION) 11

Languages: Common, Gnomish, Elvish

Proficiencies: Bagpipes, Charisma Saving Throws, Crossbow, Hand, Dexterity Saving Throws, Drum, Insight, Investigation, Light Armor, Longsword, Lute, Medicine, Pan Flute, Perception, Persuasion, Rapier, Shortsword, Simple Weapons, Tinker's Tools

OTHER PROFICIENCIES & LANGUAGES

Combat

ARMOR CLASS 11
INITIATIVE +2
SPEED 25ft

Hit Point Maximum 25

CURRENT HIT POINTS

TEMPORARY HIT POINTS

HIT DICE Total 4d8

DEATH SAVES SUCCESSES ○○○ FAILURES ○○○

ATTACKS & SPELLCASTING

NAME	ATK BONUS	DAMAGE/TYPE
Dagger	+3	1d4+1 Piercing

Equipment

- (0) Leather
- (0) Dagger
- (0) Backpack
- (0) Bedroll
- (15) Candle (5)
- (0) Clothes, Costume (2)
- Clothes, Traveler's
- Rations (1 day) (5)
- Waterskin
- Disguise Kit
- Lute

FEATURES & TRAITS

Bard:
- Bardic Inspiration (d6)
- Hit Points
- Spellcasting
- Jack of All Trades
- Song of Rest
- Bardic College
- Enthralling Performance
- Expertise
- Mantle of Inspiration
- Ability Score Improvement

Racial Traits:
- Darkvision
- Gnome Cunning
- Artificer's Lore
- Tinker

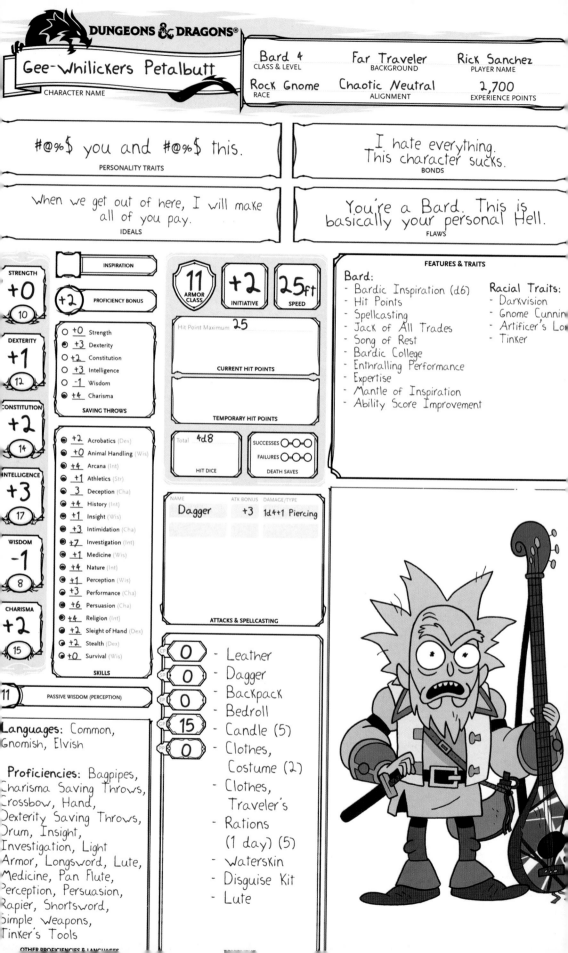

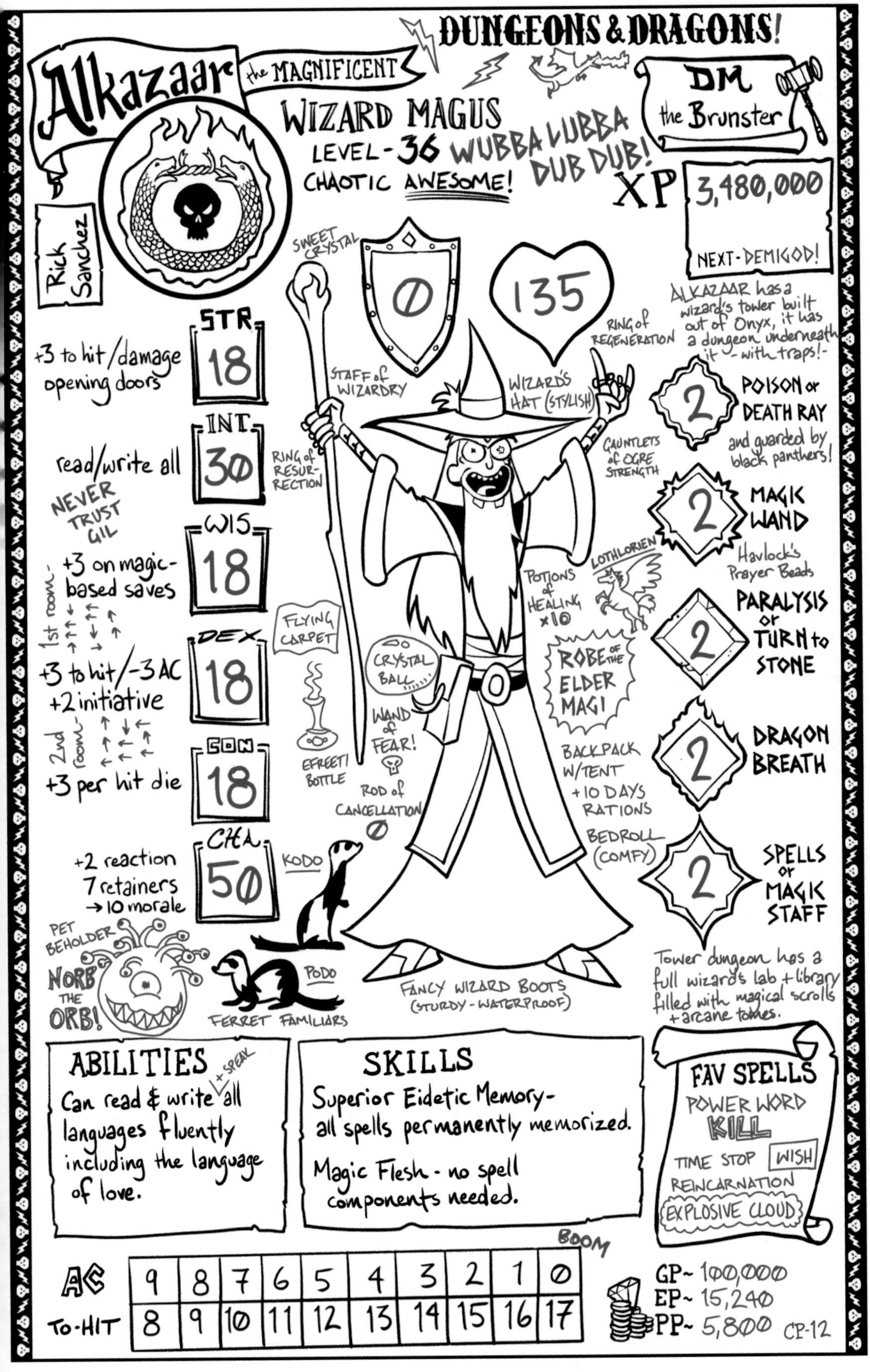
DUNGEONS & DRAGONS!
Alkazaar the MAGNIFICENT
WIZARD MAGUS
LEVEL-36
CHAOTIC AWESOME!
WUBBA LUBBA DUB DUB!
DM the Brunster
XP 3,480,000
NEXT-DEMIGOD!
Rick Sanchez
SWEET CRYSTAL
0
135
RING of REGENERATION
ALKAZAAR has a wizard's tower built out of Onyx, it has a dungeon underneath it - with traps! -
STR 18
+3 to hit/damage opening doors
STAFF of WIZARDRY
WIZARD'S HAT (STYLISH)
2 POISON or DEATH RAY
and guarded by black panthers!
INT 30
read/write all
RING of RESURRECTION
GAUNTLETS of OGRE STRENGTH
NEVER TRUST GIL
WIS 18
+3 on magic-based saves
2 MAGIC WAND
Havlock's Prayer Beads
LOTHLORIEN
POTIONS of HEALING x10
1st room
FLYING CARPET
2 PARALYSIS or TURN to STONE
DEX 18
+3 to hit/-3 AC
+2 initiative
CRYSTAL BALL
ROBE of the ELDER MAGI
WAND of FEAR!
2nd room
EFREETI BOTTLE
BACKPACK W/TENT +10 DAYS RATIONS
2 DRAGON BREATH
CON 18
+3 per hit die
ROD of CANCELLATION
BEDROLL (COMFY)
CHA 50
+2 reaction
7 retainers
→10 morale
KODO
2 SPELLS or MAGIC STAFF
PET BEHOLDER
NORB THE ORB!
PODO
FERRET FAMILIARS
FANCY WIZARD BOOTS (STURDY-WATERPROOF)
Tower dungeon has a full wizard's lab + library filled with magical scrolls + arcane tomes.
ABILITIES
Can read & write + speak all languages fluently including the language of love.
SKILLS
Superior Eidetic Memory- all spells permanently memorized.
Magic Flesh - no spell components needed.
FAV SPELLS
POWER WORD KILL
TIME STOP
WISH
REINCARNATION
EXPLOSIVE CLOUD
BOOM
AC 9 8 7 6 5 4 3 2 1 0
TO-HIT 8 9 10 11 12 13 14 15 16 17
GP~ 100,000
EP~ 15,240
PP~ 5,800
CP-12

Talking D&D with the creators of Rick and Morty vs. Dungeons & Dragons

Jim, I understand that you were initially skeptical that this crossover would ever get the green light. Can you tell us a little bit about when it was first proposed to you and how it feels now that it's actually coming together?

Jim Zub: Sarah Gaydos reached out to tell me the idea had come up during a brainstorming session and everyone at IDW and Oni were excited at the possibilities. She wanted to know if I'd be involved if they could navigate the red tape, and I laughed it off. Of course, I'd love to be on board, but it would NEVER happen. Wizards of the Coast wouldn't let the crown jewel of gaming be violated by Adult Swim™'s dimension-hopping bastards.

Little did I know that in a world of swirling media synergies and crazy memes, it's the perfect time to let these properties off the chain. I'm so glad the team at WotC realize that. This project is a warped and freakish monster, but it's also a love letter to gaming glory.

Patrick, you're primarily known for your prose work. How did you get pulled into the wild world of monthly comics? Was there any blackmail involved?

Patrick Rothfuss: It's pretty obvious when you think of it. What name screams "regular monthly content" more than Patrick Rothfuss?

Seriously though, I say, 'no' to a lot of cool projects these days. It's my main job, really. I need to turn down 95% of the offers that come my way so I can keep my head down and get work done on my next book…

But this… I just couldn't say no. These are two of my great loves. One old, one new. When they approached me, I knew I had to do it, and I knew the shape of the story I wanted to tell.

Troy, Dungeons & Dragons is known for its detailed characters across many editions, several of which are utilized in this series. Do you have a favorite creature to draw? What about one you hope to take a crack at before the series ends?

Troy Little: Oddly enough I haven't played D&D since the '80s, then just a few months ago my kids expressed an interest in trying it out. I picked up the starter set and began reading and refreshing my memory on how it all works. We've had a few sessions so far and they're hooked. I'm a bit of a rusty DM, but I forgot just how much fun you can have with this game!

When going at the cover for Issue #1 I remembered the mini dungeon from the old red cover edition I had as a kid and how funny I found the gelatinous cube to be as something to battle. I had to include that and the classic Beholder.

There's so many cool monsters to choose from! Before this series is done I better get to draw a dragon or I'm going to portal to dimension C 433. It's all dragons there.

What has your collaboration process been like? Are we talking coffee-fueled all-nighters in an armored bunker located in the forests of Bird World, or is the process perhaps a bit more grounded?

JZ: Pat and I started from a base of brainstorming things we love about D&D, from first edition all the way through to fifth—the amazing settings and scenarios that defined our childhood immersed in sword & sorcery.

Then it was about looking at *Rick and Morty*™ in the same light. Beyond all the fast-talking nihilism and wanton violence, how could

D&D emphasize what makes these characters so memorable and give us new and unexpected spins on who they are and what they embody?

Thankfully, Pat and I have synced up well on all of it. We're simpatico on what we like about both the game and the show. Pat's been a whirlwind of dialogue and emotional content and I've been channeling that into the story structure we built to make sure it reads well as a comic and gives Troy tons of wild visuals to illustrate.

PR: Writing novels (at least the way I do it) is an intensely NON-collaborative process. Yes, my editor helps. Yes, I use innumerable beta readers to gather feedback for revisions. But they are MY revisions. My book My world. I'm a madman and a monster. I am the tyranical god-emperor over all creation. Ego sum Alpha et O.

This is the opposite of that. I knew it wasn't just going to involve collaborating with an illustrator, which I've done before. It meant working with another writer. AND the characters that aren't mine. AND I'm using two sets of intelectual property I'm absolutely *not* the boss of. That means other people have the final say about what ends up in the story… That's a scary thought for me.

But so far it's been delightfully smooth sailing. I haven't lost anything worth weeping tears about. Jim knows the comic format inside and out, which I desperately need in a partner. He's better with the D&D world lore than I am in a bunch of areas, too.

Oh, and when Jim calls me a "Whirlwind of dialogue" he's being exceptionally kind. (Though I love that description.) What he should say is, "This guy doesn't understand how many words can reasonably fit into a single comic page." Luckily, Jim's been masterful at fitting as much of my funny into the script as humanly possible.

What would you consider your Alignments to be? What about your Classes?

JZ: I'd be a Rogue… Chaotic Good. I'm up for talking my way out of trouble, but not as dexterous as I'd like.

TL: I took the WotC online Alignment Test just now and evidently I am Neutral Good. I would probably be a Bard, but I'd be a lousy one. I can't play in time and would need a saving throw against tomatoes and projectiles.

PR: I'm Lawful Moist. Multiclass Paladin Bard.

Finally, is there anything you can reveal to the fans about what to expect when these worlds collide? Can you guarantee their safety during this campaign?

JZ: Morty is smitten, Rick's getting the old gang back together, and Summer's going to learn to backstab. No edition will be spared, no campaign setting is safe.

TL: I want to draw action and carnage! Monsters! Magic! Dungeons! And a dragon or two for good measure. Patrick and Jim may be the DM but I get to play in their world. This is going to be AWESOME!!

PR: I am going to break your heart.

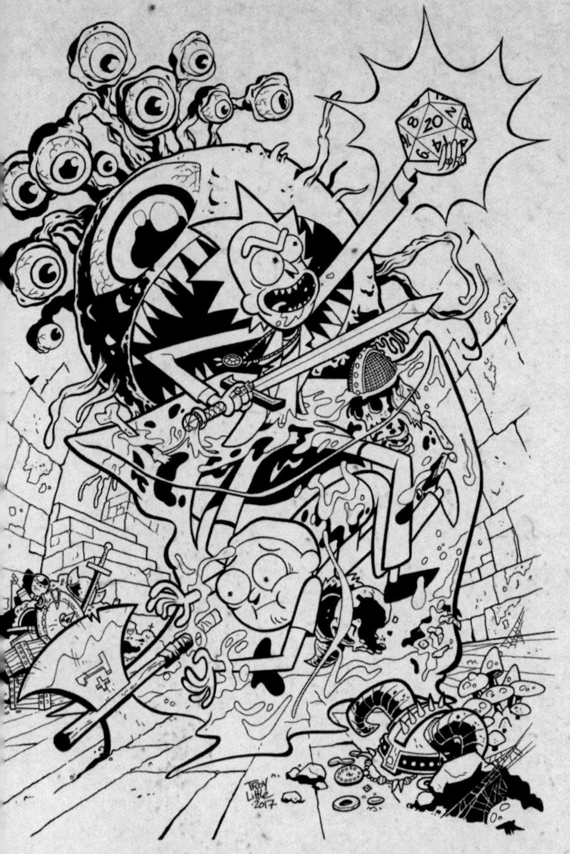

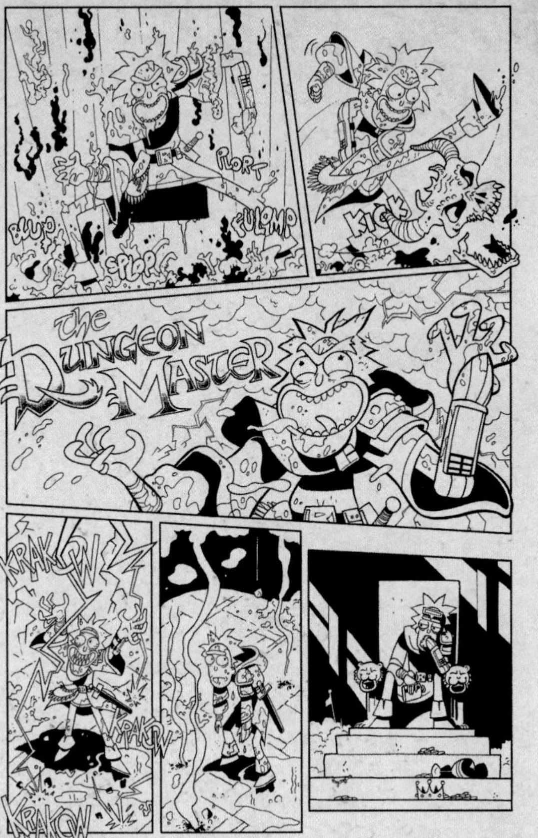
BLUP
PLORT
KICK
the DUNGEON MASTER
KRAKOW

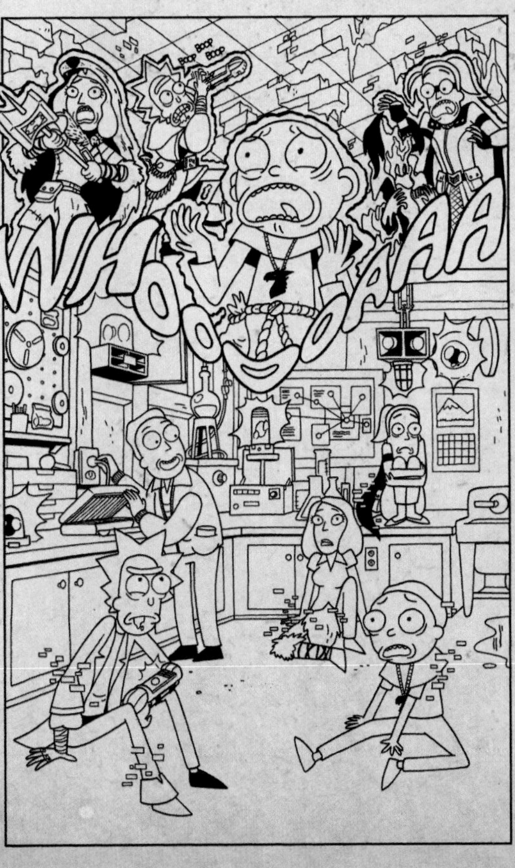
BOOP BOOP BOOP
WHOOOOAAA

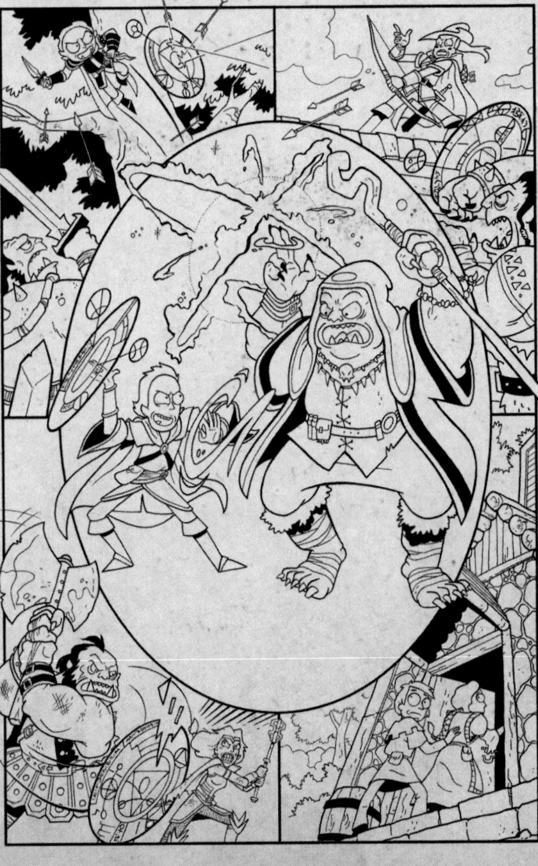

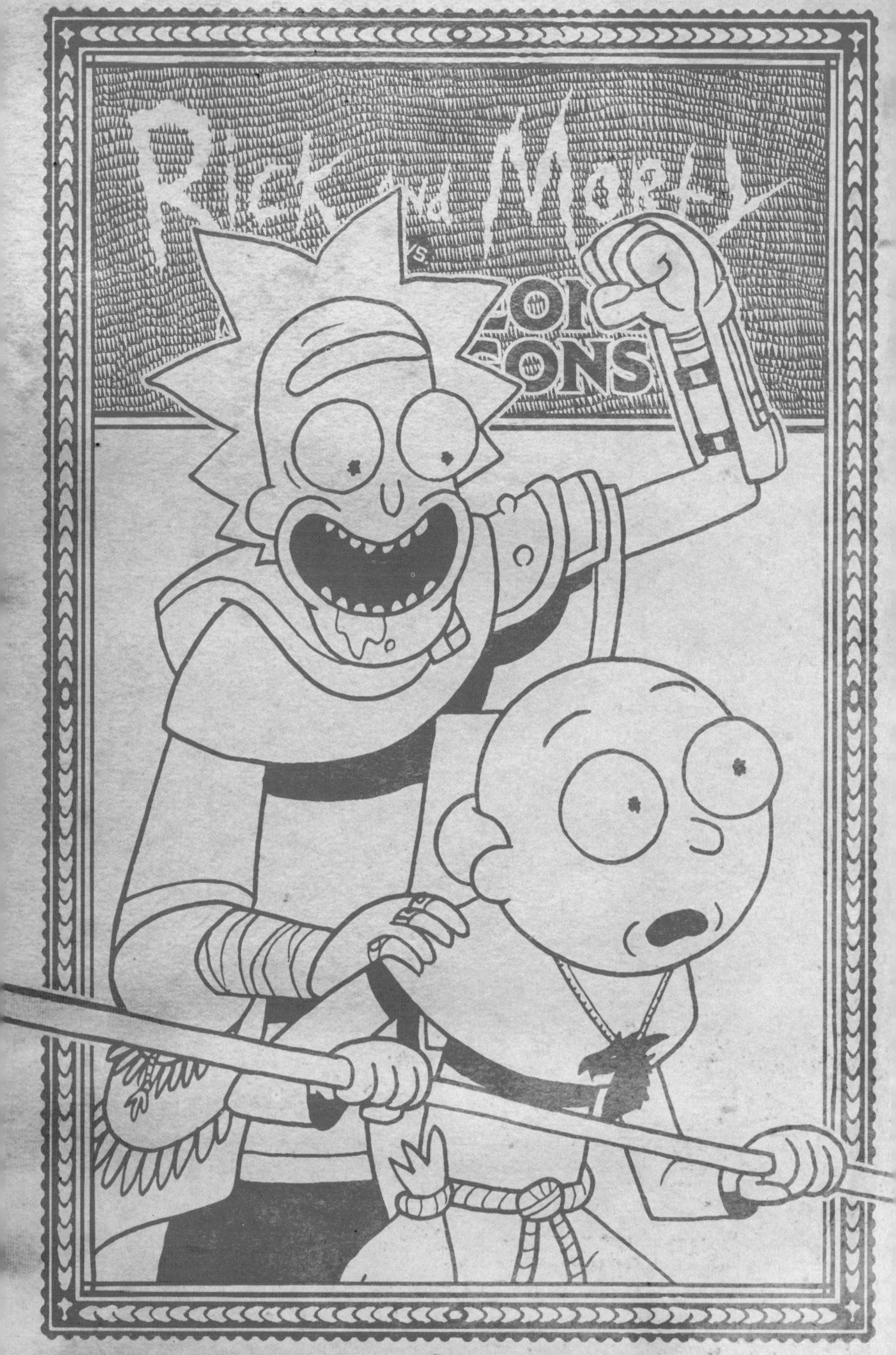
Rick and Morty
vs.